Holding the Line

U.S. Defense Alternatives for the Early 21st Century

The BCSIA Studies in International Security book series is edited at the Belfer Center for Science and International Affairs at Harvard University's John F. Kennedy School of Government and published by The MIT Press. The series publishes books on contemporary issues in international security policy, as well as their conceptual and historical foundations. Topics of particular interest to the series include the spread of weapons of mass destruction, internal conflict, the international effects of democracy and democratization, and U.S. defense policy.

A complete list of BCSIA Studies appears at the back of this volume.

Holding the Line

U.S. Defense Alternatives for the Early 21st Century

Editor
Cindy Williams

BCSIA Studies in International Security

The MIT Press
Cambridge, Massachusetts
London, England

Library of Congress Cataloging-in-Publication Data

Holding the line : U.S. defense alternatives for the early 21st century / edited
by Cindy Williams.
    p.   cm. — (BCSIA studies in international security)
    Includes bibliographical references and index.
ISBN 0-262-23215-4 (hc. : alk. Paper) — ISBN 0-262-73140-1 (pbk. : alk. paper)
    1. United States — Military policy. 2. Military planning — United States.
    3. United States — Armed Forces — Appropriations and expenditures.
    I. Williams, Cindy. II. Series.

UA23 .H53443   2001
355'.033573 — dc21   00-050082

Cover art designed by Brandi Sladek; Department of Defense photo.

Printed in the United States of America

Contents

Acknowledgments

The authors gratefully acknowledge the ideas, comments, and reviews provided by Naila Bolus, Michael E. Brown, David Burbach, Renée de Nevers, Lt. Col. Donald Falls (USAF), Michèle Flournoy, Eugene Gholz, Carl Kaysen, Charles Knight, Steven M. Kosiak, Jennifer Lind, Frances Lussier, Leo Mackay, David Mendeloff, Mary Page, Lane Pierrot, Barry Posen, Daryl Press, CAPT. John Pruitt (USN), Harvey Sapolsky, Christine Wing, Col. David Winn (USMC), Col. Brian Zahn (USA), and an anonymous reviewer for BCSIA. The authors thank Kristen Cashin and Harlene Miller for excellent administrative support during the preparation of the book, and Teresa Lawson for editorial consulting. This book was made possible by the generous support of The Ford Foundation, The John D. and Catherine T. MacArthur Foundation, the Ploughshares Fund, and the W. Alton Jones Foundation.

Holding the Line

U.S. Defense Alternatives for the Early 21st Century

Chapter 1

Introduction

Cindy Williams

The early 1990s witnessed the end of an era for U.S. defense policy. Starting with the fall of the Berlin Wall in November 1989, the Warsaw Pact and then the Soviet Union disintegrated. Communism collapsed in Europe. The Soviet threat—for decades the central focus of U.S. national security strategy—vanished. The Cold War was over, and the United States stood triumphant as the world's only superpower.

In the ten years following, the U.S. military conducted a well-organized and deliberate demobilization: it reduced combat forces by 30 to 40 percent, cut personnel levels by nearly one-third, withdrew excess forces from overseas posts, shed about one-fifth of its bases, and reduced annual spending by about 30 percent. It made the adjustments smoothly, with minimal upheaval in the lives of the men and women leaving service, and with almost wholly positive effects on the civilian economy. Moreover, it made them while preserving the strongest, best trained, best equipped, and most technologically advanced forces in the world.

But America faces two major problems as it considers the future of its armed forces. First, although smaller in size than a decade ago, today's military retains much of its Cold War shape—a shape that fails to take advantage of opportunities for innovation and is not well suited to today's missions or tomorrow's challenges. Second, after a decade of reductions, military budgets are on the rise again, in sharp contrast to the Defense Department's 1997 claims that it could hold the line on defense spending through 2003, and possibly well into the decade of 2010. By the end of the new decade, keeping the military at its current size and outfitting it with the equipment the department plans to buy will cost taxpayers $35–55 billion more a year than it does today and will return defense budgets to their Cold War levels. Adding new forces and systems that the uniformed services are now promoting would raise costs even higher.

The United States could fix this budget problem by devoting more of its tax dollars to defense every year. With huge federal surpluses in the offing, the nation can probably afford it. But increasing spending for defense means forgoing other possible uses of the surpluses that might have substantially higher economic and social payoffs for the country, such as paying down the national debt and shoring up Social Security and Medicare for the long term, investing in human capital, repairing worn-out roads and bridges, or cutting taxes. It makes no sense to revert to Cold War levels of defense spending at a time when outside threats to national security are as low as they are today. Moreover, spending extra money to hold onto forces and to purchase the weapon systems the Pentagon put on its shopping list during the Cold War will not address the deeper problem, namely that the United States is marching into the new century with forces designed for the old one.

Current law requires the Defense Department to conduct a review of national security strategy, force structure, and budgets in the opening months of every new presidential term. The 2001 Quadrennial Defense Review affords the nation an opportunity that must not be treated lightly: to reexamine U.S. national security interests, strategy, and priorities, and then to reshape the military to face the real challenges of the coming decades. Fundamental reshaping could save the military tens of billions of dollars a year in operating and procurement costs, making it possible to hold budgets at today's levels for at least a decade. Far from weakening the military, this could open the door to innovation, transforming the armed forces to be stronger and better equipped for the future they face than they are in 2000 or would be under the Defense Department's current plans.

The Defense Department asserts that current plans for the military are already innovative. The glossy vision statements of the Joint Chiefs of Staff and the individual services all point toward new ways of fighting that would capitalize on emerging technologies. Advanced Concept Technology Demonstrations (ACTDs) and joint and service warfighting experiments allow the military to explore new concepts of warfare and quick-start the development of new systems. The Army has announced a plan for transforming itself to meet future demands. The military will use "leap-ahead" weapon systems to exploit an incipient "revolution in military affairs."

A closer look at the evidence, however, reveals a much different picture. The joint and service vision statements offer conceptual frameworks, but little in the way of concrete plans. Moreover, for technical and institutional reasons, the concepts promised in the visions may not be achievable at all. In any case, tangible progress toward the visions has been slow, to the point that some in the department have taken to renaming Joint Vision 2010 "Joint Vision 2040." The ACTDs and warfighting experiments, touted as the seed corn of the revolution in military affairs, account for less than one-half of one percent of the department's budget in 2000, and often seem to be mired in bureaucracy. The Army's much-ballyhooed transformation remains largely unfunded. Most of the "leap-ahead" systems that the Pentagon advertises got their start more than a decade ago, well before the Cold War ended. In short, the "revolution in military affairs" may have won the war of rhetoric, but it has lost the war for dollars, and some supporters of military innovation despair of any revolution besides a revolution in briefing affairs.[1]

In this chapter, I outline the history of the downsizing of the U.S. military after the end of the Cold War, a subject explored in more detail by Lawrence Korb in Chapter 2. I then describe the first of the two central problems this book addresses: pressures building that will push defense budgets higher during the coming decade if the Pentagon's plans do not change. I review briefly several of the ways that are frequently proposed to restrain defense spending: reducing military infrastructure (as Chapter 3 discusses); shifting more of the burden to U.S. allies (explored by Gordon Adams in Chapter 4); and cutting nuclear weapons programs (a subject examined by David Mosher in Chapter 5). Unfortunately, the savings that are likely from all of these approaches combined fall short of halting defense budget growth over the next ten years. Gaining any real purchase on the coming budget problem will require the Pentagon to reconsider its current plans for retaining and modernizing conventional forces.

The Defense Department could continue to formulate the budget as it has in the past, letting each of the three military departments keep the same share of the budget pie that it has held for decades. If decisionmakers choose to proceed with all of the weapons procurements currently planned by the Pentagon, trimming production runs to fit the force structures that are affordable, then holding the line on defense budgets for a decade might require the services to reduce the major elements of conventional force structure by 15 to 20 percent. Such cuts would still leave the military strong, capable, and well-equipped. But reducing the services in lockstep just because it is politically expedient means passing

---

1. For a discussion of the potential cost of a revolution in military affairs, see Cindy Williams and Jennifer M. Lind, "Can We Afford a Revolution in Military Affairs?" *Breakthroughs*, Vol. 8, No. 1 (Spring 1999), pp. 3–8.

up the opportunity that the Quadrennial Defense Review affords to take a fresh look at military strategy and priorities and to ask whether a new balance among the services might foster innovation and ultimately make more sense in the world of the future than retaining the old Cold War balance.

In this book, therefore, we argue for a number of approaches to change. Fundamental to all of them is the need to recognize that many of the strains in the defense budget arise from the mismatch between official U.S. national security strategy and the way in which our forces have been used in the 1990s and are likely to continue to be used. Resolving these discrepancies, and also re-calibrating for today's realities the yardstick by which the U.S. military measures its capability for war, would give us a far better framework for shaping future conventional forces. Therefore this chapter sets out reconceived priorities for the U.S. military that more realistically reflect both the demands of the future and the forces required to meet those demands. Based on those reconceived priorities, Chapters 6, 7, and 8 each present a view of the future, a military strategy, and a force structure shaped to future demands. Rather than accepting the Cold War fiscal balance among the services as a given, each of the chapters emphasizes and capitalizes on the unique strengths of one of the military departments: for the Navy in Chapter 6 by Owen Cote; the Army in Chapter 7 by James Quinlivan; and the Air Force in Chapter 8 by Karl Mueller. Chapter 9 concludes the book with comparisons of the strategies and force structures offered in the preceding three chapters, and recommendations for decisionmakers.

The Post–Cold War Downsizing

The Pentagon's budget cuts actually began in 1986—several years before the Cold War ended—as lawmakers struggled to put the brakes on soaring federal deficits. By 1989, Defense Department budget authority declined from the Reagan-era high of $425 billion to $380 billion, a drop of 11 percent.[2]

The military downsizing made possible by the end of the Cold War freed up substantial sums for deficit reduction. From 1989 to 1998, budget

---

2. Unless otherwise stated, all dollar figures in this book are expressed in 2000 budget authority. Budget authority reflects the amount of money Congress makes available through an agency's annual appropriation to be spent that year or in future years. This chapter and the book in general treat budget authority as the basic budgetary measure for defense programs. In contrast, outlays reflect the amount of money actually spent by an agency in a given year out of the budget authority provided by Congress that year or in previous years. Outlays are used in this book and elsewhere in

Figure 1.1.   DOD Annual Budget Authority, 1947–2005.

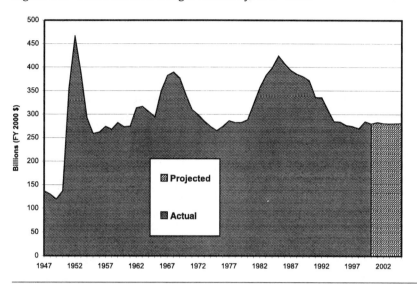

SOURCE: U.S. Department of Defense, National Defense Budget Estimates for FY 2001, March 2000, Table 6-8.

authority for the Defense Department dropped another 29 percent, to a post–Cold War low of $270 billion (see Figure 1.1). Outlays for national defense continued to rise after 1986, as programs finished spending the money authorized by Congress in top budget years; they peaked in 1989 and then fell 30 percent to the low point in 1998 (see Figure 1.2).[3] Together with the booming economy and growing tax receipts, defense cuts became a principal source of funds for balancing the budget and turning deficits into surpluses.

The military's fiscal cutbacks were dramatic. But as Lawrence Korb explains in Chapter 2, they followed the apex of Cold War military spending: not since the Korean War had the United States spent as much on the Defense Department as it did in 1985. Even after the reductions, military budgets were still about 85 percent of their Cold War aver-

discussions of federal deficits and surpluses or when comparing spending across federal programs, because entitlements like Social Security and Medicare rely on permanent laws rather than annual appropriation acts for spending.

3.   The national defense category includes spending by the Department of Defense as well as defense spending in other federal agencies, mostly for nuclear activities in the Department of Energy.

Figure 1.2. National Defense Outlays, 1965–2000 (includes DOD and other defense functions).

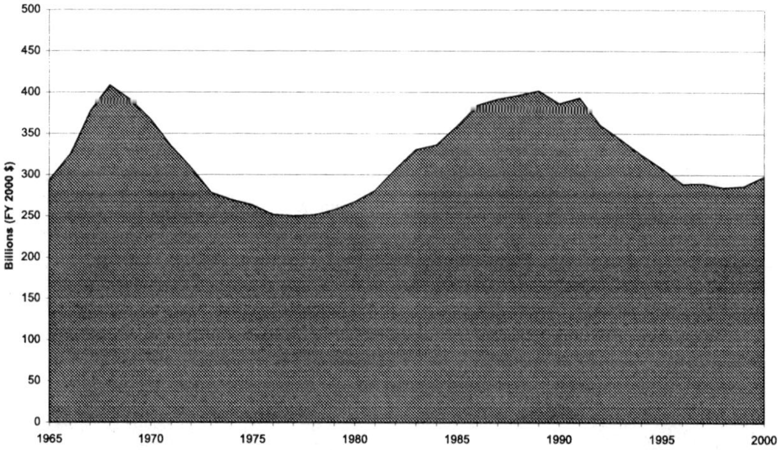

SOURCE: U.S. Government Printing Office, The Budget for Fiscal Year 2001, February 2000, Table 8.2

age—remarkable considering that no new enemy emerged to replace the Soviet Union as a major threat to American security. U.S. defense spending still far outstrips that of the next six nations combined: Russia, France, Japan, China, the United Kingdom, and Germany.

Nevertheless, in the autumn of 1998 the military complained that it could not make ends meet and that it needed $30 billion more a year to avert a coming "crisis in military readiness." Spurred on by domestic political pressures and projections of huge federal surpluses, the Clinton administration and Congress raced to give the military more money.[4] By the time the president submitted the federal spending request for 2001, the military budget commanded an extra $14 billion each year on average over 1998 levels. Even so, in the spring of 2000, the services upped the ante, arguing that they still faced an annual shortfall of $30 billion, despite the increase the nation had already provided.

The budgetary cutbacks from 1989 to 1998 had been made possible by reductions in troop strength, combat force structure, military infrastructure, and modernization plans. The number of troops on active duty declined from about 2.1 million in 1989 to 1.4 million in 1998. Civilian employment in the Department of Defense dropped from 1.1 million to

4. George C. Wilson, This War Really Matters (Washington, D.C.: Congressional Quarterly Press, 1999), provides an illuminating history of the defense budget politics of the late 1990s.

Figure 1.3   Service Shares of Total Service Spending.

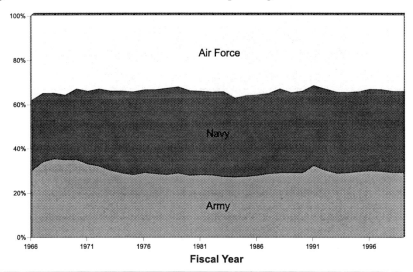

700,000. The number of active duty Army divisions fell from 18 to 10; Navy aircraft carriers from 16 to 12 and battle force ships from 546 to 333; and active duty Air Force tactical wings from 24 to 13. About 100 of the 500 military installations in the United States were closed and several major weapon systems were cancelled or delayed.

Chapter 2 describes those reductions and the strategic rationale by which they were justified in reviews during the Bush and Clinton administrations: the Base Force of 1989–91, the Bottom-Up Review of 1993, and the Quadrennial Defense Review of 1997. One striking feature of the drawdown is that the budgets of the three military departments—the Army, the Department of the Navy (including the Navy and the Marine Corps), and the Air Force—were cut back in virtual lockstep. As Figure 1.3 illustrates, each service's share of defense dollars was held nearly constant during the Cold War (with the exception of added Army appropriations during the Vietnam War). The demise of the Soviet threat did not change this allocation. This unchanging pattern of resources across the services is reflected in troop levels and force structures as well. Current plans for equipping the force also bear a strong resemblance to those of the Cold War. As Chapter 2 details, several systems planned during the Cold War have been canceled, but almost every major item in today's purchase plans was conceived during the Cold War. As a result, today's military looks like a shrunken version of the one that was built for the Cold War—despite three reviews that purported to develop force structures and allocate resources based on new strategies suited for the future world. The house may be smaller, but it still has three rooms all the same size, and furnished the same way.

Given the striking changes in the world during the past decade and the rapid advances in technologies for weapons, sensors, navigation, and communications, it would be an astonishing coincidence if the strategy appropriate to the new environment truly required exactly the same allocation of resources across the services as the one developed for the Cold War. Korb shows, in fact, that the desire to keep the allocation of resources constant drove the strategy and not vice versa. Uniformed and civilian leaders of the Defense Department decided that the services should share the cutbacks, and then outlined a strategy that would suit the forces that each service could support with a steady share of declining budgets.[5] Stuck in the Cold War pattern of force structure, organization, equipment, and infrastructure, the U.S. military has frittered away a decade of opportunity to reshape itself for the future.

The Rising Costs of Defense

The Clinton administration's five-year budget plan of January 2000 presumes that defense spending will decline somewhat after 2001 and then hold steady for several years. But in fact, budgetary pressures within the Defense Department threaten to add tens of billions of dollars to military spending over the coming decade. There is upward pressure in each of the four largest appropriation categories of the defense budget: weapons procurement; military pay; operation and maintenance (O&M); and research, development, test, and evaluation (RDT&E).

WEAPONS PROCUREMENT
The Defense Department has ambitious plans for modernization in all of the uniformed services to build advanced new airplanes, ships, submarines, helicopters and satellites. Hoping that a collection of procurement reforms instituted over the past decade will hold costs in check, the Pentagon believes it can keep the bill for these new systems below $70 billion a year over the next decade. But history shows that the costs of weapons will continue to grow, both from generation to generation and from initial estimates to actual expenses. For example, the F-22 air-to-air fighter will cost at least twice as much per airplane as the F-15 that it replaces and, ac-

---

5. See also Lorna Jaffe, *The Development of the Base Force 1989–1992*, Joint History Office, Office of the Chairman of the Joint Chiefs of Staff, July 1993; and Wilson, *This War Really Matters.*

cording to independent government analyses, nearly 20 percent more than the Air Force currently estimates. The Congressional Budget Office estimates that the multipurpose Joint Strike Fighter (JSF) being developed for use by the Air Force, the Navy, and the Marine Corps will overrun the official cost projections by 50 percent, and that the planned first-phase national missile defense (NMD) system will cost 15 percent more than the Pentagon currently claims.[6] The Navy, forced to acknowledge serious cost overruns in its shipbuilding program for 2001, still asserts that it will be able to rein in the costs of future ships. Taken together, the bill for cost overruns that the department does not yet acknowledge could raise procurement spending substantially a decade from now.

Moreover, the department's plans do not provide for replacing or extending the life of all of the military's aging equipment. If plans do not change, then workhorse utility helicopters, electronic warfare aircraft, long-range bombers such as the 1960s era B-52, and other systems will reach unprecedented ages without being rejuvenated or replaced. Replacing or refurbishing those systems to avert problems of aging across the armed forces would bring weapons bills even higher.[7]

MILITARY PAY

The military pay account covers the basic pay and allowances of current service members and also supports an accrual fund for their retirement. Military pay contributes to both military readiness and infrastructure.[8] Military leaders and advocacy organizations have voiced concern in recent years that military pay raises have fallen behind those in the private sector, saying that it adds to the difficulty of attracting and keeping talented officers and enlisted personnel during a period when low unemployment makes private-sector options plentiful. In January 2000, Congress granted the military an across-the-board pay raise that exceeds recent average pay raises in the private sector by one-half of a percentage point. In addition, current law calls for military raises to exceed those in

6.   Christopher Jehn, "Modernizing Tactical Aircraft," Statement Before the Subcommittee on Airland, Committee on Armed Services, U.S. Senate, March 10, 1999, p. 3; Congressional Budget Office, "Budgetary and Technical Implications of the Administration's Plan for National Missile Defense," April 2000.

7.   Lane Pierrot, "Aging Military Equipment," Statement before the Subcommittee on Military Procurement, Committee on Armed Services, U.S. House of Representatives (Washington, D.C.: Congressional Budget Office, February 24, 1999).

8.   Infrastructure activities are those that support the forces that would deploy in wartime, including, for example, base operations, depot maintenance, acquisition program offices, health care for military members and retirees, recruiting, and classroom training.

the private sector by one-half of a percentage point every year through 2006. Some advocates outside the military are pressing for even higher raises.

The Clinton administration's budget plan submitted to Congress in January 2000 assumes military raises for 2001 and 2002 that exceed private-sector pay hikes by half a percentage point. The plan provides for smaller increases in subsequent years, equaling the average private-sector pay raise and no more. Paying for the higher raises stipulated in the law, or accommodating the still higher boosts demanded by some, would add to the Pentagon's budget pressures.[9]

OPERATION AND MAINTENANCE

The military spends a substantial portion of its budget on operation and maintenance (O&M), a catchall category that pays for the costs of day-to-day training, upkeep, and administration of military units and bases. Like military pay, the O&M category supports both military readiness and infrastructure. The O&M account also pays the lion's share of costs of wars and other contingencies. Since the end of the Cold War, spending for O&M has not fallen in proportion with troop cuts or the lower spending for equipment. As a result, O&M now accounts for 37 percent of the Defense Department's budget, up from 30 percent just a decade ago.

Over the course of several decades, spending for O&M has varied from year to year, increasing as troop levels went up and decreasing (though not proportionately) as they fell. But O&M per active-duty service member has risen quite consistently, with increases averaging nearly 3 percent a year (see Figure 1.4). The Defense Department tried with little success to reverse this trend during the latter half of the 1990s. The Pentagon recently admitted defeat in the fight against O&M creep, acknowledging that the costs of contingencies, rising health-care costs for military employees and retirees, and additional spending to improve the quality of military life would continue to push O&M budgets up.[10] Continued growth in O&M spending is likely to exert substantial upward pressure on future defense budgets.

---

9.   Because the annual across-the-board pay hikes are considered equivalent to wage inflation for the military, these raises, no matter how they are sized or how they compare with private-sector wage inflation, typically do not show up when budgets are expressed in constant dollars. The pressure they create on defense budgets is nonetheless real.

10.   "FY 2001 Defense Budget," briefing to the press by an unnamed Defense Department official, February 2000.

Figure 1.4. O&M Spending Per Active Duty Service Member.

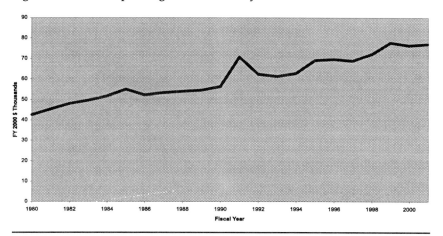

RESEARCH, DEVELOPMENT, TEST, AND EVALUATION

Current Pentagon plans assume that spending for research, development, test, and evaluation (RDT&E) can be reduced substantially in the coming years. Such a reduction may well be possible. RDT&E spending did not decline as quickly as the rest of the defense budget during the 1990s; even at the lower levels the Pentagon projects for the future, it will still exceed its Cold War average level.[11] But RDT&E plans may instead grow as the department unveils technology opportunities or works to replace aging systems that it currently plans to keep in the force. Moreover, in a rapidly changing world, RDT&E may be one area the Pentagon should not reduce. Restoring long-term spending for RDT&E to today's levels would increase annual defense budgets over the long term.

The Pentagon hopes to hold these rising costs in check. Its five-year budget plan assumes that it will be successful. But the internal pressure of rising costs is substantial, and history shows that the department will find it very difficult to control costs in all four areas—weapon procurement, military pay, operation and maintenance, and RDT&E—without changing its plans significantly. Without such changes, annual military spending can be expected to rise within a decade to a level that exceeds the current budget by $35 billion to $55 billion a year.[12]

11. Steven M. Kosiak, *Analysis of the FY 2001 Defense Budget Request,* Center for Strategic and Budgetary Assessments, Washington, D.C. February 2000, p. 12.

12. The author's estimates of the mismatch between future budgets and programs are generally consistent with those provided by the Congressional Budget Office in a

Why We Should Not Give In

Advocates of higher military spending argue that the nation can afford this extra expense. Projections of the federal budget surplus are huge, accumulating to a total of $4.6 trillion or more between 2001 and 2010. Even the so-called on-budget surplus, the part that accumulates outside the Social Security trust fund, could come to about $2.2 trillion over the decade, assuming that spending for discretionary programs grows with inflation.[13] With surpluses that large, perhaps the country can afford to spend as much money on defense as the military would like.

But the nation has better uses for the surplus than to return military budgets to their Cold War levels. Additional public investment in education, infrastructure, health care, or nonmilitary technology are likely to have higher economic and social payoffs over the long term. Using the surplus to further reduce the federal debt could put the nation in a better position to handle the rising costs of Social Security and Medicare as the baby-boom generation begins to retire during the decade of 2010. Reducing tax rates might benefit the long-term economy by putting more money in private hands.

At a time when outside threats are low and the United States already has the strongest military in the world, the nation should consider other options for the surplus before jumping to spend more on defense. Moreover, giving in to pressures to increase the defense budget makes it too easy for decisionmakers to postpone the hard choices that are needed to reposition the military for the coming century. If every service shares equally in a budget pie that expands to feed every want, neither the military nor the nation will face a strong incentive to re-examine the world, to

---

November 1997 briefing to the Senate Budget Committee and also with estimates by Steven M. Kosiak and Elizabeth Heeter, "Cost of Defense Plan Could Exceed Available Funding By $26 Billion a Year Over the Long Run," Center for Strategic and Budgetary Assessments, April 2, 1998, p. 5.

13. However, as James Horney and Robert Greenstein of the Center on Budget and Policy Priorities point out, if Medicare surpluses are placed off-limits for spending along with Social Security surpluses, and if the costs of maintaining current policies such as aid to farmers are taken into account, then the $2 trillion figure is cut in half. Ultimately the ten-year surplus available for spending or tax cuts may be more like $400 billion—just $10 billion more a year than the $30 billion the services want to add to annual military budgets in the coming years. See <http://www.cbpp.org/6-29-00bud.htm>. Unlike other dollar figures in this book, the surplus numbers are in current dollars (often referred to as "then-year dollars" by the military).

set priorities and make strategic choices, or to develop creative new equipment and ways of operating.

Miracle Cures Will Not Work

Cost pressures inside the budget mean that to hold the line, the Pentagon will need to scale back on its current plans for every year of the decade. By 2010, it will need to identify program cuts amounting to $35 billion to $55 billion compared with current projections for that year. This book uses $35 billion as a target for annual program reductions by the end of the decade.

For years, the Defense Department and others argued that savings from infrastructure and procurement reform would compensate for budget growth in other areas: if the military could run its business side more efficiently, there would be more money for things the warfighter needed, and "let's run the military more like a business" became the slogan of true believers. Others pinned their hopes on greater cooperation with allies: if we could just get our NATO partners to carry their fair share of finance, of operations, of technology investments, then the burden of shoring up stability in Europe would fall less on our military's shoulders and we could cut back. Others hoped that further reductions in the nuclear arsenal would save substantial sums: "let's stop spending money on nukes and spend it on schools instead." In fact, however, as Chapters 3, 4, and 5 show, the savings that might be achieved in these areas fall well short of the $35 billion target. Program cuts of this magnitude will not be accomplished without reining in the department's plans for conventional forces. Therefore this book explores strategic options and conventional force choices that would allow the nation to hold the line on defense spending—that is, to keep defense budgets at today's level in real terms—for at least a decade.

HOPES FOR SAVINGS FROM INFRASTRUCTURE REFORM

During the 1990s, as Chapter 3 describes, the Defense Department hoped that it could offset much of its planned increase in procurement spending through savings in infrastructure activities. Successive advisory panels outlined a broad spectrum of infrastructure reforms that might save billions of dollars a year. Some such reforms have been implemented and are already producing savings: closing military bases, consolidating defense finance and accounting activities, reengineering the business travel system, and opening some functions that the military formerly handled in-house to competition in the private sector. The Defense Department hopes to save an additional $6.5 billion annually by the end of the decade by closing about 50 more bases and by opening another 150,000 government jobs to competition, or by eliminating them entirely where that makes more sense. But Congress has refused to consider further consolidations in base infrastructure beyond the 100 facilities already closed under the base realignment and closure (BRAC) procedures of 1988–95. As Chapter 3 shows, moreover, the savings from competition and other planned reform measures may not come as quickly as the department hopes.

However, there is still room for additional savings from infrastructure reform, because the collection of politically expedient measures that the Pentagon ultimately settled on is relatively modest. Chapter 3 suggests a number of more extensive reforms, including cross-service consolidation of common functions, outright elimination of non-essential activities, substantial reductions of medical infrastructure and on-base housing, and elimination of the federal subsidy to on-base grocery stores. Taken together, these reforms might save an additional $9.5 billion a year by the end of the decade. These deeper reforms face steep political hurdles, but nevertheless we assume that the department will be able to save $10 billion a year through infrastructure reform by the end of the decade—a level between the department's current estimate of $6.5 billion and the $16 billion in savings that might be achieved if the department meets its own goals and also implements the deeper reforms proposed in Chapter 3.

GREATER BURDEN-SHARING BY ALLIES

Another path toward significant U.S. defense saving that is frequently touted is to scale back U.S. commitments to allies, and to rely on allies to provide more of the forces, equipment, or financing necessary to meet shared security objectives. Chapter 4 by Gordon Adams explores this option.

In the extreme, the United States could shun international military involvement, withdraw from most of its alliance commitments, and turn the entire burden of allied defense over to the allies. Such a strategy of restraint would allow the United States to pull forces out of Europe and Asia and greatly reduce the level of forward military presence.[14]

---

14.   Eugene Gholz, Daryl G. Press, and Harvey M. Sapolsky, "Come Home, America: The Strategy of Restraint in the Face of Temptation," *International Security*, Vol. 21, No. 4 (Spring 1997), pp. 5–48; Earl Ravenal, "The Case for Adjustment," *Foreign Policy*, No. 81 (Winter 1990–91), pp. 3–19; Eric A. Nordlinger, *Isolationism Reconfigured: American Foreign Policy for a New Century* (Princeton, N.J.: Princeton University Press, 1995).

Adopting a strategy of restraint and leaving most of the burden to others would allow the United States to reduce its military force structure significantly. One proposed posture would cut two active-duty and six reserve divisions from the Army and one active-duty division from the Marine Corps, eliminate six active-duty and four reserve wings from the Air Force, and retire about one hundred ships from the Navy, including six aircraft carriers and thirty attack submarines.[15] Cuts of this magnitude could save about $40 billion a year in operating expenses and procurement costs over the next decade. If the force structure cuts were matched by appropriate reductions in infrastructure activities, the department might save $20 billion more. If in addition the department could achieve some savings from the types of infrastructure reform discussed in the previous section, then the total savings for such a force could be as great as $65–70 billion a year, not only holding future budgets in check but bringing them back down to the post–Cold War low of 1998 or even lower.

Such a strategy of restraint is presently outside the mainstream of political thinking about U.S. foreign policy. But even without going so far, the United States might call upon its allies to handle a greater share of the burden of world security. For example, the United States might insist that its regional allies provide most of the ground forces needed for any regional war that unfolds in the near- or mid-term.[16] If, as a result, the Army could eliminate half of its ten active-duty divisions, the Defense Department might save between $10 billion and $15 billion a year in operating and procurement costs.

During the Cold War and continuing into the post–Cold War period, much of the discussion of further reliance on allies has focused on more balanced burden-sharing with European allies. But as Gordon Adams explains in Chapter 4, Europe does not share America's current strategic vision. The Europeans have fallen behind the United States in the technologies needed for warfare of the type the United States envisions, and their current spending plans will prevent them from closing the gap quickly.

Barry R. Posen and Andrew L. Ross call this a strategy of "neo-isolationism;" see Posen and Ross, "Competing Visions for U.S. Grand Strategy," *International Security*, Vol. 21, No. 3 (Winter 1996/97), pp. 5–53. But the authors identified with the strategy generally do not refer to it as isolationism, and draw strong distinctions between the economic and military isolationism of the past and the military restraint they espouse.

15. Described in Posen and Ross, "Competing Visions for U.S. Grand Strategy," p. 10.

16. Andrew F. Krepinevich, *Transforming America's Alliances*, Center for Strategic and Budgetary Assessments, February 2000, p. 81.

Adams identifies just three missions—peace stabilization operations in Europe, intra-European airlift, and naval coverage in the North Atlantic and the Mediterranean—that might realistically be met by European forces within the coming decade. Turning all three missions over to the Europeans and trimming U.S. forces appropriately could save about $7 billion a year by the end of the decade.

Over time, as new military arrangements take hold and Europe begins to close the technology gap, the United States might be able to rely to a much greater extent on its European allies, at least for operations in Europe or its immediate periphery. But as Adams explains, assuming that the U.S. proclivity for military engagement and intervention on a global scale persist into the future and that the Europeans do not greatly increase military spending, the Defense Department cannot count on the NATO allies to offset much more than a few billion dollars of its budget squeeze over the coming decade.

SAVINGS FROM THE U.S. NUCLEAR DETERRENT

Throughout the last decade, the United States has been able to reap savings from nuclear forces and missile defense programs. From 1990 to 2000, the Department of Defense and the Department of Energy reduced spending for nuclear and missile defense programs by about 40 percent. However, the peace dividend has by now largely been realized for nuclear-armed missiles, bombers, and submarines and the nuclear warheads they carry. As David Mosher details in Chapter 5, significant further savings in these areas are unlikely. Even if the United States and Russia agree to the deep reductions envisioned for START III, costs can be expected to decline very little, and may even increase to pay for required verification measures. Moreover, any savings are likely be overwhelmed by the costs of proposed missile defenses.

THE NEED FOR A NEW STRATEGY

The future holds no easy solution for the problems of the defense budget. Infrastructure reform measures might save another $10 billion a year, but they will face such steep political hurdles that they may be seen in the Pentagon as not worth the effort. Sharing the burden with allies will offer only limited relief from the budget crunch expected over the coming decade, short of a dramatic change in U.S. grand strategy and alliance relationships. U.S. nuclear deterrent forces will not yield much more in the way of savings—and in fact may add to defense costs—even if the deep reductions envisioned under START III are adopted. There is no doubt that, if the military is to live within current budget levels for another decade, it will have to reduce its plans for conventional forces.

The Defense Department could deal with the problem as it has in the past, holding each military department's budget constant for a decade and thus sharing the pain of program reductions equally across the services. The services could respond by reining in their expectations for conventional force structure, readiness, or modernization. One affordable plan would hold readiness at today's levels, trim the major elements of force structure in each service by 15 to 20 percent, and pare back planned production runs consistent with the new force size. The cutbacks would leave the Army with eight of today's ten active-duty divisions, six of the eight National Guard combat divisions, and all of the Guard's independent brigades. The Navy would retain ten of twelve aircraft carriers, ten of twelve amphibious ready groups, and more than 250 battle force ships. The Marine Corps would keep two and one-half of its three active-duty divisions. The Air Force would hold onto eleven of its thirteen active-duty tactical wings and five of its seven reserve tactical wings. The plan would provide the services with all the new weapon types they currently plan to buy, but would re-size production runs consistent with the smaller force structure, thus holding the problem of aging equipment at the same levels that the current (as yet unfunded) plan envisions.

The smaller military of this alternative would still be formidable: larger in every measure than almost any other military in the world and better equipped by far than any other armed force. With some relaxation of the ambitious timelines and unrealistic yardsticks the military has set for itself, the downsized forces would be capable in most respects of meeting the national security goals articulated during the Clinton administration. But such mindless allocation of resources across the services is not the preferred fiscal strategy for reducing the military to live within today's budgets, because it represents no coherent military strategy. Continuing to balance resources evenly across the services in this way means passing up an invaluable opportunity for the United States to reexamine its national security interests, strategy, and priorities, and then to reshape its military to face the real challenges and to capitalize on the real opportunities of this and future decades.

The next section outlines two serious mismatches in today's military thinking: one between the official U.S. national security strategy and the way U.S. forces have come to be used, and a second between the yardstick the military uses to measure its capability to go to war and the forces that would actually be needed to defend against any real-world threat. Realigning strategy to practice and re-calibrating the yardstick to reflect the world we live in would allow the United States to configure forces more realistically, eliminate some of the military's perceived readiness troubles, free thinking and resources for innovation, and clear the path toward a force structure that will not break the budget.

Mismatches in Current Strategy and Yardsticks

Senior military leaders balk at any suggestion of reducing conventional forces. In briefings, articles, and Congressional hearings, they express deep concern that U.S. operating forces are already stretched to the limit. Key units report that they are not ready for their principal missions, in some cases because of involvement in operations and deployments that are not officially their first priority. Anecdotes about overworked and dispirited troops abound.

A review of the Clinton administration's declaratory strategy and its actions reveal serious inconsistencies between the official statement of priorities for the use of military force and the actual priorities as evidenced by actions. While the Clinton strategy declares that fighting and winning in two nearly simultaneous major theater wars is the military's first priority, in actual practice the Clinton administration has engaged the military in a series of smaller-scale contingencies, some of which may last for decades. These "presence and stability" missions crowd out the major theater wars that take precedence on paper. As a consequence of this inconsistency, troops are required daily to set "second-priority" missions above the ones that officially hold first priority, and are left to struggle with the implications for their readiness to handle two wars that unfold at about the same time. Aligning declaratory strategy with today's reality could ease the pressures that cause the military to perceive its forces as less than ready, and could at the same time reduce the military's requirements for forces.

Another important inconsistency is the mismatch between the military's yardstick for sizing its conventional forces—the so-called two major theater war (MTW) standard—and the size and strength of any opposing military that U.S. forces could realistically expect to face over the next decade or more. Adjusting the yardstick to reflect the forces needed for the wars that seem likely would also significantly reduce the military's requirements for forces.

COLD WAR THREATS AND STRATEGY

From the end of the Vietnam War until the fall of the Berlin Wall, successive administrations and the Pentagon perceived the Soviet Union as the single most important threat to national and global security. Vital interests were centered at home and in the industrial capacity of Western Europe, and extended to oil resources of the Persian Gulf and to U.S. territory, trade, and alliances in East Asia and the Pacific. U.S. national security strategy focused unequivocally on deterring a Soviet attack against the United States or its allies, and defending to win should deterrence fail. Official statements made mention of other threats— terrorism, local warfare that could disrupt the world's supply of resources, and insurgencies or cross-border wars that could overthrow governments friendly to the United States—and other regions, including Latin America and Africa. But these lower-priority interests were viewed largely in the context of the global balance of power with the Soviet bloc, and the secondary threats were generally described as products of the expansion and military influence of the Soviet Union and its proxy states.

The principal declaratory mission of U.S. military forces during that period was to deter a Soviet conventional or nuclear attack. Defense policy called for forces that would also be able to operate across a spectrum of conflict: responding to acts of terrorism, protecting vital sea lanes and projecting power around the globe, supporting allies against coercion, and waging all-out global conventional and nuclear war. Being able to respond quickly across this full spectrum of demands required maintaining a forward presence of ground and air forces in Europe and Asia and of naval forces worldwide.

STRATEGIC CHOICES AFTER THE COLD WAR

The end of the Cold War spawned a lively public debate about U.S. interests and role in the world, the threats and opportunities faced by the United States, and the basic principles that should guide U.S. security policy for the future. To lend clarity to the debate, in 1996 Barry Posen and Andrew Ross identified and compared four competing visions for U.S. grand strategy.[17] The first, which they termed neo-isolationism, holds that America's single vital security interest is the political sovereignty and integrity of the homeland. Threats to that interest are minimal by virtue of the geography of the United States, the retaliatory power of its nuclear weapons, and the collapse of the Soviet Union. According to this view, the United States should avoid entanglements in the security affairs of other countries, bring its military forces home, and significantly reduce the size of its military.

A second strategy, which Posen and Ross called selective engagement, assumes that the nation's fundamental security interest is in pre-

---

17. Posen and Ross, "Competing Visions for U.S. Grand Strategy," pp. 5–53.

serving peace among the world's great powers, that is, the Eurasian industrial states with large military potential. The United States can promote peace among these powers only by remaining engaged in the world, but it should limit its engagement to those places where the risk of sparking a world war is the greatest: Europe, East Asia, and the oil-rich Persian Gulf. The United States needs a strong nuclear deterrent and conventional forces sufficient to fight and win in one major regional conflict while (at a minimum) supporting a regional ally in another.

The third grand strategy, often called cooperative security, holds that the collapse of the Soviet Union makes war among the great powers unlikely, but that the United States has a far-reaching interest in peace everywhere, and that every threat to peace in the world is a threat to the United States. The United States should, therefore, work through international institutions and use its military might to promote democracy and free markets around the globe, and to thwart aggression, whether internal or across states, anywhere in the world. Although early proponents of cooperative security supposed that U.S. forces to support the strategy could be reduced below today's levels, Posen and Ross argue that building the international credibility that would be needed to affect the calculations of potential aggressors around the world could require forces larger than today's, especially if allies in the endeavor do not increase their forces significantly, leaving the United States to do most of the heavy lifting in military operations.

A fourth strategy, called primacy, rests on the assumption that the United States has vital interests in ensuring safety at home and preserving order abroad which are best served by preserving the nation's status as the world's sole superpower. Any country that might rise to become a global peer competitor poses a threat to international order. U.S. strategy should therefore focus on precluding the emergence of any such competitor. U.S. forces must hold such an edge of superiority in size and technology that any potential challenger would be dissuaded from even entering the competition.

As the Cold War drew to a close and debate about these strategies developed, policymakers moved to redefine U.S. security strategy. Both the Bush and the Clinton administrations argued for continued engagement in international security affairs, rejecting calls for a new isolationism. President Clinton's foreign policy team entered office in 1992 with a commitment to cooperative security. But the strategy was diluted as the magnitude of the task of reshaping the world became apparent and domestic constraints forced compromise. By the end of the decade, argued Posen and Ross, the Clinton strategy appeared to be an amalgam of cooperative security and selective engagement.[18]

NATIONAL SECURITY STRATEGY OF THE LATE CLINTON YEARS

The expansive list of threats to national security articulated in President Clinton's January 2000 strategy statement strongly reflects the rhetoric of cooperative security:[19]

- Regional or state-centered threats that endanger their neighbors' sovereignty, economic stability, and access to resources, by states that may have nuclear, biological, or chemical weapons and the systems to deliver them;
- Transnational threats, including terrorism, illicit trafficking in drugs and arms, uncontrolled refugee migration, and threats to critical national infrastructures such as energy, banking, and finance;
- Proliferation of advanced weapons (including weapons of mass destruction) and weapons-related technologies;
- Failed states, which can generate internal conflict, mass migration, famine, epidemics, environmental disasters, mass killings, and aggression against neighboring states or groups;
- States that fail to respect the rights of their citizens and that tolerate or engage in human rights abuses, ethnic cleansing, or acts of genocide, which could spark civil wars and refugee crises;
- Collection of intelligence by foreign intelligence services or non-state actors;
- Environmental and health threats.

The strategy itself—termed "a strategy of engagement" by the administration—in many respects appears to be equally expansive. In addition to making U.S. citizens secure at home and bolstering economic prosperity, the strategy seeks to reshape the world as envisioned by cooperative security advocates by promoting democracy, free markets, respect for human rights, and the rule of law around the world. It aims to achieve these objectives through military, diplomatic, and economic engagement and leadership in world affairs. While acknowledging the necessity of

---

18. Posen and Ross point out that the Clinton administration's emphasis on U.S. leadership and the need to act alone in some cases suggest that U.S. strategy has strains of primacy as well.

19. The White House, "A National Security Strategy for a New Century," Washington, D.C., January 2000.

acting alone in some circumstances, the statement, consistent with a co-operative security vision, emphasizes the importance of international co-operation—working through international organizations and alliances or building ad-hoc coalitions.

Following the lead of the 1997 Quadrennial Defense Review, the January 2000 statement organizes the administration's strategy for enhancing security into three components: *shaping* the international environment, *responding* to threats and crises, and *preparing* for an uncertain future. "Shaping the international environment" includes a wide array of diplomatic and economic efforts in addition to military activities such as maintaining forward presence and mobility, conducting training and exercises with allies and friends, pursuing military-to-military contacts and retaining strategic nuclear forces for deterrence. "Responding to threats and crises" calls for diplomatic and economic measures, law enforcement, and intelligence and counterintelligence activities as well as military operations to deter or defeat the broad list of possible threats to U.S. interests. "Preparing for an uncertain future" calls for preparing diplomatic, intelligence, law enforcement, economic, and defense capabilities and institutions to anticipate and handle new opportunities and threats.

Throughout the strategy document, the rhetoric of "shape, respond, prepare" echoes the cooperative security vision, but on close inspection, the document reveals a deference to limits and priorities that place the strategy quite squarely in the camp of selective engagement, especially where the military is concerned. First, the statement acknowledges that resource constraints and the level of popular support place limits on engagement abroad: "American engagement must be tempered by recognition that there are limits to America's involvement in the world. . . . Our engagement therefore must be selective, focusing on the threats and opportunities most relevant to our interests and applying our resources where we can make the greatest difference. Additionally, sustaining our engagement abroad over the long term will require the support of the American people and the Congress to bear the costs of defending U.S. interests."[20]

Reflecting those limits, the statement's discussion of U.S. security interests and the role of the military are much more restrained and prioritized than its treatment of the threat or the overarching strategy, strongly suggesting that a strategy of selective engagement is at work. The document draws distinctions among three categories of interests: "vital" interests, including the survival of the United States or its allies, critical economic interests, and nuclear threats (reflective of selective engagement);

20. Ibid., p. 7.

"important" interests—those that do not affect national survival but may affect national well-being; and humanitarian interests. Where the military is concerned, vital interests are key, and responding to threats and crises takes priority over shaping the international environment: "Although military activities are an important pillar of our effort to shape the global security environment, we must always be mindful that the primary mission of our Armed Forces is to deter and, if necessary, to fight and win conflicts in which our vital interests are threatened." Military forces should be used decisively whenever vital interests are at stake. When the interests are important but not vital, the military should be called on only under certain circumstances. The document acknowledges that the military is generally not the best tool for humanitarian concerns, although its use might be appropriate under some conditions. In short, while the Clinton administration's rhetoric about threats and overarching strategy sound like cooperative security, the limits it acknowledges and the priorities it sets, at least for military activities, are those of selective engagement.

THE TWO-MAJOR-THEATER-WAR STANDARD
The Clinton strategy sets a clear priority for the military of responding to threats and crises rather than shaping the international environment. It also sets up a hierarchy of responses. According to the January 2000 statement, military responses can take the form of deterrence, strikes at terrorist bases or sponsors, drug interdiction, and national missile defense. They also include fighting and winning major theater wars and conducting a range of so-called "smaller-scale contingencies," from humanitarian assistance and peace operations to enforcing embargoes and no-fly zones, evacuating U.S. citizens, and reinforcing allies. But the first priority of the military is to fight and win two nearly simultaneous major theater wars (MTWs): "Fighting and winning major theater wars is the ultimate test of our Armed Forces—a test at which they must always succeed. For the foreseeable future, the United States, preferably in concert with allies, must have the capability to deter and, if deterrence fails, defeat large-scale, cross-border aggression in two distant theaters in overlapping time frames." Furthermore, "U.S. forces must also remain prepared to withdraw from [smaller-scale] contingency operations if needed to deploy to a major theater war."[21]

In short, despite the expansive rhetoric about global threats and opportunities, Clinton's declaratory strategy is clear in its priorities. Vital in-

21. Ibid., p. 25.

terests come first: the physical security of U.S. and allied territory, the safety and economic well-being of U.S. citizens, and the protection of critical infrastructures from paralyzing attack. For the military, the primary mission is to deter and, if necessary, fight and win conflicts in which vital interests are threatened. Among these conflicts, fighting and winning two major theater wars at more or less the same time takes priority for the conventional forces.

One important lesson of Clinton's declaratory strategy is that the ability to fight and win two major theater wars—which emerged during the Bush administration as a rationale for reducing the military budget by 25 percent and no more, and was later developed into a yardstick for sizing conventional forces—has been elevated to become the first priority of national security strategy for the armed forces.[22] The two-war standard, still perceived by most observers as a force-sizing tool rather than an element of strategy, is in fact much more than that, for the uniformed military as well as the administration: it is the first priority of declared U.S. military policy.

CURRENT STRATEGY IN PRACTICE

Declaratory policy and policy in practice are not, however, always the same thing. In fact, the Clinton administration has engaged the military in a round of smaller-scale contingencies, some of which may last for decades. U.S. forces continue daily patrols of the no-fly zones established after the Gulf War over northern and southern Iraq; twice during the Clinton years the military action in that region escalated to the level of a small air war. The United States also pursued two contingencies in the Balkans: a combined forces operation in Bosnia and an air war over Yugoslavia. Both Balkan operations ended with a standing commitment of U.S. military forces to support peacekeeping and nation-building operations that amount to virtual protectorates. In addition, U.S. forces have been called upon to restore democracy in Haiti, to conduct missile strikes on Afghanistan and Sudan, to assist in military operations in East Timor, and to provide humanitarian assistance elsewhere around the globe. Forces are also committed day-to-day to numerous "shaping" missions; the U.S. military maintains 100,000 troops in Europe and another 100,000 in Asia, sustains three aircraft carrier battle groups overseas, supports

---

22.   For a discussion of the emergence of the two-theater war principle and its relationship to resource planning in the Bush administration, see Lorna S. Jaffe, *The Development of the Base Force 1989–1992*, Joint History Office, Office of the Chairman of the Joint Chiefs of Staff, July 1993.

military-to-military contacts, exercises diplomacy, and conducts training exercises around the globe.

In practice, the smaller-scale contingencies and commitments to day-to-day presence take precedence over preparations for major theater war, if only by virtue of having first claim on the resources. Having been sized initially to handle nearly simultaneous wars against a remilitarized Iraq and the North Korea of a decade ago, current conventional forces seem to be more than adequate to handle either two major theater wars (as U.S. military leaders currently define them) or one major theater war and multiple smaller-scale contingencies at nearly the same time. But the military complains that it does not have enough forces to handle two major theater wars and multiple smaller contingencies at the same time. Some officers argue that the day-to-day pace of commitments taxes morale and readiness.

The Army indicates that the smaller operations sap the service's readiness for major theater warfare.[23] Air Force leaders stated during the air war against Yugoslavia that if two major theater wars unfolded, the Air Force would not be able to handle them. If two major wars over vital interests had unfolded in rapid succession during the Kosovo operation, it seems highly unlikely that the United States could or would have withdrawn its forces from Bosnia, halted operations in Yugoslavia, and (assuming one of the major wars was not with Iraq) removed its forces from the Persian Gulf in time to fight in the second major war. Thus it seems that the Clinton administration's strategy in practice—the one that actually guided its actions—assigned higher priority to smaller-scale contingencies than to the second major theater war.

Senior military leaders acknowledge privately that actual priorities differ from the ones declared in the strategy statements; they handle the contradiction by accepting what they call a higher level of risk for the second major theater war. Their understanding of actual priorities would seem to place one major theater war in first position and multiple smaller-scale contingencies in second position, with the second major theater war relegated to third place.

Some observers, including many in the military, are not happy with these de-facto priorities. They believe that the military's foremost tasks should be to deter hostile activity toward the United States through great visible strength, and to prepare for major wars. They are concerned that participation in peacekeeping operations, humanitarian activities, and

---

23.   Congressional Budget Office, *Making Peace While Staying Ready for War: The Challenges of U.S. Military Participation Peace Operations*, December 1999.

other smaller-scale contingencies steals resources from more important tasks and also raises a risk of bloodshed that is disproportionate to the potential gains.

The authors of this book hold a variety of views on the benefits of the smaller-scale contingencies the Clinton administration pursued, but all of the authors believe that such contingencies are here to stay. They also believe that conducting them requires forces that are configured and equipped differently from today's, and reduces the conventional forces available for major theater wars. One way to ease the readiness problems that the military perceives is to align declaratory policy with these realities, readjusting priorities to emphasize a single major theater war and the multiple smaller-scale contingencies and commitments that reflect the real world of today and tomorrow. Such a policy would offer an added benefit in lower force requirements, making it possible to hold defense budgets in check over the coming decade.

RECALIBRATING THE YARDSTICK FOR THE REAL WORLD

Another inconsistency in current military policy is the mismatch between the forces the Defense Department says it needs to fight and win in two nearly simultaneous MTWs and the strength of any real potential enemy. As Korb discusses in Chapter 2, the concept of retaining forces for two MTWs (also known as major regional contingencies or MRCs) originated in the Base Force that Chairman of the Joint Chiefs of Staff General Colin Powell unveiled to Congress in January 1991. Powell began with an assessment of the resources that might be available to the U.S. military after the Soviet Union collapsed. From there he determined the force structure that might be affordable, and then developed a strategic rationale— fighting in major regional wars of a specified type and size—that would match the forces.

The Bottom-Up Review, conducted under Secretary of Defense Les Aspin in 1993, refined the concept, establishing basic "building blocks" for the U.S. forces that would be needed in each MTW. One MTW was sized to thwart and counter an attack by a remilitarized Iraq against Kuwait and Saudi Arabia, the other to halt and reverse an invasion by North Korea against the south. The building block for each MTW included four to five Army divisions, four to five Marine expeditionary brigades, ten Air Force fighter wings, one hundred heavy bombers, and four to five Navy aircraft carrier battle groups.

These building blocks largely survived the Quadrennial Defense Review of 1997 and persist today as the yardsticks for planning U.S. conventional forces, even though the current actual military strengths of North Korea and Iraq do not warrant them. Since the building blocks were developed, North Korea's economy has virtually collapsed, and widespread hunger has taken its toll. Estimates of the North's gross national product have dropped, from $21 billion in 1993 to $14 billion in 1998, and its defense spending fell from $5.3 billion to about $2 billion in the same period. In South Korea, by contrast, rising defense budgets totaled $13 billion by 1998.[24] Even though the North is believed to retain large standing forces and substantial levels of equipment, and to continue to train and exercise, the South has significant advantages: a better educated and more technically trained military; geography that favors the defender in many respects; prepared defenses; significant levels of advanced equipment; and access to U.S. intelligence and reconnaissance resources.[25] Moreover, political steps toward reconciliation between North and South during 2000 seem to be decreasing the likelihood of war on the Korean peninsula.

Although military analysts inside and outside the Defense Department believe that war on the Korean peninsula would be a brutal affair, resulting in large numbers of casualties on both sides, recent studies of the conventional military balance on the peninsula find that if North Korea attacked, U.S. assistance to the South would require only half the U.S. forces currently envisioned for the MTW building block.[26] Even the 1998 *Strategic Assessment* of the National Defense University finds that North Korea is not capable of reunifying the Korean peninsula using military means.[27]

Critics of these studies argue that they assume that North Korea will engage in World War II–style combat, massing armor along two or three routes and hammering at the South in an old-fashioned attempt to break through the defenses. These critics argue that large U.S. forces will be needed, because the North will capitalize on long-range artillery, tunnels, special forces, and chemical weapons to achieve surprise and perhaps

---

24.   International Institute for Strategic Studies (IISS), *The Military Balance 1995/96* (Oxford: Oxford University Press), pp. 183–184; IISS, *The Military Balance 1999/2000*, pp. 193. Figures are in current dollars.

25.   Nick Beldecos and Eric Heginbotham, "The Conventional Military Balance in Korea," *Breakthroughs*, Vol. 4, No. 1 (Spring 1995), pp. 1–8.

26.   Michael O'Hanlon, "Stopping a North Korean Invasion: Why Defending South Korea is Easier than the Pentagon Thinks," *International Security*, Vol. 22, No. 4 (Spring 1998), pp. 135–170; Stuart K. Masaki, "The Korean Question: Assessing the Military Balance," *Security Studies*, Vol. 4, No. 2 (Winter 1994/95), pp. 365–425. Masaki argues that even less than half of the current "building block" would be required.

27.   National Defense University, *1998 Strategic Assessment: Engaging Power for Peace*, March 1998, Chapter 3.

even sneak through the defenses. But the appropriate response to such tactics is not, as presently planned, to send massive U.S. reinforcements that would take weeks or months to arrive. Rather, it is to ensure that U.S. and South Korean ground forces are well equipped with counter-battery radars and long-range artillery; that air forces have sufficient lethal munitions, that air and ground forces are equipped and trained to work cooperatively; that South Korea has sufficient well-trained security troops behind the forward defenses; and that troops and key infrastructure are provided with chemical protection, decontamination equipment, and training. In short, we should ensure that U.S. and allied forces are configured, trained, and equipped for the real wars they face rather than according to a template devised to preserve specific levels of Cold War forces.

The mismatch between the MTW building block and the real threat in Iraq is also wide. The MTW building block is predicated on an Iraq re-armed to the levels it achieved before the Gulf War. In fact, however, Iraq has been held in check by international trade sanctions and constant enforcement of two no-fly zones as well as occasional concentrated strikes by aircraft and missiles. Although Iraq retains significant levels of ground units and equipment, its air force is virtually nonexistent. Furthermore, all of its units other than the Republican Guard are thought to be operating at only 50 percent combat effectiveness, while 50 percent of its equipment lacks spares.[28] It seems highly unlikely under the circumstances that Saddam Hussein would attempt an invasion of Kuwait or Saudi Arabia, but if he did, repulsing it would not require the Desert Storm–size MTW building block that the U.S. military currently envisions for that purpose.

The uniformed military and the Defense Department understand that the 1993 building blocks are significantly larger than they need to be to check the real threats they might face in the near term. In a marked departure from previous documents, the Defense Department's February 2000 annual report barely mentions Iraq and North Korea as the specific aggressors of concern. Instead, military briefings and department documents have begun to articulate a concept of "overmatch" to justify the situation: "U.S. forces must continue to overmatch the military power of regional states with interests hostile to the United States."[29]

The Pentagon argues that it needs this overmatch to ensure success in case the enemy turns out to be larger or the circumstances more difficult

---

28. IISS, *The Military Balance 1999–2000*, p. 134.

29. William S. Cohen, *Annual Report to the President and the Congress*, Department of Defense, February 2000, p. 7.

than expected: "This is particularly important in a constantly evolving and unpredictable security environment. The United States can never know with certainty when or where the next major theater war will occur, who the next adversary will be, how an enemy will fight, who will join in a coalition, or precisely what demands will be placed on U.S. forces."[30]

Many observers would agree with the Pentagon that the United States should have such an insurance policy for one war. Some are concerned about China's military potential and its intentions toward Taiwan. Some worry that the United States needs forces capable not just of defending its allies but of accomplishing the more difficult task of overthrowing a hostile regime in a region where no strong ally can be called upon to assist. Some hold that even though no specific powerful enemy can be named today, a superpower nevertheless needs a strong military that can deter and, if necessary, fight and win a big war against a potent adversary.

But the Pentagon goes so far as to argue that the United States needs two such insurance policies, to avoid "a situation in which an aggressor in one region might be tempted to take advantage when U.S. forces are heavily committed elsewhere."[31] This "double-overmatch" insurance is excessive, considering the size and shape of actual potential adversaries today and any realistic trends for the future. Moreover, maintaining two insurance policies is expensive. Dropping just one of the insurance policies—adjusting requirements to match, not to overmatch, the real-world situation for at least one major theater war—would allow the military to reduce forces significantly.

A Strategy for the New Century

In its January 2000 statement, the Clinton administration purported to outline a national security strategy for the new century, but the military priorities it embraced are anchored in the past rather than the future. Keeping two MTWs at the top of the list of military missions denies the burden that smaller-scale contingencies have posed for the armed forces during the past decade, ignores the likely course of the next decade, and codifies a troubling discrepancy between declaratory policy and the real job that the U.S. military is being asked to do. Continuing to size the two MTWs as though the United States has two potential enemies as power-

---

30.   Ibid.

31.   Ibid.

ful as a pre–Gulf War Iraq is just one example of looking to the past instead of the future, exacerbating the mismatch between policy and reality.

To remedy this, the second half of this book focuses on military strategies that reset priorities and yardsticks for the present and the future instead of the past. The strategies presented in Chapters 6 through 8 reject the extremes of neo-isolationism and of primacy. In all three chapters, the predominant grand strategy is one of selective engagement, although the three authors vary somewhat in their leanings toward cooperative security. All three hold that the United States has two overarching security interests: protecting the sovereignty and integrity of the United States, and preserving peace among the Eurasian industrial states with large military potential. National priorities for the military should reflect these interests, first and foremost. However, for reasons not necessarily related to fundamental security interests, all three believe that U.S. leaders will continue to call on the military to intervene in civil wars, to support humanitarian activities, and to conduct peacekeeping and other smaller-scale contingencies. Military priorities therefore must be set and the military shaped to reflect this reality as well.

How should the United States shape its military to reflect these priorities? One premise of the book is that the military has a role to play in some aspects of homeland defense, particularly in maintaining a strong nuclear deterrent and responding with retaliatory force (even, under some circumstances, engaging in preemptive strikes). But other aspects of homeland defense are more appropriately handled through economic measures, diplomatic channels, law enforcement and immigration agencies, and intelligence and counterintelligence activities. National missile defenses may not be the best answer to problems of homeland defense. The range of threats they are intended to counter are quite limited, and they may not be capable of overcoming the simplest enemy countermeasures.[32] Despite these arguments, we assume that the national missile defense program the nation has embarked upon is likely to continue, for better or for worse, so discussions in this book treat the costs of the program as a given.

This book focuses on conventional forces and strategy, and holds that the first priority of the military's conventional forces should be to fight and win the nation's wars. To bolster peace among the great powers, the United States should continue to engage abroad militarily in places

---

32. See, for example, Lisbeth Gronlund, David Wright, et al., *Countermeasures: A Technical Evaluation of the Operational Effectiveness of the Planned U.S. National Missile Defense System*, Union of Concerned Scientists and MIT Security Studies Program, April 2000.

where the consequences of war could be the most serious. But the military's current insurance policy—"overmatch" for two MTWs—is overly conservative and requires more conventional forces than the United States needs.

In Chapters 6 through 8, each author emphasizes the special strengths of one of America's uniformed services to explore how its unique qualities can produce creative and efficient answers to U.S. strategic problems—Owen Cote on the Navy, James Quinlivan on the Army, and Karl Mueller on the Air Force. The authors differ in their views of the operations the military will be asked to conduct, the constraints under which it will operate, and the threats and opportunities it will face. As a result, while the grand strategies they espouse and the overall military budgets they propose are not markedly different, the specific military strategies and priorities they envision for the conventional forces are varied.[33]

In Chapter 6, Owen Cote describes a maritime-centered strategy that assumes that major theater wars of the future will occur somewhere along the Mediterranean-Indo-Pacific littoral. In that region, the United States will not be able to count on access to a developed local base structure, and thus traditional methods of rapid power projection that assume such access will be less effective. The military should therefore emphasize forces that depend less on overseas bases for rapid deployment and operation. To position the military for the world he foresees and to capitalize on emerging technologies, Cote recommends a moderately downsized and longer-legged Air Force that focuses more on exploiting air superiority rather than gaining it; an Army with significantly reduced reserves and a somewhat smaller active-duty component, better equipped to deploy rapidly and in strength; and a Navy that retains roughly its current size, but which achieves considerably more forward presence and striking power by basing an additional carrier battle group overseas and by converting eight of its Trident ballistic missile submarines into platforms for conventional precision weapons.

In Chapter 7, James Quinlivan envisions a world in which ground forces are critical for reassuring allies and deterring adversaries, in which the United States may face the challenge of expelling an adversary from defended positions and overthrowing a regime, and in which the commitment of ground forces to peace-enforcement duties on an open-ended basis continues. He recommends a new organizational structure and new equipment for the Army that will improve its ability to deploy heavy

---

33. I am grateful to Lane Pierrot of the Congressional Budget Office for suggesting this framework.

forces quickly and also accommodate the strains of smaller-scale contingencies more efficiently. He recommends a smaller and reshaped Army reserve component to provide a rotation base for open-ended peacekeeping missions; a Navy with fewer aircraft carriers; a significantly downsized Marine Corps that emphasizes its own vision of future operations; and a smaller Air Force that emphasizes multipurpose tactical airplanes at the expense of late-arriving units and ones that will not be modernized under current plans.

In Chapter 8, Karl Mueller offers a strategy of flexible power projection that capitalizes on the versatility of modern air power in order to deal with a world in which the location and the nature of future conflicts are highly unpredictable. He assumes that deployment of forces into theaters of conflict, both large and small-scale, will generally be not only possible but necessary, and that being able to deploy rapidly and then sustain these forces will often be critical to defending U.S. interests. Mueller recommends a substantial downsizing of the Army, particularly the slowest-mobilizing heavy units in the National Guard, and a reduction in the number of Navy carrier battle groups (coupled with new operational practices to enable the reduced fleet to continue to provide a level of forward presence similar to today's), while largely maintaining the size of the Navy's submarine force and the Marine Corps. To compensate for the reduced size of land and sea forces, his proposal calls for a slightly smaller but substantially more capable Air Force, better equipped with munitions, command and control systems, systems to suppress enemy air defenses, strategic airlift, unmanned aerial vehicles, and space-based sensors.

Chapters 6 through 8 represent a major departure from past and present Defense Department practice: rather than dividing the budget pie to share out constant portions among the services and then determining what forces and equipment each branch can afford, the authors let the specific forces and equipment that suit their strategies dictate the distribution of money across the services. Taken together, these chapters demonstrate that there are at least three attractive military strategies—all rooted in a grand strategy of selective engagement—that would allow the Defense Department to hold the line on defense spending while innovating to achieve a strong, better equipped, more capable military, ready for today's challenges and tomorrow's wars.

Any of the alternatives in Chapters 6 through 8 seem superior to the mindless allocation of resources across the services. Every one of them supports a greater degree of innovation across the armed forces. Every one of them eliminates force structure that is not relevant to the world it envisions and that may not be useful in any future the military really faces. Every one of them shapes a new military that looks to the future instead of the past.

Chapter 9 concludes the book with a brief summary of the military's budget problems, a comparison of the strategic choices offered in Chapters 6 through 9, and recommendations for policymakers.

Chapter 2

U.S. Defense Spending After the Cold War: Fact and Fiction

Lawrence J. Korb

When the Cold War ended in 1989, many U.S. military leaders were concerned that the defense budget would be slashed dramatically. General Colin Powell, Chairman of the Joint Chiefs of Staff (JCS) from 1989–93, feared that there would be a stampede by members of Congress arguing that since there was not a threat, there would be no need for a large military, and since we did not need so many guns, we could start shifting money to such things as schools or housing or crime prevention.[1] Even strong supporters of the military like Republican Senator John Tower, one of the architects of the Reagan buildup of the early 1980s, seemed to be willing to allow that to happen. During his 1989 confirmation hearings before the Senate Armed Services Committee in his unsuccessful bid to become Secretary of Defense, Tower agreed that if the Soviet empire collapsed we could obviously reduce our allocation of resources to defense. Tower noted that, "if there were no Soviet threat we'd be spending enormously less than we spend now. We'd be maintaining the kind of Army we had in 1938 [which was] about half the size of what the Marine Corps is now (197,000)."[2]

This did not happen. Instead, in FY 1999, defense spending exceeded $290 billion, or approximately 90 percent of its Cold War average.[3] More importantly, the United States now spends more than three times as

1.   Colin Powell, *My American Journey* (New York: Random House, 1995), p. 451.

2.   Quoted in *Defense Monitor*, Vol. 27, No. 4 (1999), p. 5.

3.   U.S. Defense Budgetary Figures come from Department of Defense Office of the Undersecretary of Defense (Comptroller), *National Defense Budget Estimates for FY 2000*, March 1999, and are expressed in National Defense (050) Budget Authority.

much on defense as all of its adversaries or potential adversaries combined, and together with its allies, accounts for nearly 80 percent of all the world's military expenditures.[4]

Yet, despite the size of the defense budget in both absolute and relative terms, the nation's top military leaders complain about their unmet needs. In the fall of 1998, for example, the five members of the Joint Chiefs of Staff (JCS) went to see President Clinton and then, with his encouragement, marched up to Capitol Hill to paint a picture of doom and gloom about massive funding shortfalls in both the readiness and modernization areas of the defense budget. Only twice in the last fifty years have the JCS taken such drastic action *en masse:* in 1958 they went to the Congress to warn about the alleged bomber and missile gaps, and in 1979 the JCS warned the Hill about the hollow military. But on both previous occasions, the United States actually was spending much less than its peer rival, the Soviet Union.

The JCS's 1998 pleas to the President and the Congress resulted in substantial additions to the FY 1999 and FY 2000 defense budgets. But in the fall of 1999, when Congress considered reducing the increase in defense spending between FY 1999 and FY 2000 from $18 billion to "only" $16 billion, JCS Chairman General Henry Shelton said that this 1 percent reduction would be devastating to the armed forces. Pentagon spokesman Ken Bacon used even more ominous tones in objecting to the proposed $2 billion reduction in a $300 billion dollar budget. He said that a reduction of that "magnitude" would mean reducing military personnel by between 39,000 to 70,000 (about 5 percent), cutting 12 percent from the already stressed operations accounts (which are over $100 billion), and cutting deeply into procurement plans ($54 billion). Shelton and the service chiefs told the Senate Armed Services Committee in November 1999 that rather than a $2 billion reduction in FY 2000, they needed an increase of $9 billion.[5] This would have brought the FY 2000 budget to over $300 billion, or about 95 percent of the real Cold War average.

In some ways, the attitude of the uniformed military is not all that surprising. As President Harry Truman noted some fifty years ago, the military is rarely satisfied even with very large, generous budgets. But what is surprising is that the JCS position has found support in most

---

4.   Budgetary totals for nations other than the United States are derived from the International Institute for International Studies (IISS), *The Military Balance 1999/2000* (Oxford: Oxford University Press, 1999).

5.   Rowan Scarborough, "Joint Chiefs of Staff Tell Hill Cutting Budget Imperils Gain in Combat Readiness," *Washington Times,* October 27, 1999, p. A1; and "Military Chiefs: Cut Would Devastate," *United Press Wires,* October 27, 1999, pp. 14, 55.

parts of the political spectrum. In January 1999, Clinton added nearly $13 billion to his projected FY 2000 defense budget and $112 billion to his own five-year defense program, the largest spending initiative of his presidency. When the Republican-controlled Congress added another $5 billion to defense for FY 2000 by taking it from non-defense (social) discretionary spending, Clinton signed the bill. Indeed, he had threatened to veto the bill when the House Appropriations Committee refused to allow the troubled F-22 to move into production because of its high costs and lack of adequate testing.

This support for increased levels of defense spending is likely to continue into the next administration, regardless of who is elected. Vice President Al Gore has said that if elected he would increase defense spending by $80 billion over the next decade.[6] The Republican nominee, George W. Bush, the governor of Texas, accused Clinton of ruining the military by underfunding it. He proposed programs that would add about $20 billion a year to the defense budget.[7] Such an increase, if enacted, would bring defense spending back to its Cold War level of $320 billion. Of the four major candidates in the primaries in 2000, only former New Jersey Senator Bill Bradley opposed further increases in defense spending. However, Bradley, the candidate of the liberal left, did not argue for a reduction, saying only that present levels would suffice if the Department of Defense were led and managed effectively.

How does a nation without a peer competitor which spends over ninety percent of its Cold War average on defense, more than it spent in the 1970s at the height of the Cold War, apparently have funding problems that some go so far as to describe as a coming train wreck? Moreover, why does the political class blindly and overwhelmingly support raising the defense budget, even while the United States is spending more than all of its adversaries or potential adversaries combined? The vote in the House to increase defense spending by $18 billion in FY 2000 was 372–55, and in the Senate, 87–11, with very little floor debate and very few hearings on the size of the budget or the proposed increase.

The answers to these questions can be broken down into two components, treated in turn below. First, despite several attempts to reinvent itself to deal with the new world order or the post–Cold War environment, the Pentagon has not yet succeeded in remaking its force structure. As

---

6.   George Hager and Ceci Connolly, "Democratic Duel's Costly Promises," *Washington Post*, October 9, 1999, p. A1; and Richard W. Stevenson, "Candidates Offer a Variety of Ways to Spend the Surplus," *New York Times*, December 27, 1999, p. A1.

7.   Governor George W. Bush, "A Period of Consequences," speech at the Citadel, September 23, 1999.

Elliott Cohen has noted, the force of 1999 is structurally little different from the force of 1989. Not only do the troops drive the same tanks, fly the same fighter aircraft, and sail the same ships as a decade ago, they are organized and operated the same way.[8] Second, members of the executive and legislative branches and many members of the informed public have uncritically accepted ten misleading assumptions—outlined below—about defense spending.

Unsuccessful Adjustments

Since the end of the Cold War, the Pentagon has tried to "reinvent" itself on three occasions: the Base Force of 1990; the Bottom-Up Review of 1993; and the Quadrennial Defense Review of 1997. In addition, Congress has commissioned its own reviews: the National Defense Panel (NDP) in 1996 and The Commission on National Security in 1998. The NDP completed its work in December 1997, while the Commission is not due to complete its review until March 2001.

The first and most important review was called the Base Force. It was begun in late 1989 and unveiled to the Congress in January 1991. It was largely the work of JCS Chairman General Colin Powell and his Joint Staff.[9] As President Reagan's assistant for National Security Affairs before moving to the JCS, Powell knew that the Soviet Union was on its last legs well before he became the nation's senior military officer. He believed that when the Soviet threat collapsed, the rationale for a large standing U.S. military would be undercut. Powell feared there would be a stampede by members of Congress arguing that since there was no threat, there would be no need for a large military, and since we did not need so many guns, we could start shifting money to such things as schools or housing or crime prevention. Powell also knew that, without a Soviet threat, the U.S. military would have to be smaller. There would be very little support within the political system for a Cold War–size military in a post–Cold War world, particularly in a Congress controlled by Democrats who had opposed the Reagan defense buildup. Powell feared that the Pentagon's political enemies would come after it with a chain saw if there was not an overarching strategy to guide the reductions. He was also aware that abstract concepts like "maintaining stability, prevent-

---

8. Elliott Cohen, "Prepared for the Last (Cold) War," *Wall Street Journal*, November 12, 1999, p. A15.

9. For a description of the process of developing and the rationale for the base force, see Powell, *My American Journey*, pp. 444–458. See also *Responding to Changing Threats* (Washington, D.C.: Defense Budget Project, June 1991).

ing chaos in the international arena, or establishing a new world order" would not resonate politically as a justification for maintaining a significant military force in the post–Cold War period. Finally, Powell did not wish to see the U.S. military diverted into such non-military tasks as peacekeeping and nation-building. In his view, and that of his colleagues, the U.S. military exists to deter potential adversaries and to fight and win the nation's wars. Powell wished to lead the U.S. Army, not the Salvation Army.

Therefore, upon taking office and before the collapse of the Soviet Union in the fall of 1989, Powell began planning for what he called the post–Cold War "Base Force." Powell's action was a reversal of the normal procedure in the executive branch. Usually the secretary of defense and his staff or the national security advisor and his staff would develop the policy and strategy and leave it to the military to execute it. However, Powell's civilian bosses, Secretary of Defense Dick Cheney and National Security Advisor Brent Scowcroft, did not believe the collapse of the Soviet Union was imminent in 1989 or 1990. In fact, even after the fall of the Berlin Wall in late 1989, Cheney had recommended that the U.S. military budget be cut by only 10 percent over the 1990–95 period.

Powell's Base Force envisioned a military about 75 percent of the size and cost of the military that existed when he took office. According to the timetable Powell presented to his superiors, the Pentagon would reduce its force structure and budget by five percent each year in real terms between 1990 and 1995. By 1995, Powell's plan would have reduced the total force of uniformed military personnel from 3.3 million (2.1 million active and 1.2 million guard and reserve) to 2.6 million (1.6 million active and 0.9 million guard and reserve). The Base Force reductions in personnel would result in parallel cuts in the number of ground divisions, ships, and tactical air wings. The essentials of the U.S. military would remain the same only somewhat smaller; that is, the forces would be organized and operated in the same way.

The Base Force represented a change in the way the U.S. rationalized its force structure. In the post–Cold War world, with no Soviet military threat, the United States would shift from a threat-based force to a threat- and capability-based force. According to Powell, while the U.S. military might no longer have a specific airlift requirement to move millions of tons of supplies and equipment to Europe to deal with a massive Soviet and Warsaw Pact invasion, it still needed the capability to move large amounts of material to several places around the world. Similarly, while the United States might no longer face the Red Army in the Fulda Gap in Germany, the nation needed to be able to project power to other places around the globe.

Powell's Base Force needed to be capable of performing four basic missions: first, it needed to be able to fight across the Atlantic; second, it needed to be capable of fighting across the Pacific; third, it needed to have a contingency force in the United States that could be deployed rapidly to hot spots, as the United States did in Panama in 1989; and finally, it needed to possess a nuclear force of sufficient size to deter nuclear adversaries.

Powell dealt with the issue of a specific enemy by arguing that his Base Force military needed to be capable of waging war by itself, i.e., without allies, against what later became known as the rogue or outlaw states.[10] According to Powell, the threat from the Soviet Union had been replaced by something quite different—demons and dangers of a regional nature against whom the U.S. Armed Forces might have to go and fight.

"Rogue states" refers to hostile third world states with comparatively large military forces and robust weapons of mass destruction (WMD) capabilities. According to those who characterize them as rogues or outlaws, these states harbor aggressive intentions against their less powerful neighbors, oppose the spread of democracy, and are guilty of circumventing international norms against nuclear, biological, and chemical proliferation. The Chairman of the JCS identified six rogue states which, in his view, posed a military threat to U.S. interests: Iran, Iraq, Syria, Libya, Cuba, and North Korea. Powell argued that U.S. forces could not be sized to defeat just one of the rogues, because that might tempt another potential aggressor, or outlaw state, to take advantage of a situation when all U.S. forces were committed against one. For example, if all U.S. forces were committed to a war in the Persian Gulf against Iran or Iraq, North Korea might believe the United States could not respond with sufficient force in a timely manner if it attempted to cross the 38th parallel. Therefore, Powell complemented his "rogue" doctrine with the two-war concept, i.e., the U.S. military should be structured to handle two major regional conflicts (MRCs) simultaneously. Finally, the United States had to assume that its allies would not automatically come to its aid in the Persian Gulf or the Korean peninsula. Accordingly, Powell believed that the United States would need a force of eleven ground divisions, ten tactical air wings, and some six aircraft carriers: about 400,000 troops in each theater. In Powell's view, the rogue doctrine and the MRC concept without allied support justified a force that was about 75 percent of the size and structure of the military maintained during the Cold War.

---

10. See, for example, Michael Klare, *Rogue States and Nuclear Outlaws* (New York: Hill and Wang, 1995).

The Base Force reductions also resulted in some reductions in the area of conventional weapons modernization. The Pentagon terminated or reduced the production of some current-generation systems (AH-64 Apache attack helicopters, F-16 multipurpose fighter planes, SSN-21 Seawolf attack submarines, and the V-22 Osprey tilt-rotor transport planes). Military leaders felt that with the reductions in force structure, current stockpiles of most major equipment categories would be more than adequate. However, the Base Force gave high priority to the development and production of several next-generation systems: the Comanche scout and attack helicopter for the Army, the F-22 stealth air-to-air fighter for the Air Force, the F/A-18 E/F multi-purpose tactical aircraft for the Navy, the new CVN-72 aircraft carrier, and the DDG-51 destroyer.

This approach to modernization put the Pentagon into an arms race with itself and was bound to cause problems by the second half of the 1990s. With the collapse of the Soviet Union, there was no real need for next-generation systems like the F-22 or new attack submarines. Moreover, since these new systems would be so expensive, the Pentagon could not replace existing systems on a one-to-one or even one-to-two basis with a procurement budget 25 percent below the Cold War average.

The Base Force also gave high priority to maintaining the readiness of the remaining force structure at Cold War levels. Since it was clear that the conventional forces would not have to face a sophisticated peer competitor like the Soviet Union on very short notice, this was a needlessly expensive extravagance. It required spending an increasing amount of operation and maintenance funding (O&M) per capita all throughout the 1990s. By the end of the decade, O&M spending per active duty troop had risen by 40 percent in real terms.

Powell also had strong ideas about the circumstances under which U.S. military forces should be committed. He argued that the U.S. military should be sent into battle only when three conditions were met: first, U.S. political objectives were clear and measurable; second, the country was prepared to use overwhelming force quickly and decisively to advance that objective; and third, military forces would be withdrawn when that objective was accomplished, that is, the political leaders had to have an exit strategy. Powell and his military colleagues did not wish to see the U.S. military become involved in more Vietnams (1960–72) or Lebanons (1982–83) where the objectives were not clear and where the military had to fight, in Powell's words, with "one hand tied behind its back." This approach to the use of military force became known as the Powell Doctrine.

For three reasons, the Bush administration accepted, uncritically, the rationale of the Base Force as well as the force structure, modernization plans, and readiness criteria proposed by Powell. First, many members of Bush's national security team did not want even as much as a 25 percent reduction in defense spending. Secretary of Defense Cheney wanted to reduce the defense budget by only 10 percent over the 1990–95 period, and reprimanded Powell for publicly revealing the Base Force concept. Second, the Bush administration did not want to become involved in peacekeeping operations around the globe. It never sent forces to Bosnia and agreed only to what it thought was a limited involvement in Somalia. Third, Bush assumed he would have a second term in which he and his team could develop their own defense strategy. Bush's single term was dominated by the Persian Gulf War and its aftermath.

One of the severest critics of the Base Force approach was Les Aspin, Chairman of the House Armed Services Committee during the Bush administration. He criticized the Powell-Cheney-Bush review as being "top-down," resulting in forces by subtraction that responded to the Pentagon's organizational needs rather than to real threats to U.S. interests. Aspin argued that a real "bottom-up review" was needed if the United States were to get the peace dividend it earned by spending $10 trillion to bring about the collapse of the Soviet empire and the Soviet Union. He presented options that could save as much as $231 billion over the FY 1993–97 period.[11]

Candidate Bill Clinton endorsed the Aspin approach, and President Clinton, "the candidate for change," appointed Aspin to be Secretary of Defense in order to change the Pentagon by conducting a real Bottom-Up Review (BUR). Aspin and his deputy and eventual successor, William Perry, did indeed carry out the BUR, but despite their best efforts, it was a bottom-up review in name only. The Aspin-Perry review resulted in a military hardly changed from the Base Force. This was not surprising given the fact that Powell remained as JCS chairman and resisted any major changes, that Aspin did not have a full team of appointees in place during the review, and that the president did not want any battles with the military.

In the BUR, the two-war concept was sanctified and the services protected their vital interests. The Navy was allowed to keep the twelve carrier battle groups it had needed during the Cold War. The Air Force did

---

11.   Les Aspin, *An Approach to Sizing American Conventional Forces for the Post-Soviet Era: Four Illustrative Options*, February 25, 1992. See also Bill Clinton and Al Gore, *Putting People First* (New York: Times Books, 1992); Powell, *My American Journey*, pp. 579–580; and Lawrence Korb, "Our Overstuffed Armed Forces," *Foreign Affairs*, Vol. 74, No. 6 (November/December 1995), pp. 22–34.

give up some 200 tactical fighters, but gained an equal number of strategic bombers for tactical use. The active Army gave up two ground divisions, but the Army National Guard and Army reserve were maintained at Cold War levels, and the Marines actually added a division's worth of ground forces.

Maintaining Cold War levels of readiness was given a top priority. Relics of the Cold War like the SSN-21 Seawolf submarine, Trident II missiles, the F-22 fighter, and the Milstar satellite communications system survived the review, even though the Soviet threat that brought about their development had gone away. In addition, the Clinton administration resurrected the Marine Corps' $40 billion V-22 Osprey transport plane, which the Bush administration had canceled. There were some changes, but they were minor: military manpower was cut by another 8 percent, and projected levels of defense spending over the FY 1994–98 period were reduced by 9 percent on the assumption that reform of the acquisition system would save substantial funds.[12]

The Bottom-Up Review pleased neither conservatives nor liberals. Conservatives argued that the reduction that Clinton made in the Bush plan, which amounted to $127 billion, or 9 percent over the FY 1994–98 period, made it impossible to prepare effectively for two nearly simultaneous major theater wars. In addition, these defense hawks were unhappy with the fact that the military began to be diverted into "operations other than war," or small-scale contingencies, in places such as Haiti and Bosnia. Liberals, on the other hand, were unhappy that Clinton had made such a comparatively small reduction in Bush's program. Their unhappiness was compounded when Clinton himself added back some of the funds he had cut and then agreed to additions the Republican Congress made to his proposals. By the end of his first term, about $100 billion of the $127 billion in cuts were restored by Clinton, or by the Congress with Clinton's assent. Over the FY 1994–99 period Clinton actually spent more on defense than Bush had projected.[13]

In order to deal with this situation, Congress mandated that the Pentagon do another review, a Quadrennial Defense Review (QDR), and Congress also set up an independent panel, the National Defense Panel (NDP), to review the QDR. As might be expected, the QDR and the NDP came up with different conclusions. But neither dealt with the central issues bedeviling the defense budget.

---

12.   Les Aspin, *The Bottom-Up Review: Forces for a New Era*, September 1, 1993.

13.   Daniel Gouré and Jeffery M. Ranney, *Averting the Defense Train Wreck in the New Millennium* (Washington, D.C.: CSIS Press, 1999), p. 55.

First, the Pentagon's QDR, like the Base Force and the BUR, reaffirmed the two-war scenario, thus leaving in place the force structure, modernization strategy, and readiness emphasis of the two previous reviews. Perry's successor, William Cohen, was no more willing than Perry, Aspin, or Clinton to take on the vested interests in the Pentagon. The QDR postulated that the U.S. military needs to be able to "respond" to two Desert Storm–like regional conflicts at the same time. Second, the United States needed to continue to "shape" the international environment by continuing to maintain over 200,000 troops forward-deployed to Europe and Asia and by providing forces for small-scale contingencies like Bosnia and Haiti. Third, the United States should continue to maintain 7,000 strategic nuclear weapons until START II is ratified by the Russian Duma and then drop that number to 3,500. Finally, the United States should "prepare" for an uncertain future by continuing to modernize U.S. weapons.

The QDR did propose some marginal across-the-board reductions in personnel and weaponry. It set a goal of reducing active-duty manpower by 60,000 or 4 percent, civilian employees by 80,000 or 11 percent, and reserve personnel by 6 percent. The QDR also proposed reductions of about 25 percent in the planned buys of the F-22, the F/A-18 E/F, and the V-22 Osprey.[14] As of the end of 1999, many of these goals had not yet been achieved. For example, the reserves still had 25,000 more personnel than the QDR goal.

The NDP, which was unveiled in December 1997, did make some useful criticisms of the QDR. First, the panel pointed out that the two-war concept is not only obsolete but is primarily a device for justifying a "Cold War–lite" force structure. Second, the NDP argued that the Pentagon is still spending too much money on yesterday's weapons such as the M1A1 Abrams battle tanks and Nimitz-class carriers. Third, the NDP criticized the Pentagon for not making ground units more mobile, and for failing to exploit unmanned aerial vehicles and other reconnaissance and communications systems. Fourth, it recommended that DOD add $5–10 billion in annual funding to support new initiatives in intelligence, space, urban warfare, joint experimentation, and information operations in order to transform itself into a twenty-first-century force.

However, when the Joint Chiefs of Staff opposed the recommendations of the NDP, Secretary of Defense Cohen also refused to support

---

14. The analysis of the QDR and NDP is based upon Michel O'Hanlon, *How to Be A Cheap Hawk: The 1999 and 2000 Defense Budgets* (Washington, D.C.: Brookings Institution Press, 1998), pp. 4–20.

them. Instead, in the fall of 1998, Cohen supported the JCS request to the president for more funding. Although the Chiefs did not receive the full $150 billion they sought over the FY 2000–05 period, Clinton gave them $112 billion over that period, and Congress added an additional $8 billion in FY 2000 and FY 2001 alone.

Table 2.1 summarizes the results of the three policy reviews conducted by the Pentagon during the past decade: the Base Force, the BUR, and the QDR. It shows that since 1991, active duty manpower has been reduced by 770,000 or 36 percent and reserve manpower by 335,000 or 29 percent. What is more interesting and significant than the size of the overall reduction is that the reductions in Army, Navy, and Air Force active manpower are almost exactly the same: 36, 37 and 37 percent respectively. Moreover, the service shares of the budget remained the same throughout the decade (Army 25 percent, Navy 31 percent, and Air Force 25 percent).

The fact that the defense force of 2000 is essentially a shrunken version of the Reagan-era Cold War force, or that the budget shares of the three military departments remained unchanged, should not be surprising. The Pentagon is a very difficult organization to change radically and the JCS are very skillful bureaucratic infighters. Moreover, Powell was probably the most influential military officer since World War II giants like Eisenhower and MacArthur, while Clinton, because of his lack of foreign policy experience and his draft history, the least likely president to bring about real change in the Pentagon. Nonetheless, by the turn of the century the Pentagon and the nation were in the worst of all possible worlds. By any reasonable comparison or historical standard, the level of defense spending was quite high, and yet the Pentagon budget was judged by the military, most politicians, and much of the public as woefully inadequate. Part of the reason for this state of affairs was that several misleading assumptions about defense spending had become accepted wisdom by the end of the decade.

Misleading Assumptions

These misleading assumptions about defense spending may be placed into four categories: assumptions about the overall size of the defense budget appropriate for the first decade of the twenty-first century, about the operations the military prepares for and participates in, about investment in equipment and military readiness, and about the spending and conditions needed to attract and retain the best people to serve in the military.

Table 2.1. U.S. Defense Policy Reviews.

	Actual Force, 1991	Base Force Recommendations, 1991	Bottom-Up Review, 1993	QDR, 1997*
Army				
Active Divisions	18	14	11	10
Reserve Brigades	57	42	42	30
Air Force Tactical Wings				
Active	22	15	13	12
Reserve	12	11	7	8
Navy				
Ships	528	450	346	306
Carriers	15	13	12	12
Marine Corps				
Active Divisions	3	2	3	3
Reserve Division	1	1	1	1
Total Uniformed Personnel				
Active	2,130,000	1,640,000	1,450,000	1,360,000
Reserve	1,170,000	920,000	900,000	835,000

NOTE: *This is the force structure that existed on July 1, 2000.

ASSUMPTIONS ABOUT THE OVERALL SIZE OF THE BUDGET

Misleading Assumption 1 is that defense spending is too low because defense consumes the smallest portion of the GDP and the smallest percentage of the overall federal budget since before Pearl Harbor. Indeed, this is an argument advanced by Governor George W. Bush in his September 23, 1999, speech at the Citadel, and it has also been put forward by Senator John McCain, former Army Chief of Staff General Gordon Sullivan, and Commandant of the Marine Corps General James Jones. While this is a true statement, it tells us more about the tremendous growth of the U.S. economy since World War II, as well as the rising cost of health care and the aging of our population. In 1940, U.S. GDP was $96.5 billion, or about $1.2 trillion in today's dollars. That compares with a 1999 GDP of more than $8.7 trillion. In effect, one percent of GDP today means eight times as much spending as in 1940.[15] Sixty years ago, spending 3 percent of

15.   Doug Bandow, "Scaling Down in a Safer World," *Washington Post,* March 22, 2000, p. A31.

GDP gave the United States a military force ranked sixteenth in the world (between Portugal and Romania), just one-tenth the size of Germany's and half the size of Japan's, and comprising only 1.6 percent of the world's military personnel.

The fact of the matter is that, in real terms, defense spending in the first Clinton term amounted to 88 percent of what this nation spent on average from the end of Vietnam through the end of the Cold War, and it is more than all of its adversaries or potential adversaries combined spend on defense. This is the real measure of what this nation should spend on defense, because Bill Clinton's military needs to deal with that of Saddam Hussein or Kim Jong Il, not that of Joseph Stalin or Adolf Hitler. Moreover, if one adds in the expenditures of U.S. allies, the spending equation favors the United States even more. Europe outspends Russia, Japan spends more than China, and South Korea outspends North Korea. The United States and all its allies account for 80 percent of the world's military expenditures. Moreover, if the Congress adds another $50 billion to the proposals of President Clinton over the FY 2000–05 period, as some in Congress have suggested, or if Governor Bush is elected and increases military spending by $20 billion a year, defense spending could be back at its Cold War average in real terms by the first part of the next century, even though the United States faces no peer competitor.[16]

Misleading Assumption 2 is that the defense budget has been reduced over the past decade because of the need to reduce the budget deficit, and now that the federal budget has a hefty surplus, defense spending should be increased.[17] It is true that the desire of Presidents Reagan, Bush, and Clinton and the majority in Congress to reduce the federal budget led them to take a hard look at defense spending. However, the fact of the matter is that the defense budget was reduced because the Cold War ended, the Soviet empire collapsed, and the Soviet Union disintegrated. Russian defense expenditures are about 80 percent less than those of the Soviet Union: Russia spends only a dollar for every five the Soviet Union spent. Moreover, during the last decade, the U.S. share of the world's military expenditure has risen by one-third. Today the United States spends twice as much on defense as all its potential enemies combined. The total defense expenditures of Colin Powell's rogue states in 1999 were $12 billion; compare that with about $300 billion for the United States.

---

16. For an estimate of the cost of a Bush defense program, see Michael O'Hanlon, "The Hole in the Bush Defense Plan," *Washington Post*, November 5, 1999, p. A33.

17. See, for example, the article by former Army Chief of Staff Gordon Sullivan, "Washington Tightwads are Creating a Hollow Military," *Wall Street Journal*, September 22, 1998, p. 22.

Misleading Assumption 3 is that defense spending should be increased because there is a $150 billion gap, claims the JCS, between defense plans and programs or between strategy and resources. Since the end of World War II, the JCS have always claimed that there was a gap. By historical standards, the $150 billion gap to which they now point is comparatively small. Even in the halcyon days of the Reagan buildup, the military leaders complained about a gap they estimated to be about $500 billion. Had we listened to the JCS during the Cold War, the United States would have spent several trillion dollars more than was, in the event, necessary, pouring large sums of money into all sorts of nonexistent gaps.

ASSUMPTIONS ABOUT MILITARY OPERATIONS

Misleading Assumption 4 is that the United States cannot be a great power unless it embraces a two-war planning scenario. Such a position defies both logic and history. When the United States was bogged down in Korea, Vietnam, or the Persian Gulf, no other nation took advantage of that fact by threatening U.S. vital interests elsewhere in the world. Even if the United States were temporarily unprepared to engage fully in a second regional conflict, the potential aggressor would have to be aware that the United States would eventually be able to bring awesome military power against it. Indeed, from the Nixon administration in 1969 through the end of the Cold War, the United States was a great power and prevailed against the Soviet empire even though it had only a one-and-one-half war strategy.

Misleading Assumption 5 is that sending our troops into peacekeeping operations like Bosnia has diverted large sums of money from core defense functions and has undermined our ability to conduct two major regional conflicts simultaneously. The fact is that peacekeeping operations have consumed less than two percent of the defense budget during the Clinton administration; only 10,000 U.S. troops are currently involved in these small-scale contingencies. Moreover, the threat from regional rogues has been wildly overestimated, and is rapidly declining. For example, as Clinton's first Secretary of Defense, Les Aspin, pointed out, in deciding how many troops the United States would need to prevail on the Korean peninsula, the Joint Chiefs of Staff assume implausibly that a North Korean fighting person is as effective as an American and 25 percent more effective than a South Korean.[18]

---

18.   Tom Philpot, "The New Bill Crowe Voices Doubts," *Naval Institute Proceedings,* October 1994, p. 90. Current U.S. intelligence estimates conclude that South Korea is capable of defeating North Korea by itself.

ASSUMPTIONS ABOUT INVESTMENT AND READINESS SPENDING

Misleading Assumption 6 is that the Pentagon needs more money because it is facing an investment shortfall. According to the Secretary of Defense and the Joint Chiefs, the Pentagon has needed $60 billion a year since 1995 to keep its forces modernized. It is true that during the past five years, the Pentagon has spent less than $50 billion on average and did not get to the $60 billion level until the FY 2001 budget. But this $60 billion figure has the U.S. military in an arms race with itself. For example, the $60 billion figure assumes that the Defense Department (DOD) must replace its current generation of tactical aircraft—the F-16, the F-15, the F-14, and F/A-18C/D—with newer, more sophisticated, and much more expensive F-22s, F/A-18E/Fs, and Joint Strike Fighters, even though the current aircraft are already the best in the world. Similarly, the Pentagon claims it needs a new generation of submarines even though the current generation, the SSN-688s, are the best in the world, have many years of useful life left, and face no threat from any next-generation Soviet submarine. The Pentagon assumes that the Army needs to continue upgrading its M1A1 tanks and buying a new heavy artillery system, the Crusader, even though its divisions are already too heavy to deploy quickly in wartime: an Army mechanized division is now 49 percent heavier than it was a decade ago.[19] Finally, this $60 billion benchmark ignores the fact that the current U.S. procurement budget is 40 percent more than those of all of our allies combined, 75 percent more than either Russia's or China's, and nine times greater than Iraq's and North Korea's together.

Misleading Assumption 7 is that the readiness of our armed forces is declining because we are not spending enough on operations and maintenance (O&M), the surrogate account for readiness. The fact of the matter is that in FY 2000, real O&M spending per capita is 40 percent higher than it was at the height of the Reagan build-up; it now exceeds $100 billion for an active duty force of 1.36 million. Moreover, the services are still using the same readiness criteria as they did during the Cold War to justify their case for additional expenditures in this area. For example, if the mission-capable rates of tactical aircraft have declined by five or even ten percentage points compared to 1985, as some have claimed, is that a problem? Not unless the North Korean military or the Iraqi military were at least 90 to 95 percent as capable as the Soviet military. If an Army tank unit drives only 500 miles a year, instead of the prescribed 800, how can

---

19. Congressional Budget Office, *Moving U.S. Forces: Options for Strategic Mobility* (Washington, D.C.: CBO, February 1997), p. 7.

that be a problem, if none of our potential adversaries is driving even 100? Moreover, it is not clear that raising O&M spending would actually increase readiness. In the first Reagan term, during the largest peacetime buildup in history, readiness rates for Army and Air Force units actually dropped between 1980 and 1984.

A further problem in this line of argument is that the O&M account pays not just for readiness, but also for military infrastructure and administration as well. In 1998, for example, infrastructure spending accounted for fully 60 percent of the O&M budget. This spending covers activities like the upkeep of military bases, managing payroll and financial accounts, cleaning up environmental problems, and paying for the health care of military families and retirees, functions quite unrelated to military readiness.[20] (See Chapter 3 for a discussion of the military's spending for infrastructure.) In short, judging military readiness based on levels of O&M spending makes no sense.

ASSUMPTIONS ABOUT MILITARY PEOPLE

Misleading Assumption 8 is that the services are failing to meet their recruiting goals even though they have lowered the quality standards they maintained in the 1980s. The fact of the matter is that today all the armed services have a higher percentage of high-quality accessions—high school graduates and people scoring average or above average on the armed forces qualification test (AFQT)—than at any time during the Reagan years. For comparison, in FY 1989, 60 percent of the Navy's recruits had a high school diploma, 58 percent scored in categories I through IIIA on the AFQT, and 11 percent were in category IV (below average). In FY 1999, by contrast, 95 percent of the Navy's enlistees had high school diplomas, 66 percent were in category I-IIIA, and no category IVs were accepted. The situation is similar in the other services. If the services used the same quality standards they used in building the force that performed so well in the Persian Gulf, or that supported the Reagan buildup, the military could meet its recruitment goals much more easily, even in this robust economy.

Misleading Assumption 9 is that the services are having retention problems because a much higher percentage of the force is deployed overseas than during the Cold War. Some have claimed that the military has deployed somewhere outside the United States once every nine

---

20. For a discussion of post–Cold War trends in O&M spending and the relationship between readiness and O&M, see Congressional Budget Office, *Paying for Military Readiness and Upkeep: Trends in Operation and Maintenance Spending* (Washington, D.C.: CBO, September 1997).

weeks in the last decade.[21] The fact of the matter is that in the 1980s over 500,000 people (or 25 percent) out of an active duty force of 2.1 million were deployed outside the United States. Today, however, that number is about 235,000, or about 17 percent of an active force of 1.36 million. A decade ago, only 58 percent of the active Army was in the United States. Today that figure is over 75 percent. Sailors today spend about the same amount of time at sea as they did a decade ago. The net effect of long or hostile duty on retention rates is actually positive for the Army and Marines, and statistically insignificant for the Navy and Air Force.[22]

Of the 235,000 people deployed outside the United States today, 200,000 of them are on regular deployments in Europe and Asia. That means that just 35,000 men and women, or 3 percent of the remaining active force not on routine planned deployments to Europe and Asia, are being sent to places like the Balkans and the Persian Gulf, or on other unplanned deployments. Moreover, when counting these operations the military makes no distinction between sending a handful of people to Southeast Asia for a few days to try to recover servicemen still unaccounted for from the Vietnam War, or to Africa to deliver some food, and deploying thousands of troops to the Balkans for several years. This is hardly a demanding requirement, and if, even so, it is causing problems for selected units, they should be solved by good management, not by spending more money. For example, units that go on unplanned deployments regularly, like Army Civil Affairs Brigades or Air Force Search and Rescue Units, should be in the active component rather than in the reserves.

Finally, the Pentagon has lightened the load on the active forces by using substantial numbers of troops from the reserve components to handle part of these unexpected deployments. For example, of the 150,000 people who have served in Bosnia since 1995, over 30,000 have been reservists and over 10,000 of the 56,000 who have deployed to Kosovo are reservists.

Misleading Assumption 10 is that there is a pay gap between the military and civilian sectors and that therefore pay and benefits for all military people must be increased substantially. This is what the Pentagon and Congress did in the FY 2000 and 2001 budgets when they raised base pay by about nine percent across the board and increased the percentage

---

21.   See, for example, Governor Bush's Citadel Speech.

22.   Office of the Undersecretary of Defense for Acquisition, Technology and Logistics, *Defense Science Board Task Force on Human Resources Strategy,* February 2000, p. 68.

of base pay a retiree would receive after 20 years from 40 to 50 percent. As evidence of the gap, proponents of a pay raise claim that the military suffers a 13 percent pay gap relative to the private sector and this has resulted in such problems as the deploying forces of the Navy being short 15,000 people, 12,000 military people being on food stamps, and a severe pilot shortage in the Navy and Air Force.

In reality there is no pay gap. The majority of the men and women in the armed services earn more money than 75 percent of their civilian counterparts. An entering recruit with a high school diploma makes $22,000 in basic pay, food, housing allowances, and tax benefits, while an officer earns $34,000. After 20 years, the total pay of an enlisted person exceeds $50,000, while that of high-ranking officers tops $100,000. In addition, throughout their careers military personnel are eligible for a wide variety of bonuses and a generous package of fringe benefits such as free health care and generous non-contributory retirement. Moreover, there is no evidence to support the contention that raising the retirement benefit to 50 percent after 20 years will have an impact on retention.[23]

The consequences of the pay gap are also overblown. The Navy is at or very near its authorized end strength; its problem is that the sailors are not in the correct place. Moreover, the fact that the Navy fell 6,892 short of its recruiting goals in FY 1998 should not be surprising. It actually recruited as many people in FY 1998 as it did in FY 1995 and FY 1996. The problem was that the Navy increased its numerical goal for FY 1998 by 15 percent over FY 1996 without making the corresponding increases in recruiters and advertising in a timely manner. For example, in FY 1998 the Navy had fewer recruiters than in FY 1996 and FY 1997, and the advertising budget for FY 1997 was below FY 1996 in current dollars. An adequate number of recruiters and a robust advertising budget should go a long way toward curing the shortfall, and indeed, with additional recruiters and more advertising, the Navy actually met its recruiting goal in FY 1999.

Similarly, while it is true that some 12,000 military people are technically eligible for food stamps, the majority of these (60 percent) are individuals in the lower ranks (E3-E5) who have large families and live on base. Because they live on base in rent-free quarters, they do not receive a housing allowance. If they lived off base or if the Agriculture Department counted the fair market value of their housing in its calculations of eligibility, most of these military people would not be eligible for food

23. Cindy Williams, "Our GI's Earn Enough," *Washington Post*, January 12, 2000, A19; and Congressional Budget Office, *The Effects of the Military Retirement Reform Act of 1986 on Mid-Career Retention*, February 1999.

stamps. Correcting for these distortions reduces the number to 750–1,000, or about 0.08 percent of the force.[24]

Finally, it is true that the Air Force and the Navy are short some 2,000 pilots, but this is the result of two factors. In the first part of the 1990s, the military reduced the number of pilots it trained below what is needed to sustain an appropriate level, as Air Force Chief of Staff General Michael Ryan conceded: "We made a terrible mistake six years ago when we reduced our pilot training to such a low level."[25] This accounts for 80 percent of the shortage.[26] Second, the remaining 20 percent of the short-fall is occurring because the civilian airlines are hiring in unprecedented numbers. There is no way that the military could match the compensation or lifestyle of a civilian pilot for Delta, American, or United Airlines, even by doubling its pilots' pay and never deploying them. Training more pilots until 2003, when airline hiring is projected to slow down, will be more effective than just throwing more money at the problem.

The military does indeed have personnel problems, but they result not from the amount the Pentagon spends on pay and benefits, but on how it spends its dollars. The Pentagon is going into the twenty-first century with a pay and personnel system more suited to the nineteenth. A one-size-fits-all pay system will no longer enable DOD to recruit and retain the people it needs. To compete in today's market, it must make three changes. First, it should reform its retirement system. DOD should allow earlier vesting than the current 20 years and should permit military men and women to control their retirement funds, as is the case with federal civil servants. This would not only be more advantageous to the service members, but would save the government money. For example, in FY 1999, the retirement accrual charge to DOD for its defined benefit plan (50 percent after 20 years service and 75 percent after 30) will be $9.7 billion. This is about 30 percent of FY 1999 outlays for base pay. If DOD switched to a defined contribution plan, even using very conservative rates of return, $4 billion a year would be more than sufficient to provide individuals who retire after at least 20 years of service with larger benefits than they receive under today's annuity system.[27] Moreover, this defined contribution plan could vest after five years and thus

24. Greg Jaffe, "Military Food Stamp Problem Seems Less than Feared," *Wall Street Journal*, March 17, 2000, p. A20.

25. *Armed Forces Journal International*, November 1998, p. 31.

26. Carl Conetta and Charles Knight, *The Readiness Crisis of the U.S. Air Force: A Review and Diagnosis* (Cambridge, Mass.: Project on Defense Alternatives, April 23, 1999), p. 12.

27. *Defense Science Board Task Force on Human Resources Strategy*, pp. F1–5.

would allow service personnel who leave before 20 years to receive something. This earlier vesting would no doubt help with first-term retention because military personnel, completing their first four-year commitment, would no longer face an additional 16-year commitment to receive an annuity.

Second, the military should privatize its housing system. At the present time, 200,000 units, or two-thirds of the military's existing family base housing, is inadequate. To renovate the existing or construct new housing would take 30 years and cost $20 billion. If DOD privatized the construction and maintenance of housing, it could cut the backlog in ten years at half the cost, and also deal with one of the main reasons for unhappiness among service families.[28] (See Chapter 3 for a proposal to rely more the private sector for military family housing.)

Third, dependents of military people should be placed in the federal employees' health benefits program (FEHBP). This would give better care and increase retention, and would also reduce the cost of health care by about $5 billion a year by allowing excess military hospitals to be closed.[29] (Chapter 3 outlines such a proposal as one possible way to reduce military infrastructure.)

Conclusion

An FY 2000 budget of about $300 billion should be more than adequate to safeguard U.S. interests in the world. However, the money must be spent more wisely. As former Army Chief of Staff General Edward Meyer noted in late 1999, "Every year we are probably wasting money [because today's spending] isn't going to the force we necessarily will need in the future."[30] Even if the current budgetary surplus does allow the defense budget to increase somewhat, the increase will not be enough to close the gap between the current defense program and likely budget totals. Moreover, throwing more money at the Pentagon would legitimize the failure of its leaders to come to grips with the post–Cold War world. The remainder of this book offers suggestions about choices to spend this money more effectively and efficiently.

28. Congressional Budget Office, *Budget Options for National Defense*, March 2000, pp. 78–86; and *Defense Science Board Task Force on Human Resources Strategy*, pp. 65–66.

29. Congressional Budget Office, *Budget Options for National Defense*, pp. 66–75; and *Defense Science Board Task Force on Human Resources Strategy*, pp. 66–68.

30. Thomas Ricks, "Military Must Change for 21st Century—The Question is How," *Wall Street Journal*, November 12, 1999, p. A1.

Chapter 3

Holding the Line on Infrastructure Spending

Cindy Williams

Every year, the Defense Department spends more than two-fifths of its budget on infrastructure activities that support the combat forces but are not closely related to them, such as recruiting soldiers, disbursing pay, providing medical care to families, operating military bases, conducting basic research, and testing and maintaining equipment. For more than a decade, analysts and advisory groups have offered proposals for cutting the cost of these activities to free up money for investment and other military priorities.

Infrastructure activities seem like prime candidates for reform. For one thing, the military's infrastructure did not shrink as rapidly as force structure during the drawdown of the 1990s. While the number of active-duty Army battalions, Navy ships, and Air Force squadrons fell by about 30 percent, the number of military installations in the United States declined by just 20 percent and floor space in military facilities by only 22 percent. While the number of troops on active duty declined by one-third, the number of people employed in infrastructure activities fell by 28 percent and the number employed in headquarters by just 18 percent. Although the military's projections of wartime casualties declined dramatically, the number of military medical personnel decreased by just 13 percent.

Even in areas that were cut back substantially, the Defense Department retains significant excess capacity. For example, although one-half of the major maintenance depots owned and operated by the government in 1988 no longer function as government entities, the ones that do remain have about 50 percent excess capacity.[1] Similarly, the Defense Department retains about 35 percent excess capacity in research and development laboratories and 50 percent excess in test and evaluation centers, even after numerous closures and consolidations in these areas.[2] Thus infrastructure looks to many people like fat waiting to be cut.

Moreover, proponents of infrastructure reform point to recent vast productivity gains in private-sector businesses and argue that by adopting the types of reforms that paid off for private industry—reducing excess capacity, consolidating duplicative activities, eliminating functions that are no longer needed, outsourcing activities that do not constitute core competencies, and reengineering to streamline business processes and take advantage of new technologies—the Defense Department could improve support to the warfighter and cut costs.

Cutting fat and improving efficiency sound great in theory. But in practice, whole categories of reforms that might yield big savings engender strong resistance from powerful constituencies. Some changes are blocked by law or regulation. During the 1990s, the Pentagon embraced some reform proposals whole-heartedly. It rejected many of the more politically difficult ones. Unfortunately, even the relatively limited reforms that the Pentagon did embrace ran into resistance and got off to a slow start. It seems unlikely that the savings the department hoped to achieve will match its projections. Infrastructure reform will not be the miracle cure for the Pentagon's budget woes.

Yet it makes no sense that a military that reduced so much of its force structure should continue to be saddled with a support structure that no longer fits. It seems premature to give up on infrastructure reform without further considering some of the proposals the Pentagon passed up when it adopted its more limited but politically more expedient reforms. The political barriers to implementing these ideas are steep, but savings could be substantial.

In this chapter, I explore several proposed approaches to assess their potential for savings and the obstacles that stand in the way of implementing them. I offer some examples of the Pentagon's failure to take up difficult approaches and then review the relatively limited prospects for

---

1. Congressional Budget Office, *Budget Options for National Defense*, March 2000, p. 99; David R. Warren, *Defense Outsourcing: Challenges Facing DoD as It Attempts to Save Billions in Infrastructure Costs* (Washington, D.C.: General Accounting Office, GAO/T-NSIAD-97-110, March 12, 1997), p. 3.

2. General Accounting Office, *Best Practices: Elements Critical to Successfully Reducing Unneeded RDT&E Infrastructure* (Washington, D.C.: General Accounting Office, GAO/NSIAD/RCED-98-23, January 8, 1998).

success of the measures that the Pentagon has adopted. I conclude by identifying some promising avenues that the Pentagon has neglected, calculating their potential savings, and identifying some of the political reasons why they will continue to meet resistance.

If the department continues on its current path, it is unlikely to reap more than a few billion dollars in annual savings from infrastructure reform. Widening the reform agenda to include the proposals suggested here might increase the level of savings to $16 billion a year, freeing up more than half of the extra $30 billion that the chiefs of the military services argue they need to make ends meet. It still, however, will not be nearly enough to solve the budget problems that the Pentagon faces over the long term.

Approaches to Infrastructure Reform

Experts have offered a variety of approaches to streamline infrastructure and support the military more efficiently. Some proposals would reduce support functions or eliminate them entirely. Others would reduce excess capacity or consolidate work, either within a single service or among services or agencies. Still others would have the military turn to the private sector for functions currently handled by the government, or reengineer the way the work is done, introducing modern business practices and tools to do it more efficiently. The various approaches overlap significantly. For example, reducing capacity by closing Hanscom Air Force Base would also eliminate the base support activities—maintaining buildings, keeping up the lawn, running the library and fitness center— associated with the base.

All of the approaches offer potential for savings. But the approaches differ in the way they achieve savings, and also in the institutional barriers they face.

Eliminating functions outright—for example, closing the military's medical school, reducing headquarters, or getting rid of activities added to funding bills through pork-barrel politics—probably offer the most direct route to savings. But such elimination can raise resistance from the communities, contractors, and government workers who stand to lose jobs. And of course Congress may never outgrow its need for pork. Similarly, while realigning bases or closing maintenance depots that no longer bring in enough work costs the government money up front, reducing excess capacity offers great potential for direct savings and can help the department meet targets for personnel reductions. The economic effects of facility closures on surrounding communities have not been nearly as severe as forecast. [3] But communities, contractors, and government workers all typically fight to keep their bases open.

Consolidation and collocation offer the potential for substantial savings after a period of initial investment. Consolidating or collocating work can reduce overhead and improve efficiency. Consolidating under a single manager may offer the added benefit of breaking down institutional barriers to change, making it easier to eliminate excess capacity, resize the workforce, and eliminate unneeded activities. [4] But perhaps more than any other approach to infrastructure reform, the threat of consolidation—especially across service or command lines—can raise fierce opposition from the military leaders faced with downsizing their organizations and possibly losing control of critically important functions.

Turning to the private sector for goods and services currently provided by government workers offers significant benefits. Activities that could benefit from competition in the private sector range from routine upkeep such as painting buildings, to accounting services, to training courses or maintenance of military equipment. Another form of privatization is to substitute cash payments to military families for some of the in-kind goods and services that military members currently receive as part of their compensation package, allowing them to purchase services from the competitive private sector.

Outsourcing can boost productivity and free the military to focus on its core competency, fighting the nation's wars. Opening work to competition in the private sector can also save substantial sums. Studies by the Center for Naval Analyses indicate that public-private "competitions" have saved the government an average of 30 percent—20 percent when the government team won and 40 percent when a private contractor got the work.[5] Of course, using competitions to save 20 to 40 percent of current costs is not the most effective choice if the work being competed for is redundant or obsolete.

To safeguard the government's interests and protect federal workers, current laws and regulations limit the types and amount of such work

3.   Michael Dardia, Kevin F. McCarthy, Jesse Malkin, and Georges Vernez, *The Effects of Military Base Closures on Local Communities: A Short-Term Perspective* (Santa Monica, Calif.: RAND (MR-667-OSD), February 1996); James Kitfield, "Baseless Concerns," *National Journal*, April 12, 1997, pp. 703–705.

4.   Congressional Budget Office, *Easing the Burden: Restructuring and Consolidating Defense Support Activities*, July 1994; Congressional Budget Office, *Paying for Military Readiness and Upkeep: Trends in Operation and Maintenance Spending*, September 1997, p. 51.

5.   Alan J. Marcus, *Analysis of the Navy's Commercial Activities Program* (Alexandria, Va.: Center for Naval Analyses, July 1993).

that the government can turn over to the private sector. One law requires that at least 50 percent of depot-level maintenance work must be performed by federal employees. Others require the department to keep work that is "inherently governmental" in-house and to notify Congress before outsourcing most activities.[6] In addition, federal regulations require that for activities involving more than ten federal employees, the government team must be allowed to compete against private firms to determine who will do the work.

Opening an activity to competition means displacing or laying off federal civilians and reducing the size of the military team. Thus local communities can have powerful incentives to resist these competitions. Although most military families stand to benefit from substitution of cash for payments in kind, others would fare less well; as a result, such changes are generally opposed by military families and retirees and the military's uniformed leadership. But commanders are often pleased with the improved productivity and responsiveness that follow other public-private competitions. Thus competition and outsourcing—except for changing the structure of compensation to military members—typically face vastly less resistance from the uniformed military than consolidation across services.

Examples of reengineering include modernizing the military's system for business travel, using government credit cards for small purchases, reducing paperwork, and ordering goods for delivery "just in time." Reengineering has the potential to save money and will be necessary if the government is to realize the full potential of consolidation or outsourcing. When carried out in small chunks under the discretion of individual commanders, reengineering can be the path of least political resistance of any of the reform mechanisms.

Action and Advice in the 1990s

The 1990s opened with impressive measures to downsize and streamline military infrastructure. As the decade wore on, some voices outside the Pentagon continued to call for consolidating activities across services, closing operations outright, reducing the size of support organizations, and substituting cash payments for some of the in-kind benefits provided to military families. But inside the Pentagon, the vision for achieving infrastructure savings became increasingly limited: seek Congressional

---

6. Work is "inherently governmental" if it requires the exercise of discretion in applying government authority or the use of value judgments in making decisions for the government.

support for closing more bases; reduce the number of personnel at service and command headquarters and in organizations that report directly to the Secretary of Defense; pursue more public-private competitions; conduct limited internal consolidations; and eke out whatever savings are possible from adopting business practices that have become common outside government.

BASE CLOSURES AND AGENCY CONSOLIDATIONS OF THE EARLY 1990S

Some of the boldest infrastructure initiatives of the post–Cold War period were set in motion before the Berlin Wall fell. The BRAC process that ultimately led to the closure of about one hundred bases in the United States was instituted late in the Reagan administration. The Bush administration moved to consolidate several functions previously performed within the individual services: supply under the Defense Logistics Agency (DLA), contract administration under a new Defense Contract Management Command, payroll and financial reporting under a new Defense Finance and Accounting Service (DFAS), commissary systems under a Defense Commissary Agency (DeCA), and many computer operations under the Defense Information Systems Agency (DISA).[7]

Some observers argue that the consolidations of the early 1990s plucked the low-hanging fruit by combining mundane business operations that the uniformed services might be grateful to be rid of. Service leaders would be hard pressed to argue that their needs for payroll accounting, common supplies, or groceries were so special that a consolidated defense agency could not provide for them. Thus resistance from the uniformed military was kept to a minimum. Nevertheless, the consolidations and base realignments of the first half of the decade saved money, contributed to downsizing, and resulted in the only significant cross-service consolidations the military has achieved since the Cold War ended.

THE ROLES AND MISSIONS DEBATE OF THE EARLY 1990S

Several reform proposals emerged in the early 1990s as part of a wider debate about the proper roles and missions of the four services. Proponents of reform saw an opportunity to reorganize responsibilities, in part to reshape the military for the future, but also to save money by eliminat-

7.   Report of the President's Blue Ribbon Commission on Defense Management, July 1989; Dick Cheney, Annual Report to the President and the Congress, January 1991, pp. 28–35; General Accounting Office, Defense Reform Initiative: Organization, Status, and Challenges (Washington, D.C.: General Accounting Office, GAO/NSIAD-99–87, April 1999), p. 18.

ing outmoded missions and reducing overlap. Many of the initial suggestions were related to combat missions, such as reducing the inefficiencies associated with retaining "four separate air forces." But other ideas focused on restructuring and consolidating support activities.

In 1992, Senator Sam Nunn urged the services to explore a variety of options for consolidation and restructuring. On the support side, the services should consider combining maintenance workloads, closing depots with duplicative workloads, consolidating training, merging legal services, and consolidating the medical and chaplain corps.[8] But the Chairman of the Joint Chiefs of Staff responded that most of the Senator's suggestions would be undertaken very slowly if at all. For example, the services would not consolidate chaplaincy or legal services because, he said, combining them would be harmful to morale.[9]

The Senator's proposals thrust into areas that raised deeply held concerns for the uniformed military. Seeking evaluations from experts outside the Pentagon, Congress directed the department to establish an independent Commission on Roles and Missions and also asked the Congressional Budget Office (CBO) to examine opportunities for rebalancing among the services. The CBO offered a $4 billion savings plan to centralize leadership of the health care system, increase reliance on the private sector for family housing, consolidate acquisition functions and flight training, organize depot maintenance under central management, and streamline the intelligence community.[10]

The Commission on Roles and Missions, in contrast, shifted the debate away from the allocation of responsibilities among the services. Only a few of its suggestions were aimed at eliminating the duplication the commission was charged with addressing. Instead, its infrastructure recommendations focused on tapping into the private sector for commercial-type support.[11]

The commission estimated that subjecting most of the department's commercial activities to competition could reduce spending by $3 billion annually. The commission recognized that overturning the laws and reg-

---

8.   Sam Nunn, "The Defense Department Must Thoroughly Overhaul the Services' Roles and Missions," *Congressional Record*, Washington, D.C., July 2, 1992, pp. S9559–S9565.

9.   Chairman of the Joint Chiefs of Staff, *Report on the Roles, Missions, and Functions of the Armed Forces of the United States*, February 1993.

10.   Congressional Budget Office, *Easing the Burden: Restructuring and Consolidating Defense Support Activities* (Washington, D.C.: Congressional Budget Office, July 1994).

11.   Department of Defense, *Directions for Defense: Report of the Commission on Roles and Missions of the Armed Forces*, Arlington, Va., May 1995, chap. 3.

ulations that stood in the way of wholesale outsourcing would pose a challenge and that resistance related to displacing government civilians could make outsourcing difficult. But compared with a realignment of service roles and missions, outsourcing seemed a happy solution—one that might avoid the uniformed military's opposition to further cross service consolidation as well as the inter-service warfare that further attempts to consolidate might spawn. Thus the commission shifted and significantly narrowed the range of possible options it was charged with studying, steering clear of a whole class of institutional barriers in the process.

THE SHIFT TO OUTSOURCING

Shortly after the commission released its report, the Defense Department launched a privatization initiative and also asked the Defense Science Board (DSB), a group of civilian advisors to the Pentagon's acquisition chief, to examine opportunities for infrastructure savings. The DSB conducted two studies, both focused on the potential benefits of privatization and outsourcing. The first concluded that subjecting a broad range of commercial-type activities to private-sector competition would improve performance and cut costs by 30 to 40 percent, resulting in projected annual savings of $7 billion to $12 billion. The second argued that the military should look to the private sector for a much wider range of activities, retaining government workers only in jobs immediately connected to core competencies: warfighting, direct battlefield support, policymaking and decisionmaking, and oversight. In addition to business-type functions, the study recommended privatizing logistics and maintenance, test and evaluation facilities, commissaries, family housing, and health care. It also recommended closing more bases, adoption of private-sector accounting methods, and investments in technology to improve efficiency. The second study projected savings as high as $30 billion.[12]

The savings estimates in the second DSB study appear to be dramatically overstated. Nevertheless the two studies reinforced the depart-

---

12. Department of Defense, "Improving the Combat Edge Through Outsourcing," Washington, D.C., March 1996; Carl J. Dahlman and C. Robert Roll, "Trading Butter for Guns: Managing Infrastructure Reductions" in Zalmay M. Khalilzad and David A. Ochmanek, eds., *Strategic Appraisal 1997: Strategy and Defense Planning for the 21st Century*, RAND 1997, p. 286; Office of the Under Secretary of Defense for Acquisition and Technology, *Report of the Defense Science Board Task Force on Outsourcing and Privatization*, August 1996; and Under Secretary of Defense for Acquisition and Technology, *Report on the Defense Science Board 1996 Summer Study on Achieving an Innovative Support Structure for 21st Century Military Superiority: Higher Performance at Lower Costs*, November 1996.

ment's enthusiasm for outsourcing. Base closures and outsourcing became the largest sources of savings in the Pentagon's plans to improve the efficiency of infrastructure and support.

THE DEFENSE REFORM INITIATIVE

The Pentagon's plans for infrastructure improvements were codified in the Defense Reform Initiative (DRI) of 1997. The DRI groups its support initiatives into four categories: reengineering, consolidation, competition, and elimination.[13] But while these categories sound bold and comprehensive, some of the actual initiatives they represent bear only a passing resemblance to the broader reforms the terms would suggest.

For example, most of the consolidation that the DRI envisions would take place in the Office of the Secretary of Defense, the defense agencies, and the department's field activities—in other words, the organizations that the Secretary of Defense controls most directly—rather than within or among the uniformed services or combatant commands. None of the so-called consolidations would cut across services or commands. Thus consolidation, as interpreted by the DRI, would seem to create little bureaucratic resistance but also not much savings. The DRI does not include savings estimates for reengineering or consolidation, and the department does not plan to track savings from those measures.

In the area of competition, the report calls for opening some depot maintenance to competition, along with "commercial functions" such as civilian and retiree payroll operations, disposal of surplus property, management of leased property, and laboratory evaluation of drug tests. But it fails to take on two of the bolder recommendations of the expert panels: reducing the government's role in providing groceries, and providing health care to military families. Thus while its competitions would need to overcome resistance from local communities and government employees, they would not face the more orchestrated institutional challenges posed by military family and retiree organizations.

The DRI calculates that the department can eventually save $2.5 billion a year by opening about 150,000 government positions to competition. More recently, the department expanded this element to a concept it calls "strategic sourcing," which includes the possibility of eliminating government positions outright—rather than setting up public-private competitions—when consolidation, reengineering, or elimination of ob-

---

13. William S. Cohen, *Leading Change in a New Era*, Report of the Defense Reform Initiative, November 1997. Savings estimates appear on pp. 28, 30, and 40.

solete functions makes sense. The department now projects eventual savings of $3.5 billion a year from strategic sourcing.[14]

The DRI envisions eliminating excess infrastructure by closing additional bases, demolishing buildings, and privatizing utility systems. It also calls for internal consolidations within DFAS and DISA, "regionalization" of some support services (for example, combining base support services in regions that have multiple military installations), and some internal consolidation or restructuring of laboratories and test facilities within the services. In addition, the report calls for "privatizing family housing construction," though the intent of this initiative is largely to seek private-sector capital rather than to reduce the number of families living in government-provided housing.

The DRI projects that two additional rounds of base closures would save about $3 billion. It makes no estimate of savings from the other areas of elimination. By counting on base closures for the lion's share of estimated savings, it essentially shifts much of the burden of reform to others. If Congress agrees to more closures, an independent commission will shelter the department and the administration (as well as members of Congress) from responsibility for specific decisions on which bases to close. If not, the department can fault Congress for the excess infrastructure it continues to carry. Thus despite the fierce resistance that can be expected from local communities and others who might be affected, proposing more base closures seems to be nearly risk-free for the department from a political point of view.

Prospects for Savings

The Pentagon's current goals for infrastructure savings are modest. In addition to savings from the hundred bases already closed, the department now projects eventual annual savings of about $6.5 billion from strategic sourcing and two more rounds of base closures. It also continues to rely on out-year savings from reengineering, headquarters reductions, and other measures, though it does not announce or track specific estimates of savings from those reforms. Unfortunately, it is unlikely that the department's initiatives will save even these relatively modest amounts.

---

14.   William S. Cohen, *Annual Report to the President and the Congress,* February 2000, p. 140; Randall A. Yim, Remarks at the Installations Commanders' Conference, Washington, D.C., August 3, 1999 <www.defenselink.mil/dodreform/yim081999.html>, p. 12; Department of Defense, "FY 2001 Defense Budget," briefing by a "senior defense official," February 2001 <http://www.defenselink.mil/news/Feb2000>.

The Pentagon's plans for cutting the fat from infrastructure do not come close to setting the budget straight.

The DRI's reengineering initiatives may result in savings. The department indicates that purchase cards have already saved hundreds of millions of dollars a year and also bring in rebates from the commercial banks that issue the cards.[15] Similarly, electronic purchasing, paperless offices, and other reengineering measures are likely to save the government money. Since the department has decided not to target specific levels of saving or keep track of savings from specific reengineering efforts, however, the benefits will be difficult to estimate.

"Consolidation" encompasses the least ambitious of the department's DRI goals: reorganizing and reducing the workforce in the Office of the Secretary of Defense, the defense agencies and field activities, and other headquarters. By and large the department has met those goals, reducing staff levels as planned and on schedule. But those reductions may bring little in the way of savings. For example, many of the positions that the Office of the Secretary of Defense placed on the chopping block were vacant anyway, or held by military incumbents who rotated to other jobs.[16]

Strategic sourcing and opening work to competition may yield less savings than the Pentagon predicts. For one thing, competitive sourcing studies are taking longer to complete than planned.[17] Also, the competition studies cost money to conduct and implement, some of which the services have failed to include in their budgets.[18] Another problem is that the department's estimates of future savings are based on competing

---

15.   William S. Cohen, *Leading Change in a New Era,* Report of the Defense Reform Initiative, November 1997, p. 5; William S. Cohen, *Annual Report to the President and the Congress,* February 2000, p. 140.

16.   General Accounting Office, *Defense Headquarters: Status of Efforts to Reduce Headquarters Personnel* (Washington, D.C.: General Accounting Office, GAO/NSIAD-99-45, February 1999).

17.   General Accounting Office, *Quadrennial Defense Review: Status of Efforts to Implement Personnel Reductions in the Army Materiel Command* (Washington, D.C.: General Accounting Office, GAO/NSIAD-99-123, March 1999), pp. 6–7; Edward G. Keating, Frank Camm, and Christopher Hanks, *Sourcing Decisions for Air Force Support Services: Current and Historical Patterns,* RAND Project Air Force (DB-193-AF), 1997.

18.   Randall Yim, Deputy Under Secretary of Defense for Installations, Acquisition and Technology, "Remarks at the Installations Commanders' Conference, Washington, D.C.," August 3, 1999 <http://www.defenselink.mil/dodreform/yim081999.html>, p. 12; and General Accounting Office, *DOD Competitive Sourcing: Questions About Goals, Pace and Risks of Key Reform Initiative,* February 1999.

work in low-skill areas that require limited capital investment and un-
skilled labor, and can be described to bidders in simple work statements.
It is not clear that future competitions will be as straightforward or find
such a competitive marketplace on the outside. Finally, some government
teams may already be operating more efficiently because of the 1990s
downsizing than earlier estimates reflect, leaving less room for improvement.[19]

As for base closures, although some observers believe that Congress
will concede to closing more bases when Clinton is out of office, the evidence from congressional hearings is mixed.[20] Some in Congress are concerned that real estate, once given up, is difficult or impossible to regain;
they argue that the military needs to keep some excess base capacity as a
hedge against future needs. Moreover, three of the service chiefs of staff
have expressed reservations about cutting more bases.[21]

If the additional base closures that the department has asked for are
allowed, they may save less than the Pentagon anticipates. The department's projections of costs and savings assume that future base closings
will be similar in size and character to the 1993 and 1995 rounds. But the
Pentagon has never been able to track specific savings from those rounds,
because it is difficult to separate BRAC savings from other downsizing
measures. Moreover, it is possible that earlier rounds already picked the
"low hanging fruit."[22]

It is not clear how much money the DRI's other elimination initiatives might save. Demolishing unneeded buildings might save a significant amount. But the department failed initially to budget adequately for the up-front costs involved, and demolition efforts got off to a
slow start. Even the limited initiative to obtain outside financing for

---

19.   David R. Warren, *Defense Outsourcing: Challenges Facing DOD as It Attempts to
Save Billions in Infrastructure Costs*, General Accounting Office (GAO/T-
NSIAD-97–110), p. 8; General Accounting Office, *DOD Competitive Sourcing: Questions
About Goals, Pace, and Risks of Key Reform Initiative* (GAO/NSIAD-99–46), February
1999, p. 4.

20.   Many in Congress are still angry over President Clinton's decision to honor campaign promises he made in 1996 by keeping two Air Force maintenance depots open,
against the recommendations of the 1995 base closure commission. Although those
bases were later put up for closure, members of Congress viewed the President's 1996
action as undermining the BRAC process.

21.   "Joint Chiefs Cool to Renewed Base Closings; Cohen Pushes Plan," *National Journal's Congress Daily AM*, March 2, 2000.

22.   General Accounting Office, *Future Years Defense Program: How Savings From Reform Initiatives Affect DOD's 1999–2003 Program*, February 1999, pp. 5–6.

family housing is off to a slow start and may not result in savings in any case.[23]

Deeper Reforms Could Save More

Current plans to close more bases, open work to competition, reengineer processes, and streamline some organizations internally represent much needed reform and can save money. But they fall far short of the goal the department once had: to capture enough savings from infrastructure reform to pay for much of the planned increase in procurement spending. Without additional changes in infrastructure, spending for support will rise in the coming years, rather than falling as the department previously hoped. But if defense budgets are to be held in check, then every dollar added to infrastructure is a dollar taken away from readiness, force structure, or modernization. Rather than accept the department's budget problems as inevitable, perhaps it is time to revisit some of the approaches to reform that the Pentagon shied away from in recent years: eliminating or reducing activities; consolidating activities across service or command lines; and increasing the role of the private sector in providing goods and services to members of the military and their families.

ELIMINATING ACTIVITIES

The Defense Department plans to eliminate some unneeded functions through process reengineering and strategic sourcing. But it still conducts many activities that are only loosely related to its core mission and could be handled just as well in the private sector, by another government agency, or not at all. Many of these activities find their way into the budget as congressional pork: support for colleges and institutions linked loosely, if at all, to military needs; youth development programs targeted to specific communities; construction on bases fearful of future BRAC rounds; research on breast cancer and prostate disease. Others are vestiges of the past that may not be appropriate in a streamlined military.

For example, the department operates its own elementary school system for children of military families living on some of its bases in the United States: a leftover from the days of segregation, when some public schools did not serve the needs of the integrated military. The schools are of high quality but they cost the government more per pupil than typical public schools, and serve only a very small segment of the military popu-

---

23.   Barry W. Holman, *Defense Infrastructure: Challenges Facing DOD in Implementing Reform Initiatives*, (Washington, D.C.: General Accounting Office, March 18, 1998).

lation. Eliminating the schools would save the government more than $50 million a year.[24]

Another candidate for elimination is the military's medical school. Established in the mid-1970s, the Uniformed Services University of the Health Sciences trains medical students for the military and conducts medical research. Although its cost per student is higher than what the military pays to train medical personnel in the private sector, the military's medical community argues that the investment pays off in doctors who stay with the military longer and are better prepared for wartime. But the school may represent excessive overhead if the military's medical system is downsized to meet wartime needs. Closing the school would eventually save about $90 million a year.

Overcoming political barriers to elimination of activities will not be easy, especially when the interests of powerful members of Congress are concerned. Senator John McCain and others have tried shaming the sponsors by shining a light on pork-barrel activities in each year's appropriations, but with no noticeable reduction in the number or cost of such activities. In cases like the medical school or the children's schools, however, the action for change may come from inside the services as the rising costs of support erode budgets for force structure and modernization. Although the combined savings from these two eliminations sound small compared with the overall defense budget, they would easily offset the purchase of two Joint Strike Fighters for the Air Force each year, even given JSF cost overruns anticipated by independent analysts.

CONSOLIDATING ACROSS SERVICES OR COMMANDS

The department already enjoys benefits and savings from consolidations carried out early in the 1990s. For example, the Defense Finance and Accounting Service, formed in 1991, reported savings through consolidation alone of six percent by 1995, even though according to the General Accounting Office, consolidation of infrastructure within the agency did not begin in earnest until that year.[25] The Defense Department says DFAS has saved about a billion dollars since 1991 through consolidation and other

---

24.   Defense Department savings would be higher, but would be offset by increases in impact aid spending by the Department of Education. Congressional Budget Office, *Budget Options for National Defense*, March 2000, pp. 86–87.

25.   Congressional Budget Office, *Paying for Military Readiness and Upkeep: Trends in Operation and Maintenance Spending*, September 1997, p. 52; General Accounting Office, *Defense Infrastructure: Challenges Facing DOD in Implementing Reform Initiatives* (GAO/T-NSIAD-98–115), March 18, 1998, p. 14.

reforms.[26] Savings from combining the services' separate commissary systems under the Defense Commissary Agency are less clear, but that consolidation did result in significant non-monetary benefits, such as more uniform standards of quality across the services. Other consolidations have the potential to save significant sums while improving cooperation and joint thinking among the services.

For example, the General Accounting Office estimates that the Defense Department has about 35 percent excess capacity in research and development laboratories and 50 percent in test and evaluation centers. Annual spending in these facilities totals over $35 billion.[27] If reductions in overhead and duplicated activities could eliminate just six percent of the cost of these facilities, savings would exceed $2 billion a year. In some cases, such as laboratories and acquisition centers for command and control systems, consolidation might also improve the likelihood that military services and commands will be able to operate jointly in wartime.

Some analysts are concerned that Defense Department plans to reduce spending for research and development will shortchange the one area where the military needs to concentrate resources in the coming years. Streamlining the R&D infrastructure could help the department modernize and get more bang for the R&D buck, thereby reducing the impact of planned reductions on future innovation.

Excess capacity in the department's maintenance depots is as high as 50 percent.[28] Consolidating workloads in areas of overlap and closing several depots could eventually save about $300 million a year.[29]

Another area ripe for consolidation is individual training. The military currently spends about $20 billion a year for such training. Some of it, such as initial training for operating or maintaining common types of systems, electronics courses, and leadership courses, overlap across the services and also between the active and reserve components. Some ob-

26. William S. Cohen, *Annual Report to the President and the Congress*, February 2000, p. 143. According to the report, consolidation and reengineering have also increased productivity and improved standardization and customer service.

27. General Accounting Office, *Best Practices: Elements Critical to Successfully Reducing Unneeded RDT&E Infrastructure* (GAO/NSIAD/RCED-98-23), January 8, 1998.

28. David R. Warren, *Defense Outsourcing: Challenges Facing DoD as It Attempts to Save Billions in Infrastructure Costs* (General Accounting Office, GAO/T-NSIAD-97-110), March 12, 1997, p. 3.

29. Congressional Budget Office, *Budget Options for National Defense*, March 2000, p. 99.

servers argue that even basic training overlaps sufficiently that the services should consider consolidating it.

The services maintain large administrative agencies to conduct training in classrooms. Combining some of these agencies would reduce overlap and cut overhead. Moreover, combining schools or sending students to the closest school regardless of service or component (active or reserve) can save more than 20 percent of the costs associated with students' travel and time away from home, factors that together account for the lion's share of the expense of training.[30] Lowering the cost of training by just six percent through consolidation of overlapping functions across services and components would save the department $1.2 billion a year.

The four services also retain separate cadres of lawyers and clergy. Combining these separate corps under one service could reduce duplication and overhead. Estimates of the savings from such cross-service consolidation are not available to the author.

The uniformed services fiercely oppose most attempts at consolidation. One way to relax the opposition would be to set up an explicit trade-off between infrastructure consolidation and modernization: the service that saves money by consolidating across service lines gets to keep more of its modernization money than the service that does not.[31] If defense budgets were held constant for a period of years, the services might even adopt the trades implicitly, preferring consolidation of support activities rather than the larger cuts in force structure or procurement that they would otherwise face.

Local communities and businesses can also be strong opponents of consolidation. Base closure commissions dealt with that opposition through the impartial review of the military role of each base considered for closure. Because the closure lists developed under BRAC were to be accepted or rejected in toto, the process shielded the services, the Defense Department, the President, and Congress from responsibility for choosing specific installations for closure. A similar process, involving an independent commission of experts, could be set up for other consolidations: one for depot maintenance, another for the acquisition corps and the sci-

---

30.   John F. Schank, John D. Winkler, et al., *Consolidating Active and Reserve Component Training Infrastructure* (MR-1012-A), RAND, 1999; Congressional Budget Office, *Easing the Burden: Restructuring and Consolidating Defense Support Activities*, July 1994, pp. 67–79.

31.   Carl J. Dahlman and C. Robert Roll offer a more lucrative version of this exchange, based on a game-theoretic analysis, in "Trading Butter for Guns," Zalmay M. Khalilzad and David A. Ochmanek, eds., *Strategic Appraisal 1997: Strategy and Defense Planning for the 21st Century*, RAND, 1997, pp. 273–347.

ence and technology infrastructure, a third for individual training, and even one for specialty areas like legal services.[32] A fair and independent panel of experts could make choices based on considerations of military effectiveness and efficiency. Local communities as well as the military organizations affected might find decisions easier to accept if arrived at through a BRAC-type evaluation. Such a mechanism would at least protect Congress and the administration from the political pressures that make such choices nearly impossible today. With potential annual savings of about $3.6 billion—enough to pay for the Army's Comanche and Crusader programs combined even with expected cost overruns—finding ways to overcome the political hurdles seems worth the effort.

INCREASING THE ROLE OF THE PRIVATE SECTOR IN PROVIDING GOODS AND SERVICES TO MEMBERS

Changing the structure of benefits to families may seem like swimming upstream: the services are finding it difficult to recruit and hold the people they need in a booming economy and the leveling out of personnel requirements that followed the downsizing. As a result they are clamoring for expanding current benefits rather than altering the way benefits are provided. But providing goods and services in kind to military families is inherently inefficient. Substituting cash payments and getting the government out of these businesses could save substantial sums and provide most families with a better overall compensation package.

Lawmakers have set plans in motion to improve retiree pay and grant military raises for several years that exceed private-sector wage inflation. The extra wages are widely viewed as a catch-up measure to make up for a pay gap that many believe has eroded the competitiveness of military pay. But the increase in cash pay also affords the nation an opportunity to review the way it compensates its military, and even to regard a portion of the extra cash as a substitute for some of the benefits the government currently provides in-kind.

Changing the structure of compensation and services provided to military members and retirees can profoundly affect their perception of the way they are treated. Although many service members say they would prefer cash in their pockets rather than in-kind goods and services, others may feel that the in-kind benefits foster a sense of community that attracted them to the military. Even under reforms in which most members and retirees would be better off, some would fare less well

---

32. Congressional Budget Office, *Budget Options for National Defense*, March 2000, p. 99.

than they currently do, leading to concerns about equity across the population.

Although such changes are generally opposed by military leaders, they might look attractive compared to the cutbacks in force structure and modernization suggested in later chapters. An added benefit is that they would reduce the military's role in activities that the private sector performs very well, thus freeing the armed forces to focus on warfighting needs.

For example, the Defense Department currently owns and operates about 216,000 family housing units in the United States, serving as landlord to about one-third of active duty families. Housing on base is typically a good deal more valuable than the cash housing allowances the families forgo when they choose this in-kind compensation, and it costs about 35 percent more for the military to provide the housing than for families to rent comparable units in the private sector.[33] According to a recent RAND survey, most of the military families who choose to live on base do so because it is more economical for them. In general, surveyed families scoffed at the notion that on-base housing is inherently preferable because it comes with military neighbors or offers a better sense of community. They say that if the allowance were somewhat higher, they would choose the allowance instead and rent or buy housing off-base.[34]

The Defense Department has announced plans to increase housing allowances in the hope that most military families will choose to live off base, thus relieving the department of the burden of revitalizing and replacing much of its aging housing stock.[35] A proposal from the Congressional Budget Office would take the department's plan a step further by giving the allowance to all military families and requiring that they pay rent for units on base, thus setting up a competition between base housing and private-sector housing. The government would pay to revitalize units only if the rent that the market would bear allowed it to recover all costs of operation and construction. Adopting this proposal would save more than $600 million a year, dramatically reduce the military's role as a landlord, and improve housing and housing choice for all military families.[36]

---

33.   Ibid., pp. 79–80.

34.   Richard Buddin, Carole Roan Gresenz, et al., *An Evaluation of Housing Options for Military Families* (MR-1020-OSD), RAND, 1999.

35.   Department of Defense, "FY 2001 Defense Budget," briefing by a "senior defense official," February 2001 <http://www.defenselink.mil/news/Feb2000>.

36.   Congressional Budget Office, *Budget Options for National Defense*, March 2000, pp. 79–80.

Another idea is to change the way the nation provides medical care to military families and retirees. During the Cold War, the military built a large medical infrastructure, ostensibly sized to handle the military casualties expected in the event of war. To make use of that infrastructure during peacetime, the military provided health services to military families and retirees as an in-kind fringe benefit. Studies conducted by the Office of the Secretary of Defense in the early 1990s indicate that wartime needs have shrunk dramatically since the Cold War ended, yet the military retains far more hospitals and medical professionals than it needs to treat soldiers in wartime. Downsizing the system to handle the casualties anticipated under today's war plans would save billions of dollars a year.

Those savings would be offset by the costs of closing facilities and providing alternative health care coverage for military families and retirees. In one example examined by the Congressional Budget Office, the government would offer private sector insurance to active duty families and retirees under age 65 through the Federal Employees Health Benefits Program (FEHBP) that already insures federal civilians. Older retirees would continue to rely on Medicare, as they typically do today. [37]

If coverage is provided free of charge, it will attract people who are eligible but currently do not demand care from the department because they have other insurance options. This is especially true for younger retirees, many of whom currently opt out of the military system and instead share the cost of health insurance with their employers in a second career. One way to ameliorate this problem is for the government to share the cost of the insurance premium with the family. In the CBO's example, retirees under age 65 and active-duty families pay the same share of the premium as federal civilians, but active-duty families receive a voucher to compensate for their share.

The CBO calculates that reducing the military's medical infrastructure and changing the structure of health care coverage in this way would save the government more than $5 billion annually, after an initial period of investment. The plan would provide the nearly free medical care that active-duty families have come to expect as part of their compensation and might improve medical services for many families. It would provide a more uniform benefit and open a wider range of choices for active-duty families and younger retirees. For active-duty families, out-of-pocket health care costs would generally be limited to the co-payments charged under their chosen insurance plan for specific services (and could be held

---

37. Ibid., pp. 66–74.

to a minimum by choosing one of the more comprehensive plans). For younger retirees, the costs would be higher, since they would not receive vouchers to cover their premiums.

For older retirees, the Medicare improvements being contemplated for all of America's elderly might ameliorate concerns that the CBO plan would not improve their coverage. Alternatively, offering a mail order prescription service or similar benefit for retirees who are eligible for Medicare might sweeten the deal for them and would reduce government savings by about $500 million a year.

A third proposal is to drop the current subsidy to the military's commissaries as a trade-off for part of the raises above inflation that the military hopes to receive in the coming years. Currently Congress appropriates about $1 billion a year for these grocery stores. The appropriation covers about three-quarters of operating costs, allowing the commissaries to provide low-cost groceries to current and retired military personnel. Commissaries are a popular benefit with military families and retirees, and the Defense Department views low-cost groceries as part of its compensation package. But running grocery stores is far from a core competency of the military. Both the subsidy and the government operation foster economic inefficiencies, while highly competitive commercial stores operate in close proximity to nearly every U.S. base. Moreover, the Defense Department has reported that the subsidy will have to increase significantly in the coming years to refurbish and revitalize stores.

Dropping the subsidy would force commissaries to compete with private grocery stores on a more equal footing, leaving it for customers to decide whether they survive. The change would save the government a billion dollars a year (more as the costs of maintaining the commissary complex increase), but would reduce the in-kind grocery benefit for members and retirees. Increasing military pay at rates higher than inflation, as currently stipulated in law, will more than offset the loss for members in uniform, though not for retirees.[38]

The savings suggested in this category would exceed $6 billion a year, twice as much or more than the Navy will need for the three new DD-21 surface ships it plans to build every year beginning mid-decade. The ideas offered here could expand choices and improve compensation for most active-duty families and many retirees. But changes in this category face significant opposition from family and retiree groups, the mili-

---

38. Congressional Budget Office, *The Costs and Benefits of Retail Activities at Military Bases*, October 1997; Congressional Budget Office, *Budget Options for National Defense*, March 2000, pp. 83–84.

tary's uniformed leadership and medical community, and contractors who provide goods and services through the current system.

One problem with in-kind compensation is that many in the military do not view it as compensation at all. When asked how much they are paid, soldiers in military housing rarely include the value of the housing they live in or even the allowance they forgo to live on base. Another problem is that the perceived inadequacies of in-kind compensation—substandard housing, long waiting times for appointments at military clinics—become a constant source of irritation, even when members choose the in-kind pay explicitly because it benefits them financially. Changing the structure of compensation to look more like the structure of pay in the private sector could make troops feel better off, remove a constant source of complaints, and improve morale across the board. But the value of the changes will need to be made explicit (for example by increasing housing allowances, adding sweeteners for changes in retiree benefits, or linking additional pay raises above inflation to the reduction of the commissary subsidy), and they will still meet resistance.

A suggestion offered by the Congressional Budget Office might help to soften resistance from some quarters: realign appropriation categories so that all the costs of attracting and retaining military personnel—from basic pay to housing, health care, commissaries, educational benefits, and day care centers—appear in a single account. The change would force Congress and the department's uniformed and civilian leadership—if not individual members and retirees—to recognize the relative costs of choices, from cash compensation to in-kind benefits.[39]

Greater Savings Are Possible, But Still Not Enough

Savings from these examples in categories of reform that the Pentagon has virtually ignored could exceed $9.5 billion a year. Additional measures suggested by the Congressional Budget Office, the General Accounting Office, and others could bring further savings. Combined with the $6.5 billion that the Defense Department hopes to save through strategic sourcing and two more rounds of base closures, it is conceivable that within a few years the military could save $16 billion or more annually from infrastructure reform alone. But this estimate may double-count savings that the department already includes in its projections for base closures. Moreover, the department's estimates may overstate the level of savings that are actually achievable from its planned initiatives. Finally,

39. Ibid., pp. 77–78.

political stumbling blocks may make some of the additional measures too difficult.

Since the Cold War ended, the Defense Department has shed bases and depots, reduced its logistics and training infrastructure, combined some business functions across services, reduced medical infrastructure, and streamlined headquarters. But these reductions in infrastructure have generally not kept pace with cuts to force structure or troop levels. Nor has the U.S. military matched the large productivity gains reaped by the private sector by changing its approach to functions that are not directly related to core competencies.

The department hopes to improve its warfighting effectiveness and achieve further savings through a collection of infrastructure reforms. Current plans call for closing additional bases, outsourcing some business-type functions and eliminating others, consolidating some activities within organizations and reengineering business processes. But actual savings will take longer to achieve and will almost certainly be lower than the Pentagon projects. They will not be enough to compensate, as the Pentagon once hoped, for the expanding procurement programs the department envisions.

Greater infrastructure savings are possible, but only if the department revisits categories of reform that it shunned during the late 1990s to avoid internal and external opposition and wars between the services. Instituting these reforms will not be easy; rather it will require sustained leadership from the administration, active congressional support, and bipartisan commitment to change. BRAC-like mechanisms, the substitution of cash payments or alternative benefits, and the stark choice of other reductions may soften or counter resistance to some of the ideas. But like any change, the reforms will leave some individuals, communities, and interests worse off than they are today.

This book assumes that the next administration and Congress will work together with the uniformed military to bring about at least some of these reforms. It also assumes that the next administration and Congress are successful in establishing two additional rounds of base closures and that the department ultimately achieves a significant share of the savings it is counting on from strategic sourcing. If the department could save $3 billion a year from additional base closures, $3.5 billion from strategic sourcing (as it currently projects), and $9.5 billion from the deeper reforms suggested in this chapter, the eventual total infrastructure savings would exceed $16 billion a year. But recognizing the political barriers to further reform and the problems in reaching even the limited savings goals from the reforms the department has already embraced, the subsequent chapters in this book assume that eventual savings in the support area are not more than $10 billion a year.

Some in the Pentagon believe that the prospect of saving $10 billion from a budget that exceeds $300 billion is not worth the political effort it would take. That is probably true from the perspective of the services and the department, as long as the consequences can be passed on to the tax-payer in the form of higher defense budgets. But $10 billion amounts to more than three percent of the department's budget. It is enough to pay the Army's entire procurement bill for FY 2000. If the department finds it is expected to hold the line on defense budgets and has to choose be-tween giving up infrastructure and reducing its force structure and mod-ernization goals, then $10 billion in infrastructure savings might seem worth fighting for.

Chapter 4

Seeking Strength in Numbers: The European Allies and U.S. Defense Planning

Gordon Adams

For fifty years, political figures in the United States have urged the European NATO allies to contribute more fully to the common defenses of the alliance. Advocacy of greater "burden-sharing" has risen and fallen over those decades, but never disappeared from the transatlantic defense dialogue.

With the end of the Cold War, U.S. forces stationed in Europe fell by two-thirds, providing an inviting opportunity for its NATO allies to assume greater responsibility for European regional security. At the same time, however, European armed forces also shrank, as did European defense budgets. While the European Union (EU) made significant treaty commitments to harmonize defense and security policies (especially the Common Foreign and Security Policy [CFSP] decreed by the Maastricht Treaty of 1991), there was very little change in the downward trend in European defense capabilities and spending.

The major European allies moved to reverse course sharply at the end of the last decade. The decision by the British government to join in creating a common European security policy, combined with the European military capability shortfall exposed by the Kosovo air campaign, led the European Union to make a more concrete commitment to develop a common European Security and Defense Policy (ESDP) within the framework of the European Union.

The author wishes to thank the following people for useful comments on this chapter: the members of the MIT study group, Robert Bell, Michael Brown, Eugene Gholz, David Gompert, Steve Kosiak, Harvey Sapolsky, and Alan Platt.

For the first time since the NATO alliance was created, there is a real prospect that the distribution of the defense burden across the Atlantic might change, with greater responsibility being borne by the European NATO allies. This shift could open up opportunities for the United States to conserve its own defense resources through greater reliance on European military capabilities. This chapter explores the reality behind these changes.

Fundamentally, while there may be opportunities to shift some of the defense burden to the European allies, they are unlikely to bear significant near-term fruit. U.S. defense planners should not count on reaping a large burden-sharing harvest over the next decade as a result of the development of more common defense policies and capability in the European Union. Rather, the United States should do what it can to foster and support the emerging ESDP, recognizing that, with the best of intentions, the promise is more than a decade off and perhaps even further.

There are four principal reasons for the slow payoff for U.S. defense planning from the European Union's ESDP: strategic differences, political tensions, technological gaps, and economic competition.

First, major differences in strategic vision between Europe and the United States will limit the value of future European force planning for U.S. planning purposes. Europe's security vision is largely limited to Europe; the U.S. security responsibilities are more self-consciously global. European strategy, doctrine, and force planning are unlikely to place priority on missions outside the NATO area (and its Balkan fringe). European defense capabilities are unlikely to take on an expeditionary orientation. Nor will European doctrine focus on the high-intensity combat operations at the heart of U.S. force planning. While British and French force planning provide partial exceptions, neither country is likely to develop an expeditionary capability in the near term that would permit the United States to achieve savings by relying on their contributions. Moreover, British and French forces are unlikely to be used outside the NATO area in any other than a "coalition of the willing," making it difficult for U.S. defense planners to assume they will provide capabilities for more global operations that the United States could safely forgo.

Common European defense capabilities in the EU may provide a welcome opportunity for the United States to devote less planning time and fewer forces to the mission of ensuring stability in Europe. To the extent that the Europeans are prepared to take on the peacekeeping, peace enforcement, and regional stability missions that will be needed in less stable parts of Europe, the United States may be able to forgo some part of its own land forces dedicated to such missions. The difficult planning issue for the United States will be whether to remove that part of its land capability from its force structure as a result, or simply to redirect and reshape it for the high-intensity combat missions it anticipates in non-European theaters.

Second, critical political differences between U.S. and European defense planning may delay any near-term savings that could result from greater interoperability between U.S. and European forces. Those tensions, clear at the diplomatic level, are now being experienced at the level of force planning. The relationship between the emerging EU military capability and the military requirements of the NATO alliance poses one of the most difficult near-term diplomatic challenges across the Atlantic. It is increasingly clear that the ESDP project is a political requirement for the Europeans, as much as a military one. Some of the strongest supporters of the ESDP, notably the French, would prefer that EU defense capabilities be put in place in isolation from discussions in the NATO context. Meanwhile, NATO is intensely involved in its own effort—the Defense Capabilities Initiative (DCI)—to close the military gaps exposed by the Kosovo air campaign.

Keeping these two planning processes separate will exacerbate tensions between the EU and NATO; within each organization, it will limit the synergy and interoperability that could be created between the two efforts; and it is likely to lead to unnecessary duplication between the two forces. As a result, U.S. defense planners could be less than enthusiastic about relying on an emerging European capability, and large U.S. savings will not materialize.

Third, at best, the Europeans will only slowly close the technology gap with U.S. forces or shift to a more expeditionary capability, given the serious limitations on European defense budgets. There is every reason to think that the transatlantic technology gap could be closed. Increasingly, military capability depends on technologies that are both more commercial and more global in character, and, therefore, more readily available to all partners in the alliance. The gap between the two sides is more budgetary than technological. Given the limits on overall defense budget growth, the cost of shifting from conscript to professional militaries, and the low level of European investment in defense R&D, however, the biggest risk is that the Europeans will promise a capability they are unable to afford, hence to deliver. These resource limitations are unlikely to be overcome in the near term. Without redirected and, arguably, greater European defense spending, the Europeans could fall further behind the Americans, develop too few forces or advanced technologies and platforms, and lose the industrial and technological capacity required to keep the pace.

Even assuming adequate investment, the payoff from European military technological progress is likely to be very slow. Moreover, given the differences in strategy, doctrine, and missions, it is not clear that the United States will want to forgo any technical capabilities in the near term, in the expectation that the Europeans will provide them.

Fourth, the technology and interoperability gaps could be closed if a more open transatlantic defense market for technology and equipment emerges over the next few years. The promising industrial trends of recent years have stalled, however, and a dangerous trend toward creating defense industrial and technological fortresses on both sides of the Atlantic has appeared. Here, the greater responsibility must lie with the United States, given the size of the U.S. defense market and the barriers to entry posed by U.S. policies. The number of significant, joint transatlantic defense programs has dwindled to a handful, and even those are threatened. The United States constrains defense technology exports, even to relatively reliable NATO allies, and discourages direct European investment in defense industries in the United States.

Apart from British firms, the Europeans have made only limited efforts to move in a transatlantic direction in the face of these obstacles. On the continent, governments and the EU have encouraged a more fortress-like process within industry. The result has been the emergence of two European industrial champions, one based in Britain (BAE Systems) and the other primarily Franco-German (European Aeronautic, Space and Defense Company, or EADS), with participation by the Spanish and Italian industries.

Greater transatlantic defense industry and technological cooperation carries obvious advantages. At best, however, this market will only emerge slowly. The Europeans will spend time integrating these two firms and defining a European Union–level set of rules for the defense industry and defense exports. The U.S. rules of the road will take some time to change. Thus, an economically logical and militarily beneficial trend could be frustrated by political logic, setting back technological cooperation and military interoperability and delaying the payoff for defense planners on both sides of the Atlantic.

Despite these reservations, the Europeans could, in the relative near term, take on greater responsibility in certain areas: peace stabilization operations in Europe and intra-European air transport and naval coverage in the North Atlantic and Mediterranean. Shifting greater responsibility for these activities to European NATO, while eliminating U.S. forces and programs that currently handle them, could save U.S. taxpayers as much as $7 billion a year, though not until about 2010. But even if the Europeans take over these responsibilities, it may be prudent for the United States to retain the forces and equipment for use in other areas, rather than eliminate them.

In sum, the payoff from greater European commitment to enhancing Europe's defense capabilities will be some time in coming, and will not be a source of large near-term savings for U.S. defense planners. Over a longer term, assuming greater European involvement in out-of-area missions and technological progress, a more ambitious burden-sharing arrangement might be possible.[1]

The Promise: Defense Planning in the European Union

Since the NATO alliance was created in the late 1940s, there has been constant discussion about the need for greater burden-sharing across the Atlantic. This persistent debate produced relatively little visible change, however, until the Cold War—the contingency for which the alliance was created—ended in 1989. As part of a broader effort to expand the political character of the European Union in 1991, the EU member states made a common commitment to "define and implement a common foreign and security policy" (CFSP), including "the eventual framing of a common defence policy, which might in time lead to a common defence."[2] There was, however, limited progress toward this objective throughout the decade, especially when it came to discussing the prospect of common European defense capabilities.[3] The Maastricht goal, as applied to defense, foresaw using the Western European Union (WEU) as "the defense com-

---

1. This chapter focuses deliberately on the potential for greater burden-sharing across the Atlantic. There may be reasons, as well, to focus on U.S. savings that might result from greater Japanese, South Korean, and Australian assumption of defense responsibilities in Asia. None of these cases of burden-sharing is, however, likely to result in significant U.S. budgetary savings over the next decade. The absence of a region-wide security agreement in Asia and the importance of a continuing U.S. military presence, both to reassure Japan and to ensure a sense of security amongst China's neighbors, argues for continuity of U.S. policy, not for a near-term reduction in U.S. forces. A major change in the North Korean government or the collapse of the regime might lead to some changes, but not necessarily to a U.S. military withdrawal from the region or a demobilization of the forces withdrawn, given these longer-term regional security issues.

2. Article J.1, Treaty of Maastricht.

3. For an early, pessimistic prognosis for a Common Foreign and Security Policy in Europe, see Philip Gordon, "Europe's Uncommon Foreign Policy," *International Security*, Vol. 22, No. 3 (Winter 1997/98), pp. 74–100.

ponent of the European Union," but made limited efforts to strengthen the WEU to that end.[4]

The collective commitment of the EU to a CFSP was reiterated in the Amsterdam Treaty of 1997, which also provided for the appointment of a High Representative for the CFSP. In Amsterdam, the Europeans also described the missions Europeans might consider for a European military force (commonly referred to as the "Petersberg tasks"): "humanitarian and rescue tasks, peacekeeping tasks, and tasks of combat forces in crisis management, including peace-making."[5] While these missions fell short of all-out combat, they represented a considerable expansion of intended responsibilities for any common European military capability.

By and large, no significant progress was made in implementing the defense part of the CFSP until late in the 1990s. The December 1998 meeting between Britain's new Prime Minister, Tony Blair, and French President Jacques Chirac in St. Malo, France marked a watershed for British policy on European defense, and clearly set a common European process in motion. The St. Malo declaration stated that the two governments wanted to "make a reality of the Treaty of Amsterdam." The agreement committed the EU to creating "the capacity for *autonomous* action, backed up by credible military forces, the means to decide to use them, and a readiness to do so, in order to respond to international crises." In order to make decisions and approve military action, the Union would "need to have recourse to suitable military means," which were defined as "European capabilities pre-designated within NATO's European pillar or national or multinational European means outside the NATO framework."

The process initiated by the British-French agreement received additional impetus from the European military performance during the Kosovo air campaign. It was already clear during the Gulf War and the deployment to Bosnia that a gap was opening between European and U.S. military capabilities. The United States clearly had better capabilities for intelligence, surveillance, and reconnaissance, more accurate precision-guided munitions, significantly better air and sealift resources and logistics, and greater capacity to communicate among the services.[6]

---

4. Declaration No. 30 of the Western European Union. The WEU members who are also EU members include the United Kingdom, France, Germany, Italy, Belgium, Netherlands, Luxembourg, Spain, and Portugal.

5. Treaty of Amsterdam Amending the Treaty on European Union, the Treaties Establishing the European Communities and Certain Related Acts, Article J.7.2. The "Petersberg Tasks" were first laid out by the WEU at a June 1992 meeting in Petersberg, near Bonn, Germany.

6. James P. Thomas, "The Military Challenges of Transatlantic Coalitions," Adelphi

The Kosovo campaign showed that this gap had become a chasm. The U.S. forces had clearly become more capable for high-intensity air operations, were well supplied in precision munitions (apart from a cruise missile shortfall in the Air Force), and had a strikingly more advanced ability to handle the communications and information requirements of modern, high-technology warfare.[7]

As a result of the Kosovo air campaign, the European allies, especially the British, French, and Germans, realized that they lacked the flexible, agile, and technically capable forces they would need to operate in tandem with the United States in high intensity combat, or, for that matter, to conduct an effective, autonomous operation as envisaged by the Petersberg tasks or the St. Malo agreement.

At the June 1999 EU summit in Cologne, the European Union agreed that the EU must have the capacity for autonomous action, backed up by credible military forces, the means to decide to use them, and a readiness to do so, in order to respond to international crises without prejudice to actions by NATO.[8] The Europeans also decided that, by the end of 2000, the machinery of the Western European Union would be absorbed into the EU itself, and the European Union would take on the "Petersberg tasks."

The Cologne commitment to develop military forces was strongly re-enforced six months later at the EU's December 1999 Helsinki summit. The EU committed itself to what has been described as a "headline goal": the creation of a specific military capability by a specific point in time. According to the Helsinki agreement, by 2003 the members "must be able to deploy within sixty days and sustain for at least one year military forces of up to 50,000–60,000 persons capable of the full range of Petersberg tasks."[9]

Paper No. 333 (London: International Institute for Strategic Studies [IISS], 2000), chap. 2.

7. See, e.g., IISS, "A Common European Military Policy," *Strategic Comments*, Vol. 5, No. 6 (July 1999), p. 2; J.A.C. Lewis, "Building a European Force," *Jane's Defence Weekly*, June 23, 1999, p. 22; Carla Anne Robbins, "Display of U.S. Might Makes Allies, Adversaries Doubt Their Relevance," *Wall Street Journal*, July 6, 1999, p. 1; Thomas, "The Military Challenges of Transatlantic Coalitions," See also Secretary of Defense William S. Cohen and General Henry H. Shelton, "Joint Statement on the Kosovo After Action Review," October 14, 1999, p. 8. François Heisbourg, "Questions sur une paix," *Le Monde*, June 19, 1999, p. 20.

8. "Presidency Conclusions: Cologne European Council, 3 and 4 June 1999," para. 1.

9. Presidency Conclusions, Helsinki European Council, 10 and 11 December 1999," para. 28.

By the end of 1999, the Europeans had come a substantial distance from the Maastricht Treaty and appeared ready to make a serious commitment to creating a European military capability that might be able to act autonomously from the United States. In principle, at least, the headline goal force and the new EU institutions, which have come to be known as the European Security and Defense Policy (ESDP), contain the promise of real burden-sharing, in contrast to prior statements of principle.

Strategy and Force Planning: Can the EU and the United States Converge?

STRATEGIC DIVERGENCE

The ability of a European defense force to support, interoperate with and substitute for U.S. defense capabilities will depend on the degree of convergence in the transatlantic strategic relationship. The individual European militaries or the new EU rapid reaction force may not fit with U.S. strategic plans. Thus, as the details of European force planning evolve, they may have only partially overlapping missions with U.S. forces, making it difficult for the United States to rely on those capabilities as a substitute for its own.

Sharp divergences in strategic vision will reduce the incentive for close coordination in force planning and equipment acquisition. Convergence, on the other hand, would give the allies the incentive to create more interoperable forces for coalition missions, which could in turn stimulate greater interest in the acquisition of interoperable or common military hardware.

The strategic relationship across the Atlantic contains decidedly mixed signals. With the end of the Cold War and the loss of the Soviet Union as a common adversary, the unity of strategic vision in the NATO alliance has been replaced by a complex set of agreements and disagreements over regional and global security strategies and objectives.

Given the more complex international realities of the twenty-first century, Americans and Europeans have very different visions of the scope of their security concerns. By 2000, the Clinton administration had clearly accepted a global mission for its armed forces, supporting a global national security strategy.[10] U.S. force deployments and defense planning

---

10. See *A National Security Strategy for a New Century*, White House, December 1999. As discussed in Chapter 1, the United States has already reaped a significant budgetary dividend from the end of the Cold War, regardless of the actions of its European allies. See Office of the Undersecretary of Defense (Comptroller), *National Defense Budget*

refocused from the Cold War to regions more distant than the European continent. The 1991 Gulf War, the North Korean crisis of 1994, the Taiwan Straits crisis of 1996, military strikes in the Perisan Gulf region, and the multiple peacekeeping and peace enforcement deployments of U.S. forces over the past decade have been global. As Chapters 1 and 2 discuss, by the early 1990s, the central focus of the Defense Department's force planning had shifted from Europe to regional wars, with the Persian Gulf and Korea as the proxies for defense planning purposes.[11]

U.S. strategy for Europe has taken on a clearly different character after the Cold War. Rather than large forward deployment of heavy conventional forces to deter a major Soviet attack, the United States has focused on expanding the NATO alliance to include former Warsaw Pact countries, the use of high-technology warfare in the former Yugoslavia, and the temporary deployment of U.S. forces as part of peace enforcement and regional stability operations in the Balkans.

Although there is still not one common European view on security strategy, the European outlook is clearly more regional than global. At the global level, European concerns have been economic rather than military, with trade negotiations and international finance at the top of the list. The British have disengaged entirely from military involvement in Africa, with the French close behind. In South Asia, the Europeans have virtually no military presence or mission, and they are absent almost entirely from the debates over security issues in Asia.

Even close to Europe, in the Middle East, the Europeans have played a secondary role to the United States. In the peace process, the Europeans have a marginal diplomatic impact, while providing financial assistance.[12] Although most European allies supported the Gulf War, only the British and the French made significant military contributions.[13] Since

Estimates for FY 2000 (Washington, D.C.: Department of Defense, March 1999), Table 6.8, "Department of Defense BA by Title," and Table 7.5, "Department of Defense Manpower." See also Office of Management and Budget, *Budget of the United States Government, Fiscal Year 2001* (Washington, D.C.: Executive Office of the President, February 2000), p. 151, Table 9–1.

11.   See Secretary of Defense Les Aspin, *Report of the Bottom-Up Review* (Washington, D.C.: Department of Defense, Office of the Secretary of Defense, October 1993); and Secretary of Defense William Cohen, *Report of the Quadrennial Defense Review* (Washington, D.C.: Department of Defense, Office of the Secretary of Defense, 1997).

12.   See Philip Gordon, *The Transatlantic Allies and the Changing Middle East*, Adelphi Paper No. 332 (London: IISS, September 1998).

13.   In military terms, the European contribution in the Gulf War was comparatively small. The United States supplied 1,376 aircraft and 532,000 ground troops, while the British contributed 69 aircraft and 35,000 ground troops, and the French, 42 aircraft

1991, many allies have favored lifting the sanctions regime against Iraq, which the United States has resisted. European and U.S. views on dealing with Iran diverge substantially, and the Europeans make little direct military contribution to Gulf security arrangements. Europe has shown minimal concern about the potential ballistic missile threat from the Middle East and Gulf region, while the United States is rapidly pursuing missile defense technologies to protect both forward-deployed forces and the U.S. homeland.

The distance between the U.S. and the European strategic visions was clear during the preparations for the NATO fiftieth anniversary summit of April 1999. The European allies strongly resisted any U.S. proposals that NATO ought to consider an extension of its mission to security issues beyond the territory of the Alliance. European willingness to consider "out-of-area" strategic issues extended no further than the Balkans.

The shared concern over the Balkans points to the one significant area of convergence in strategic vision across the Atlantic. The U.S. government has come to the view that Balkan stability is an important goal and a crucial test for the Atlantic alliance. After some hesitation at the start of the decade, Europeans have come to a similar view, and have shown a willingness to deploy military force to meet that goal. As will be explored below, a predominant European responsibility for regional stability on that continent may be one area that provides limited opportunities for U.S. defense resource savings.

Some analysts have argued that the Europeans will increasingly come to share the Clinton administration's concern about such problems as potential future Russian military capabilities, the proliferation of nuclear arms and ballistic delivery vehicles, African political stability, Middle East oil, a globalized economy, terrorism, narcotics and cyberwarfare.[14] However, there do not seem to be near-term opportunities for U.S. savings as a result of greater European willingness to partici-

---

and 13,500 troops. The British deployed these forces slowly, using largely their own transport. The French relied heavily on U.S. transport and were so lightly armored that they were put on the left flank and supplied with U.S. artillery support. See David C. Gompert, Richard L. Kugler, and Martin C. Libicki, *Mind the Gap: Promoting a Transatlantic Revolution in Military Affairs* (Washington, D.C.: NDU Press, 1999), p. 18. See also Michael O'Hanlon, "Transforming NATO: the Role of European Forces," *Survival*, Vol. 39, No. 3 (Autumn 1997), p. 9; and Thomas, "The Military Challenges of Transatlantic Coalitions," chap. 2.

14. More broadly, Gompert, Kugler, and Libicki, *Mind the Gap*, p. 20, suggest that the Europeans and Americans do share basic interests, which "reflect the underlying vulnerabilities and opportunities of a society, and its economic vitality, relative to developments elsewhere in the world. In this sense, Europeans do have global interests—in-

pate in such global missions. While such interests may be shared, they are not shared at equal intensity. More important, while the United States may consider military force as one option for addressing such problems, it is far from clear that the Europeans are willing to do so. In the near term, only British and French strategic thinking appears to extend past the European theater, and even then, not past the Gulf. Moreover, their forces may not yet match even these limited ambitions. Should force become an ingredient in common European policies for such problems, it is unlikely that this policy synergy and the forces to match will be achieved in the near future.

FORCE PLANNING: A U.S.-EUROPEAN MISMATCH

Even with full strategic convergence, force planning will determine the extent to which European military capabilities can operate with or substitute for U.S. capabilities. European and U.S. force planning have diverged considerably throughout the decade of the 1990s, as the Kosovo air campaign revealed. The U.S. investment in sizable, technologically advanced forces is driven, in part, by its global security strategy. Given the more restricted European strategic focus and the collapse of the Soviet threat, the incentive for force restructuring has been absent. To a large extent, the Europeans became "prisoners of inertia," locked in a Cold War defense paradigm.[15]

The force planning gap is not purely technological, although there is a growing separation between U.S. technical capabilities and those of the European allies, which is discussed below. There are also differences in doctrine and in more traditional capabilities, such as logistics, sustainment, and transportation. Europeans began to come to terms with these differences only late in the decade, and it is not clear that these gaps can be closed within the next ten years. Moreover, to some degree, the Europeans may need to choose between creating forces that are capable of the Petersberg tasks and emphasizing those that can engage in the high-intensity, long-distance combat for which U.S. forces are being designed.[16] The Europeans may not be able to do both in the near term.

---

deed interests quite similar to those of the United States." They note that "the transatlantic disparity in strategic outlook is not really about interests: it is about whether and how to protect them."

15. Gompert, Kugler, and Libicki, *Mind the Gap*, p. 10.

16. David Gompert describes the intensity/projection gap as crucial. It is "the ability to send forces nearly anywhere with little warning to conduct rapid and highly destructive operations in a dangerous environment" that distinguishes the U.S. capability from that of Europe. Communication with the author, December 13, 1999.

THE UNITED STATES. Since 1990, the Pentagon has had to cope with both types of requirements, but has focused principally on developing high-intensity power projection forces. Base Force (1991) and Bottom-Up Review (1993) planning sought capabilities that could respond to two major regional contingencies (MRCs) at nearly the same time, using the Gulf and the Korean peninsula as proxies. The less intense peacemaking, peacekeeping, and humanitarian interventions were described as Operations Other Than War (OOTW) and were treated as contingencies that could be covered by forces designed for the major contingencies.

The 1991 Gulf War, the 1994 crisis with North Korea, and the 1996 tensions in the Taiwan Strait suggested that the two-MRC scenario was rooted in geostrategic reality. However, the operations that consumed the bulk of the Pentagon's operational attention in the 1990s were the OOTWs: Somalia, Rwanda, Bosnia, Haiti, and, following the air war, Kosovo.

Despite some inertia in the Pentagon and the commitment of the services to legacy systems and doctrines, U.S. forces had already moved substantially toward greater mobility, agility, and precision, even before 1990. The U.S. military, while declining 32 percent in end strength, has continued to move in this direction over the past decade; it has started to redesign military units (wings, divisions, and battle groups), and move down the road toward integrating advanced information and communications technology.

The slowest adaptation has been by the Army. Even there, Army Chief of Staff General Eric Shinseki has acknowledged publicly that the Army needed to reshape itself to become more agile, lighter, and more flexible if it is to arrive early in a crisis and be militarily effective.[17] This planning has only begun in the Army, but points toward significantly different forces. The Air Force, facing demands for ever-longer-term projection of air power, with resulting retention and morale problems, has moved toward creating more integrated expeditionary air wings, which will combine close air support, air interdiction, air superiority, jamming, and long-range bombing under a common command, along with deployments of specified rather than unlimited duration. Air Force planning has also begun to focus on long-range air operations, including both bombers and fighters, with appropriate tanker capability. The Navy and Marines

---

17. See Army Chief of Staff General Eric Shinseki speech to Association of the U.S. Army, October 11, 1999; George I. Seffers, "Shinseki Unveils All-Wheeled Vision for U.S. Army," *Defense News*, October 25, 1999, p. 12.

had operated for decades as a global force, and thus have faced the least wrenching adjustment. Even for the Navy, however, doctrine and force planning begun to focus more on the requirements of littoral operations, rather than the traditional blue water design.

The U.S. military has continued the progress it made in the 1980s in integrating advanced technology into its force design and doctrine: precision-guided munitions, sophisticated interoperable communications, satellite and drone-derived intelligence, data linkages, and the information systems that tie operations and equipment together.

U.S. planning has focused on achieving synergy with the Europeans. Throughout the 1990s, despite much discussion in NATO, the bulk of U.S. planning for agility, flexibility, and global power projection has been conducted with only minimal attention to coalition interoperability. Although U.S. forces have largely been used in coalitions, especially in the Balkans, the underlying assumption of the 1997 Quadrennial Defense Review (QDR) was that the U.S. military would need to be able to accomplish its principal missions—two major theater wars—unilaterally. The NATO allies were not directly involved or systematically consulted during the QDR planning process.

THE EUROPEANS. Only late in the decade have the Europeans begun to recognize the technology gap, the divergence in expeditionary capabilities, and the need for renewed attention to such fundamentals as logistics, sustainability, and transport. The European NATO allies spend amounts roughly equal to 60 percent of the U.S. defense budget, but with this they maintain more than 1.8 million soldiers under arms, 1.3 million of these (nearly the size of the active duty U.S. forces) in British, French, German, and Italian uniforms.[18] Spending on military equipment, including both procurement and research and development, generally consumes smaller shares of European defense budgets. While Britain and France devote roughly a quarter of their defense resources to equipment (the comparable U.S. share is one third), the Germans spend only 13.6 percent on equipment, and Italy and Spain just over 12 percent.[19] Because European nations do not coordinate force and equipment planning, at least some of this spending is redundant.

---

18. This excludes Greek and Turkish personnel and includes the new NATO members in Central Europe. NATO, "Financial and Economic Data Relating to NATO Defence," Press Release M-DPC-2 (December 2, 1999), p. 152, Table 6.

19. Equipment expenditures include procurement and research and development spending and use NATO definitions. IISS figures indicate the same trends. See IISS, *Military Balance, 1998–99*, Table 46, p. 295.

Although European defense forces and budgets fell with the end of the Cold War, personnel levels remain quite high. European NATO manpower declined just over 20 percent between 1990 and 1999, while U.S. manpower declined over 32 percent.[20] While this decline is consistent with the decline in budgets, European militaries remain fairly personnel-heavy.

In general, as the Soviet threat disappeared, European force planning and spending did little to adapt to the changing face of war. The training, doctrine and equipment for European forces continued to focus on European regional defense, Cold War–style:

Because the threat had receded, it . . . led the allies to de-emphasize readiness and modernizations. Within their declining defense budgets, the Europeans have stressed quantity (i.e., force structure and end strength) over quality (technology); defensive capabilities over projection and strike capabilities; and meeting payrolls and other current expenses over investment for the future.[21]

Although the key European allies—Britain, France, and Germany—have begun to adapt their forces, the crucial questions are how long that adaptation will take and whether the emerging forces are designed for missions that are compatible with U.S. planning, allowing potential savings for the United States.

The defense reviews that preceded the Blair administration reduced funding for defense sharply, shrank the forces, and began a process of defense management reform, but did little to redirect force structure toward post–Cold War missions and capabilities. Between 1990 and 1998, military manpower declined by 32 percent, RAF aircraft by 30 percent, infantry battalions by 27 percent, tanks by 45 percent, and destroyers and frigates by 27 percent.[22] Then, after nearly a decade of inertia and defense budget cuts, British force planning began to move toward the creation of

---

20.   NATO, "Financial and Economic Data Relating to NATO Defence."

21.   Gompert, Kugler, and Libicki, *Mind the Gap*, p. 18; they note (pp. 39–40) that only the British could deploy a division in an expeditionary mission, along with a few other European brigades from NATO's Rapid Reaction Corps. In total, Europe could deploy perhaps two division equivalents, three to four air wings and 20–30 naval combatants. Heisbourg argues that European land forces would only be able to deploy 40,000 soldiers in a power projection mission. François Heisbourg, "L'Europe de la defense dans l'Alliance atlantique," draft article for *Politique Etrangere*, June 7, 1999, pp. 3–5.

22.   Ministry of Defence, *Strategic Defence Review: Modern Forces for the Modern World*, "Supporting Essay Six: Future Military Capabilities," June 1998, p. 1

expeditionary capabilities through the Strategic Defence Review (SDR) of 1997–98.

While the SDR continued the government's commitment to acquire 232 Eurofighters and to retain the Trident missile and submarine program, it emphasized the goal of creating lighter, more deployable forces for expeditionary missions. The most demanding mission was to be "the challenge of conducting two concurrent medium scale operations—one a relatively short warfighting deployment, the other an enduring non-warfighting operation."[23]

The Ministry of Defence plans to create a Joint Rapid Reaction Force by 2001, with the command and control, lift, and logistics that would allow the United Kingdom to move two brigade-sized forces with air and naval support "at short notice." The SDR also pointed toward greater expeditionary capabilities for the Royal Navy, with the lessons of the Gulf War in mind. It projected buying two new, larger carriers capable of supporting 50 aircraft, a significant improvement over the smaller, *Invincible*-class carriers used in Gulf operations. The review described the new carriers as supplying "increased offensive air power and an ability to operate the largest possible range of aircraft in the widest possible range of roles." This Naval force should have the "independent ability to deploy a combat force from the sea."[24] This capability will arrive slowly, however, since the carriers are unlikely to be available before the second decade of the twenty-first century.[25]

The Army would add a sixth deployable brigade to make the projected two-brigade deployments possible. Five airborne brigades would also be made heavier, and a new air maneuver brigade would be created. Roughly 3,000 soldiers would be added to the Army to provide needed signals, engineer, medical, and logistics capabilities. The Royal Air Force would shift its focus from the defense of British airspace to deployability for crises, and British aircraft would be armed with next generation air-to-air and air-to-ground missiles.

The SDR underlined the British intention to use these forces primarily in coalition with allied forces: "This means that we do not need to hold sufficient national capabilities for every eventuality, just as we did not plan to defeat the Warsaw Pact on our own. But it also means that we

---

23. Ibid., p. 2.

24. MOD, *Strategic Defence Review*, Supporting Essay Six, p. 10.

25. See Humphry Crum Ewing, "Strategic Defence Review: Now That We Have the Review, What do We Do Next?" Bailrigg Debating Point No. 6, July 1998, Center for Defence and International Security Studies, Lancaster University.

need balanced, coherent forces which are capable of operating effectively alongside forces from other countries."[26]

Although the British Army intended to buy the U.S. Joint Tactical Information Distribution System and digital radios to improve communications interoperability with the United States, the SDR generally gave only minimal endorsement to investing in advanced military technologies

On the whole, British force planning is taking significant steps toward an expeditionary doctrine that parallels that of the United States. The United Kingdom also intends to buy capabilities to transport and sustain that force. It is less clear that the British intend to make the technology investments that would give them the capability for high-intensity combat operations. Moreover, the time frame for delivering transportation capabilities of any magnitude or of buying advanced technology do not suggest near-term compatibility with U.S. forces. The United States can, in all likelihood, count on British capabilities to support most U.S. operations in Europe and in the Gulf. Alone, however, British capabilities do not appear adequate to allow the United States to eliminate forces or investments.

France has also begun to transform its forces. Since 1966, when they opted out of the NATO military structure, the French have maintained some capability for autonomous operations, including a small blue-water navy and modest airlift. The Gulf War brought home the lesson that the French land force was light, minimally interoperable, and difficult to deploy and sustain at a distance. The French capacity to operate autonomously had virtually disappeared. This realization led to a significant change in French defense planning: the 1994 decision that French forces in the future would have to operate in coalition with others.[27] From this decision, it was logical for the French to urge an autonomous European defense capability.

In 1996, the French began to move in the direction of expeditionary forces as well. France abolished conscription by 2003 and created a joint Land Action Force Command for expeditionary operations. There are 23 percent fewer French military personnel since 1990. Driven by the goal of autonomy, moreover, the French have gone further than the British in investing in advanced technology, acquiring a Helios reconnaissance satellite (for autonomous intelligence), and making plans to purchase more rapidly deployable communications, stand-off precision strike weapons,

---

26. MOD, *Strategic Defence Review,* Supporting Essay Six, p. 4.

27. Ministère de la Defense, *Livre Blanc sur la Defense,* Paris: *Services d'Information et de Relations Publiques des Armées,* February 1994, pp. 46–47.

transport aircraft, and air refueling aircraft. The French will also deploy a new carrier.[28]

Expeditionary capabilities (twice the size of those deployed in the Gulf War), coalition operations (with the Europeans), and advanced technology are integral parts of French planning. Although the French forces operated with the United States during the Kosovo air campaign, however, it is not clear how predictably the United States can rely on those forces to handle missions that the United States could then avoid, in order to achieve budgetary savings. Moreover, given budget limitations discussed below, it is not clear how soon the French capability will be fully available.

Germany's adaptation may be the most gradual and difficult of the major European powers. The German forces are designed for coalition warfare, but of the old school: the defense of the central European front. Personnel levels have shrunk by 39 percent since 1990, but the force remains large, almost entirely conscript in nature, and heavily armored. It is conceivable that this force could play a central role in the Petersberg tasks (particularly large-scale peace enforcement missions). Short of major restructuring, however, German military capabilities will diverge sharply from U.S., British, and French plans for lighter, more mobile, expeditionary capabilities armed with advanced technology.[29]

Political considerations and history have contributed to the German reluctance to restructure their military for a full-spectrum military capability or agile, highly mobile forces for out-of-area combat operations. In general, peacekeeping, peace enforcement, and humanitarian operations have been more politically acceptable. Slowly, however, German thinking appears to be changing. Germany agreed to participate in NATO deployments outside the NATO region in 1994, a decision declared constitutional by the German constitutional court that year. While retaining conscription, German planning targeted the creation of a professional, inter-service Crisis Reaction Force (CRF) by 2000, consisting of roughly 54,000 soldiers in six brigades, with eighteen air squadrons and three transport wings, giving it greater mobility, and a separate command headquarters. Germany also participated in a small way in coalition operations in Somalia and Bosnia, and flew combat aircraft in the Kosovo air campaign.[30]

---

28. Thomas, "The Military Challenges of Transatlantic Coalitions," pp. 17–23.

29. Franz-Josef Meiers, "A German Defense Review?" paper for the Seminar on European Force Structures, WEU Institute for Security Studies, Paris, May 27–28, 1999, p. 1.

30. Thomas, "The Military Challenges of Transatlantic Coalitions, pp. 17–23."

The German government has recognized that it must move in a more expeditionary direction, despite budgetary and political constraints. The 1999–2000 review of German defense capabilities, conducted by the independent Commission on Common Security and the Future of the Bundeswehr, recommended a significant transformation of the German military, reducing troop strength by more than 100,000, increasing significantly the number of volunteers, restructuring the forces toward coalition expeditionary operations, and calling for a greater investment in advanced technology, airlift, intelligence, communications, and logistics. It did not, however, propose increases in the German defense budget, but rather urged that savings through personnel reductions and management reforms be dedicated to the necessary acquisition programs. The government accepted the recommendations overall, but decided to retain higher conscript levels and settle for force structure cuts of about 60,000. It will take time before this restructured force is ready and equipped to be fully interoperable with its European partners or NATO.[31]

Overall, the force planning of the major European allies appears to be slowly evolving toward smaller, lighter, more expeditionary capabilities. This transformation has not yet reached the point where it complements U.S. defense plans sufficiently to permit a U.S. decision to forgo some capabilities, knowing the Europeans will supply them. It will be several years before full expeditionary capabilities are achieved by the British and French, and even more before the German forces reach that goal. Moreover, much of the transport, communications, and logistical capabilities needed to deploy those forces will be some years away, suggesting that Europe will continue to rely on the United States for these important capabilities.

NATO or the EU: The Dilemma of Coalition Planning

A key issue for European force planning and for the transatlantic relationship will be the framework for military planning. The Europeans recognize they must operate in coalitions. The struggle at the end of the 1990s was to define the framework for that coalition activity: a European identity in NATO or a European Union defense identity that could act with

---

31. Ralph Atkins, "Berlin Earmarks Funds to Update Germany's Forces," *Financial Times*, June 15, 2000, p. 3; Ministry of Defense, *Common Security and the Future of the Bundeswehr: Report of the Commission to the Federal Government*, May 23, 2000; Rudiger Moniac, "Leaked German Report on Armed Forces Sparks Policy Row," *Jane's Defence Weekly*, May 17, 2000; Cecilie Rohwedder, "Germany to Modernize Military, Trim Defense Spending by 2.5%," *Wall Street Journal*, June 15, 2000, p. 22.

some autonomy from NATO. The greater the separation between NATO and the EU's ESDP, the more difficult it will be for the United States to rely on the European capability to fulfill defense requirements.

NATO and the EU have grappled with this relationship since the end of the Cold War, reviving persistent tensions over burden-sharing in the Alliance.[32] NATO has endorsed the goal of a stronger European defense capability within the Alliance. The NATO Council formally agreed in 1996 to support a European Defense and Security Identity (ESDI) that could call on NATO military assets, including its new Combined Joint Task Forces, logistics, transport and intelligence for separate military operations if the North Atlantic Council agreed. Since the EU at that point had no institutional capacity for defense policy or operations, the NATO link for these missions was to be with the Western European Union, which would coordinate European operations.[33]

As the EU became the locus of European defense planning, U.S. concern grew that the search for greater European autonomy in defense operations could divide and weaken the NATO alliance. Rhetoric on both sides of the Atlantic tended to exacerbate this concern. In the eyes of some Europeans, particularly the French, autonomy for an EU defense capability was essential, given the need to balance the United States as the sole remaining superpower.

U.S. rhetoric about European defense capabilities and planning has been ambivalent. On the one hand, the Kosovo experience reinforced a U.S. sense that the United States was, once again, bearing the principal burden of alliance military operations in Europe, to the detriment of its more global responsibilities.

On the other hand, the United States was worried that the goal of European defense autonomy articulated in the St. Malo agreement could bring into being a European capability that was decoupled from the alli-

---

32. See Gordon Adams and Eric Munz, *Fair Shares: Bearing the Burden of the NATO Alliance* (Washington, D.C.: Defense Budget Project, 1988).

33. The ESDI is a NATO concept, as distinguished from the ESDP concept in the EU context. The WEU, largely moribund since its creation in 1954, includes ten countries that are fully members of NATO, with another 18 associated countries, observers and partners. It has conducted few operations during its existence and relies entirely on NATO for the capacity to do so. After the 1996 agreement with NATO, the first opportunity for the WEU to take action using the new authorities was the collapse of government in Albania in 1997. The members could not agree to act under the WEU charter and created a small coalition of the willing (France, Greece, Romania, Spain, and Turkey) under Italian leadership, which conducted a five month policing operation in that country. See Antonio Missiroli, *CFSP, Defence and Flexibility*, Chaillot Paper 38 (Paris: Institute for Security Studies of the Western European Union, February 2000), pp. 21–22; and Gordon, "Europe's Uncommon Foreign Policy," p. 88.

ance and the United States. The result would be a weaker NATO and a loss of security on both sides of the Atlantic.

Both NATO and European Union planning and statements in the late 1990s have generally dismissed or papered over the divergence between the alliance and European Union defense planning. The April 1999 NATO summit welcomed the goal of a European defense capability and acknowledged "the resolve of the European Union to have the capacity for autonomous action so that it can take decisions and approve military actions where the Alliance as a whole is not engaged."[34]

The Washington summit grappled with the details of the relationship between EU and NATO defense planning. The alliance statements also made it clear, however, that NATO intended to keep a fairly close rein on ESDI actions, to ensure that they were organized inside the alliance and with the agreement of the NATO partners, even if they were conducted without the full participation of all countries in the alliance. ESDI would "continue to be developed within NATO," and the alliance would "assist the European Allies to act by themselves as required through the readiness of the Alliance, on a case-by-case basis and by consensus, to make its assets and capabilities available for operations in which the Alliance is not engaged militarily under the political control and strategic direction either of the WEU or, as otherwise agreed, taking into account the full participation of all European Allies if they were so to choose."[35]

Under U.S. leadership, NATO has also initiated the Defense Capabilities Initiative (DCI), a concerted effort within the alliance to close the gaps—both in low and high-technology capabilities—that were exposed by the Kosovo air campaign:

Many Allies have only relatively limited capabilities for the rapid deployment of significant forces outside national territory or for extended sustainment of operations and protection of forces far from home bases. Command and control and information systems need to be better matched to the requirement of future Alliance military operations which will entail the exchange of a much greater volume of information and extending to lower levels than in the past. . . . Increased attention must be paid . . . to the challenges posed by the accelerating pace of technological change and the different speeds at which Allies introduce advanced capabilities.[36]

---

34. NATO Communiqué, S(99)64, April 24, 1999, para. 9a.

35. NATO, "The Alliance's Strategic Concept," Press Release NAC-S(99)65, April 24, 1999, para. 30.

36. NATO, "Defense Capabilities Initiative," Press Release NAC-S(99)69, April 24, 1999, p. 2. The DCI is intended to improve NATO capabilities in several key areas: the deployability and mobility of Alliance forces, their sustainability and logistics, their

The NATO planning efforts are deliberately designed to link EU plans to improvements in NATO's capability to conduct coalition operations. At the same time, the European Union planning efforts in the framework of the ESDP have moved, at least rhetorically, to close the gap between the two. The EU language about this crucial relationship had clearly evolved between the Cologne and Helsinki summits, in part in response to U.S. pressure. In Cologne, the objective of EU planning was to "have the capacity to autonomous action . . . in order to respond to international crises without prejudice to actions by NATO." By Helsinki, the EU goal had evolved to the capacity to act autonomously "where NATO is not engaged." Moreover, this process "will avoid unnecessary duplication and does not imply the creation of a European army."

U.S. statements echoed the European rhetoric. Deputy Secretary of State Strobe Talbott noted that the Americans were "for" a stronger Europe, one that "can act effectively through the Alliance or, if NATO is not engaged, on its own." He welcomed the recognition in Helsinki of "NATO's central role in collective defense and crisis management" and noted explicitly the EU language that European actions would take place "where NATO as a whole is not engaged."[37]

The evolution of this relationship will be critical to the ability of the United States to rely on the EU to carry out missions the United States is willing to forgo. If EU planning is conducted separately and without communication with NATO, the link between the developing European capability and the DCI will be unclear. As of early 2000, no procedures had been established to coordinate the two exercises.[38]

Moreover, the meaning of "autonomy" will be critical to the long-term relationship between the two. There are indications that to some Europeans, notably the British, autonomy does not mean seeking to duplicate all intelligence, communications, and logistical capabilities of the alliance, but rather, to be able to rely on the United States for some of these. For the French, autonomy may mean being able to act independently, even if the United States does not approve of the action. From the

---

survivability and effective engagement capability, and command and control and information systems. Ibid., p. 3.

37.   Strobe Talbott, "The State of the Alliance: An American Perspective," Speech to the North Atlantic Council, December 15, 1999, p. 3. Skepticism about the long-term relationship between the two efforts remains, however. See, e.g., John-Thor Dahlburg, "Plan for Europe Strike Force Worries U.S." *Los Angeles Times*, December 6, 1999, p. 1; and Michael Evans, "U.S. Skeptical on Euro-Force," *London Times*, December 8, 1999.

38.   See Brooks Tigner, "U.S. Seeks Talks With WEU Before It Disbands," *Defense News*, February 21, 2000, p. 4.

French perspective, it is important, therefore, to establish European force planning and technology goals before coordinating this effort with the NATO alliance.[39]

Negotiating the relationship between the EU and NATO will be critical to future U.S. defense planning, and the outcome is far from clear. To the extent that these two planning processes diverge, the United States will find it difficult to rely on Europe for military capability. To the degree they converge, with European capability improvements re-enforcing the DCI effort, the United States may become more comfortable with Europe taking direct and increasingly sole responsibility for European regional security. Moreover, if the full range of DCI objectives is met, the United States may also become more secure about the ability of European forces to operate in coalitions outside the NATO area. It will be some years, however, before this relationship is clearly defined.[40]

Technology: Can Europe Close the Gap?

While strategic, force planning and political differences separate the United States and Europe, the gap in defense technology exposed by the Kosovo air campaign is a major obstacle to force interoperability across the Atlantic. Should it prove impossible to close this gap, coalition operations within NATO will become increasingly difficult. In the worst case, the United States may be able to rely on Europe only for low-intensity operations that do not draw on the revolution in defense technology. Even there, communications among the cooperating forces could prove difficult without significant European investment. The Europeans have declared the intention of closing the defense technology gap, but given the global U.S. mission, decades of investment and the disparity in research and procurement investments, it is not clear how quickly this goal can be reached.

The defense technologies used in the Gulf War and the Kosovo air campaign and increasingly deployed throughout the U.S. force structure

---

39. For a detailed analysis of Franco-British differences in EU defense planning, see Jolyon Howorth, "Britain, France, and the European Defence Initiative," Survival, Vol. 42, No. 2 (Summer 2000), pp. 33–55.

40. One critical issue to be resolved is how NATO European members who are not in the EU are to be included in the European planning. This issue has caused some internal European tensions. See Peter Finn, "Six in NATO Upset over EU Corps Plan," Washington Post, April 9, 2000, p. 16; Joshua Muravchik and Lawrence F. Kaplan, "Western Europe Tells the East: Keep Quiet," Wall Street Journal Europe, April 3, 2000; William Pfaff, "Falling Out Over European Defense," International Herald Tribune, April 13, 2000.

are frequently referred to as constituting a Revolution in Military Affairs (RMA): sophisticated command, control, communications, computers, intelligence, surveillance, and reconnaissance (C4ISR), data links, and precision-guided munitions.[41] This package of technological capabilities is one of the great force multipliers of the twenty-first century, and its impact on military operations will only grow.

The impact of this technological revolution will be quite profound, distinguishing advanced forces from less capable ones. Successful combat operations will depend on possessing accurate, real-time surveillance, and the ability to communicate target and activity information in real time to war planners and, in turn, to air, ground, and naval-based shooters. These, in turn, will translate that data into operational decisions about where, when, and how to launch sophisticated, highly accurate weaponry (manned and unmanned), carefully protected by stealth and electronic defenses. Real-time information will be needed about the results of those strikes, to plan future phases of more thoroughly integrated air, land, and naval campaigns. U.S. defense doctrine is increasingly influenced by the possession of such capabilities.

The RMA manifests itself in rapid force deployment, decisive force employment, and reduced vulnerability. The first comes from lift assets and lean mobile units. The second results from advanced C4ISR systems, joint doctrine, and strike capabilities. The third comes from dispersing forces, exploiting greater weapon ranges without sacrificing weapons accuracy, and using information dominance to render the other side incapable of inflicting damage.[42]

Although some RMA advocates argue that the U.S. military is taking advantage of these technologies too slowly, the U.S. military has been at the cutting edge compared to the Europeans. Deliberate attempts to use improved technology to multiply force began during the Cold War, to

---

41. See, e.g., Thomas A. Keaney and Eliot A. Cohen, *Revolution in Warfare? Air Power in the Persian Gulf* (Annapolis, Md.: Naval Institute Press, 1995); Michael G. Vickers, *The Military Revolution and Intrastate Conflict* (Washington, D.C.: Center for Strategic and Budgetary Assessment, 1997); James Blaker, "Understanding the Revolution in Military Affairs: A Guide to America's 21st Century Defenses," Defense Working Paper No. 3 (Washington, D.C.: Progressive Policy Institute, January 1997); Laurent Murawiec, *La Guerre au XXIe Siecle* (Paris: Editions Odile Jacob, 2000).

42. Gompert, Kugler, and Libicki, *Mind the Gap,* p. 33. Air and sealift do not necessarily qualify as RMA technologies, though they are critical to expeditionary operations in the post–Cold War world. See also John Deutch, Arnold Kanter, and Brent Scowcroft, "Saving NATO's Foundation," *Foreign Affairs,* Vol. 78, No. 6 (November/December 1999), p. 61: "These C3I technologies make possible sweeping air superiority, successful combined air-and-land attacks, and effective naval power projection."

compensate for NATO's manpower and land force inferiority.[43] With the end of the Cold War and the U.S. commitment to global defense missions, rapid deployment over long distances and the application of precision force remained essential to U.S. military operations. Possessing the technology and adequate budget resources (even at a reduced level), the U.S. military has made progress in integrating the RMA into its military capabilities. The major European militaries, by contrast, have invested more heavily in personnel, shrinking their technology investments over the past decade.

It is not impossible to imagine that the Europeans can close the RMA gap. It is not a gap of technology, *per se.* At its core, the RMA integrates into military applications technologies, many of which were initially developed in the commercial, rather than the defense-specific sector: information systems, communications, computers, data links, and software. While the adaptations, integration, and refinements are defense-specific, the businesses that generate these technological inputs are increasingly global; they converge across the Atlantic and around the world in a market, which knows little of nationality or the desire of governments to have exclusive ownership and control over technology.[44]

The growing application of global, commercial technology to military requirements constitutes a fundamental change in the traditional defense industrial base. It is no longer composed primarily of companies that provide technologies and equipment exclusively to the military as their primary business. For the firms generating advanced communications and information technologies, defense is a small share of total business: just another market for a product or technology they sell commercially in a global market.[45] The global character of this technology base draws the European and U.S. economies together, making it increasingly difficult

---

43.   See Gompert, Kugler, and Libicki, *Mind the Gap,* pp. 12, 29–31.

44.   "Most of the basic information technologies behind the RMA arise in the commercial world. They may therefore be purchased by anyone with the means to pay—and prices are declining." Gompert, Kugler, and Libicki, *Mind the Gap,* p. 49. This view is shared by a National Defense University study, written before the Kosovo air campaign: Robbin F. Laird and Holger H. Mey, *The Revolution in Military Affairs: Allied Perspectives,* McNair Paper 60 (Washington, D.C.: Institute for National Strategic Studies, National Defense University, April 1999), pp. 9–10. See also John Alic et al., *Beyond Spin-Off: Military and Commercial Technologies in a Changing World* (Boston: Harvard Business School Press, 1992) chap. 1.

45.   "Advanced military systems are chock-full of information technology. Yet non-military market segments dominate the information technology market. Defense contracts account for a mere 2 percent share of today's purchases of information technology." Gompert, Kugler, and Libicki, *Mind the Gap,* pp. 68–69.

for any government, including the United States, to maintain exclusive control or create a technology "gap."[46]

What distinguishes the United States from the Europeans is the greater ability of the U.S. military to exploit these technologies for defense applications. Europe falls short because of the long-term low level of its investments in defense research and development, the absence of research coordination among the European militaries, and the relative scarcity of large, system-integrating defense contracting firms in Europe.[47]

The commercial character of the RMA technologies offers hope for greater intra-European and transatlantic technological cooperation. The consolidation of European defense system–integrating companies should allow the Europeans to take greater advantage of those technologies and to eliminate some of the European R&D duplication within a single company framework. Moreover, they should be able to take this advantage in a transatlantic way, given the U.S. defense investment and the global character of the technology market. This process is already underway at the subcontractor level, where a component and supplier market of roughly $12 billion is already estimated to exist across the Atlantic, roughly equal in each direction.[48]

The Budgetary Dilemma: Can Europe Afford to Transform Its Military?

Resources are the heart of the matter if Europe is to create a defense capability that can inter-operate with the United States, conduct expeditionary operations, buy adequate advanced technology, and provide itself

---

46.   The opposite argument is made by Deutch, Kanter, and Scowcroft, "Saving NATO's Foundation"; they argue that advances in communications, computers, and software are areas where "the United States has a considerable advantage (but by no means a monopoly) over Europe." (p. 61) Gompert, Kugler, and Libicki, *Mind the Gap*, make a similar argument (pp. 74–77), claiming that U.S. commercial firms, such as Motorola and Oracle, are far ahead of Europe and there are significant barriers to commercial exchanges across the Atlantic that reinforce this advantage. It is not clear, however, that these firms operate exclusively in the U.S. market; all of them research, produce, or market on a global basis. The know-how in these businesses is widely disseminated and available in Europe, while European firms are not backwards, as the successes of Ericsson and Nokia suggest. See "FT Telecoms: Financial Times Survey," *Financial Times*, October 8, 1999, pp. I–L. U.S. DoD studies in the 1990s suggest that the U.S. military might benefit from significant technical capabilities that exist in Europe.

47.   See Damian Kemp, "R&D Funding Disparity Widens Capability Gap," *Jane's Defence Weekly*, April 5, 2000, pp. 16–17.

48.   IISS, *The Military Balance, 1998/99*, p. 273.

with the logistics, transportation, and sustainment it needs. The ability of the Europeans to create compatible capabilities within the EU or NATO will depend on their ability to provide adequate funding for the purpose. Barring adequate, coordinated defense budgets in Europe, the United States will be hard pressed to rely on European capabilities to supplement its own.

The gap between U.S. and European defense budgets is large. While the European NATO allies spend 60 percent of the U.S. budget level, the investment gap is greater. Overall U.S. defense budgets for procurement and research and development are almost certain to exceed $100 billion a year over the next five years, more than twice the level of spending by the European NATO allies.[49]

If the European goal of autonomy is to be met, at the very least the shortfall in investment funding will need to be redressed. A failure to augment European defense investment would mean relying even more on U.S. logistics, transportation, communications, and intelligence. Continued dependence of this sort could exacerbate, rather than heal, transatlantic tensions. Some European countries could resent the dependency, while Americans could react even more strongly to a Europe which could not "share the burden."

Budgets could prove to be the Achilles' heel of European defense efforts. The costs of significant European investment in command, control, communications, intelligence, surveillance, and reconnaissance will be high. European plans for enhanced logistics, sea and airlift, meaningful inventories of precision-guided munitions, all weather, day-night aircraft, in-flight refueling, and search and rescue aircraft will add to the costs. While the total price tag cannot be easily estimated, it could add billions annually to current European defense budgets.

All European allies face severe budgetary constraints, making overall increases in the level of defense spending unlikely. Defense budgets, especially those of the largest allies, declined sharply between 1985 and 1999: Britain by 34.5 percent, Germany by 28.4 percent and France by 16.1

---

49. As Chapter 1 discusses, even this level of funding may not support the Defense Department's planned modernization program. See also General Accounting Office, *Future Years Defense Program: Funding Increase and Planned Savings in Fiscal Year 2000 Program Are at Risk*, NSIAD-00–11 (Washington, D.C.: GAO, November 1999). Daniel Gouré and Jeffrey M. Ranney, *Averting the Defense Train Wreck in the New Millennium* (Washington, D.C.: Center for Strategic and International Studies, 1999), believe that the Department will need vastly more money than Chapter 1 indicates. But see a telling critique of the CSIS study: Steven M. Kosiak, "CSIS 'Train Wreck' Analysis of DOD's Plans-Funding Mismatch is Off-Track," *Backgrounder*, Center for Strategic and Budgetary Assessments, March 28, 2000.

percent.[50] Spending for defense equipment, which will be critical to meeting European defense planning objectives, is a small proportion of defense spending for most European allies: 13.6 percent in Germany, 12.2 percent in Italy, 16 percent in the Netherlands. Only France at roughly 25 percent, and the United Kingdom at 28 percent, are close to the U.S. level of more than 30 percent. Moreover, equipment budgets have been declining, not rising. From 1994 to 1998, French equipment expenditures declined 24.7 percent in constant dollars; German equipment spending fell 7.5 percent. Only Britain went the other direction, increasing equipment spending by 15.5 percent.[51]

Research and development spending will be critical if the Europeans are to acquire advanced defense technologies. European spending on defense R&D has been especially low, compared to U.S. spending, for many years. By 1998, the combined R&D spending of the European NATO allies was $9.7 billion (in 1997 dollars), 90 percent of that spent by the British, Germans, and French. The U.S. investment was nearly four times as great, at $35.9 billion. Moreover, there is substantial duplication in European defense R&D investment, given the lack of any sustained coordination among the European allies in this area.

There is little expectation that this overall trend in European defense budgets will be reversed. Throughout the 1990s, EU governments generally held down budget growth of any kind, notably lowering deficits as a proportion of gross domestic product, in order to meet the criteria that would permit entry into the European Monetary Union. Currently, none of the major European countries is proposing defense budget increases.[52]

---

50. These calculations use NATO definitions and data and are made in constant local currency to avoid the problem of changes in currency values. Outside of the Aegean, only Denmark, Norway, and Portugal have increased defense budgets over this period. Greece and Turkey have both increased their defense budgets over this period, but much of this is driven by their local rivalry, not by NATO requirements. For comparison, U.S. defense budgets declined 27.8 percent over the same period. Author's calculations based on NATO, "Financial and Economic Data Relating to NATO Defence." According to IISS data, the average decline in NATO Europe defense budgets has been 26 percent since 1986. The new NATO allies do not reverse this trend; according to IISS data, their budgets have declined since 1990 at twice the average rate for the western European NATO allies. IISS, *The Military Balance, 1998/99.*

51. Author's calculations, based on IISS data. For comparison, U.S. equipment spending declined 6.1 percent over this period. Italy also increased its spending 41.4 percent, while the new allies, preparing for NATO entry, increased it significantly, albeit from a low starting point: the Czech Republic by 115.9 percent, Hungary by 30.7 percent, and Poland by 89.8 percent.

52. See Colin Clark, "Lack of European Spending Threatens DCI," *Defense News*, December 13, 1999, pp. 4; Douglas Barrie, "Defense Budgets Remain Tight Throughout

The British Strategic Defense Review of 1997–98 proposed significant changes in force planning and hardware, with the goal of creating a more expeditionary force. At the same time, however, the British Treasury was proposing to reduce defense budgets by 3 percent in real terms between 1998–99 and 2001–02, to be achieved through "efficiency savings." Moreover, British commitments to continuing military operations were further tightening the squeeze on defense resources. The defense committee of the House of Commons reported in February 2000 that the Ministry of Defense was facing severe pressures with "cancelled exercises, delayed equipment programmes and resources apparently insufficient to reverse the problems of overstretch and undermanning."[53] In the absence of compelling reasons for major defense budget increases, the British Treasury is likely to put primary focus on domestic spending priorities.

In France, non-defense requirements place very real constraints on increasing defense resources. The French unemployment rate has remained over 10 percent for much of the past decade, a problem to which a socialist government feels constrained to respond with increased spending on job creation and social welfare programs. The French government must also respond to continuing pressures to absorb a large immigrant population, primarily from North Africa. As a result, the French defense budget for 2000 fell below that of 1999, while procurement spending declined 3.5 percent.[54]

Budgetary pressures are especially acute in Germany. Unemployment has remained significant at levels around 10 percent, while the population is aging rapidly. The Social Democratic government has found it necessary to respond to these social stresses by increasing spending for pensions, health, welfare, and immigration programs, while continuing to support the costs of absorbing the former East Germany. The need for fiscal discipline led German Finance Minister Hans Eichel to demand across-the-board reductions in the German budget. These would reduce the Bundeswehr's projected funding by at least $1.6–2.3 billion per year over the next five years, from a 2000 base proposal of $22 billion, setting the budget at its lowest level in real terms since 1970.[55] Investment budgets would be particularly hard hit, with cuts of $10 billion in planned

Europe," *Defense News*, December 20, 1999, p. 26; David R. Sands, "Bid to Create EU Army Stalled; Lack of Euros Hinders Progress of Defense Force," *Washington Times*, January 9, 2000, p. C11.

53.   As reported in Reuters, *BBC Online*, February 10, 2000.

54.   Douglas Barrie, "Defense Budgets Remain Tight Throughout Europe," *Defense News*, December 20, 1999, p. 26.

55.   Jack Hoschouer, "German Industry Hamstrung by Government Policies," *De-*

funding between 2001 and 2004. These reductions could delay the introduction of advanced technology into German forces, as well as plans to buy a new transport aircraft, a light combat vehicle and an air-to-air missile for Eurofighter. The German Defense ministry argues that the budget should actually increase by at least $900 million per year, in order to accommodate the procurement requirements.[56]

Overall, European defense budgets are unlikely to grow. As a result, it will be difficult to meet force and technology goals set by EU defense planning or the DCI unless there is much closer coordination between national budgets to eliminate redundancies across countries, and a reallocation of priorities in national budgets away from personnel and overhead and toward investment. There are no current plans to coordinate defense budgeting in the EU context, suggesting that more efficiencies through the elimination of cross-European redundancies is not likely in the near term.

Moreover, it will not be easy to reallocate resources within national defense budgets. Germany could achieve budgetary savings by further reducing manpower, a proposal that has been made by the commission examining the structure of the Bundeswehr.[57] Moreover, given the important role of conscription in maintaining a democratic military and providing social services through alternative service options for potential conscripts, moving to a professional army will be difficult for the Germans. French military personnel remain large in number. Although end strength will decline with the end of conscription in 2003, increased funds will be needed to pay higher salaries for a professional military.[58] The British have encountered over-stretch as they have shrunk forces 35 percent since 1985, freeing funds for hardware purposes. The SDR actually proposed adding personnel. For both Britain and France, shrinking the force beyond a certain point could make it more difficult to provide adequate expeditionary forces to complement U.S. capabilities.[59]

Both defense budget increases and reallocations will be politically and economically difficult for the Europeans. U.S. officials have urged the

---

fense News, October 18, 1999, p. 78; Barrie, "Defense Budgets Remain Tight Throughout Europe."

56.   Rudiger Moniac, "German MOD Fights Cuts," Jane's Defence Weekly, February 23, 2000, p. 14; Moniac, "Debate Heats Up on Shape of German Armed Forces," Jane's Defence Weekly, April 5, 2000, p. 10.

57.   Moniac, "Debate Heats Up on Shape of German Armed Forces."

58.   Barrie, "Defense Budgets Remain Tight Throughout Europe."

59.   See, for example, "Defense: The Battle of Whitehall," Economist, January 29, 2000, p. 67; and "German Defence: Achtung!" Economist, December 18, 1999, p. 44.

Europeans to overcome these obstacles,[60] but it seems likely that the Europeans will have a hard time shaping common programs and equipment plans, especially plans that seek to achieve greater autonomy from the United States. The shortage of European resources and growing U.S. investment budgets could exacerbate transatlantic tensions and make it unlikely that the United States can count on European capabilities in the near term.

Consolidating Industry: The Creation of Two Fortresses

As already suggested, defense technology has changed dramatically over the past decade, drawing increasingly on a global and commercial information and communications technology base. At the same time, the declines in both defense budgets and the global market for defense equipment have stimulated significant change in the defense industrial and technology base on both sides of the Atlantic. While technological and economic trends are leading to greater transatlantic integration in dual-use technologies, however, defense firms on both sides of the Atlantic have consolidated into national and European champions. There is a marked trend toward the emergence of two defense industrial fortresses. Combined with a search for European defense autonomy, this trend could frustrate military interoperability between Europe and the United States and pose a further obstacle to synergies that allow savings on the U.S. side. It may be some time before these obstacles can be overcome, particularly on the U.S. side.[61]

A more global, consolidated defense industry has been developing steadily since the end of the Cold War. In some countries—France, Italy, and Spain—the major defense firms have been wholly or largely state-owned and closely tied to domestic and international policies. In others—Britain, Germany, and especially the United States—they are privately owned or have been privatized, leading the firms to respond more fully to market forces. The large contractors—Lockheed Martin, Raytheon, Northrop Grumman, Boeing, Matra, Aerospatiale, British

---

60. "In the final analysis, allies will have to spend more on defense, if they are to measure up to NATO's military requirement and establish a European Security and Defense Identity that is separable but not separate from NATO." Secretary of Defense William S. Cohen, "Europe Must Spend More on Defense," *Washington Post*, December 6, 1999, p. 27.

61. For more discussion of the transatlantic industry process, see Gordon Adams, "Convergence or Divergence: The Future of the Transatlantic Defence Industry," in Simon Duke, ed., *Between Vision and Reality: CFSP's Progress on the Path to Maturity* (Maastricht, Holland: European Institute of Public Administration, 2000), pp. 161–208.

Aerospace, CASA, Saab, DASA, Finmeccanica, Thomson CFA—performed defense system integration and final assembly or built major components of military hardware: missiles, aircraft, helicopters, and satellites.

The consolidation process took place fairly quickly in the United States, once the Defense Department sent out a clear message in 1993 that the prime contractors should merge or exit the market. National consolidation of the industry in Europe at the national level actually preceded the U.S. process. In some cases, it involved both privatizing and consolidating businesses, leading in Britain to the emergence of two major firms: British Aerospace (BAe) and General Electric Co./Marconi. In Germany, the government similarly stimulated the emergence of one major firm—Deutsche Aerospace (DASA)—a subsidiary of Daimler-Benz (now Daimler-Chrysler). In other cases, such as Italy and Spain, state-owned defense facilities were consolidated under state-run holding companies—Finmeccanica and CASA, respectively. In Sweden, Saab and Celsius provided the two poles for industry consolidation.

In France, where the industry was largely government-owned and industrial autonomy was seen as a vital goal, consolidation proceeded more slowly. French state holdings were gradually centralized in Aerospatiale and Thomson CSF and these were, in turn, slowly being watered down through public offerings and mergers.

While cross-national defense programs and corporate joint ventures had become increasingly common in Europe (Airbus, Tornado, AlphaJet, Eurofighter, Typhoon, and Tiger helicopter), before 1999 there was relatively little in the way of cross-border mergers and acquisitions among the more prominent European firms.

The vision of a trans-European defense firm strong enough to compete with the major U.S. firms emerged from government discussions in the late 1990s. In December 1997, the French, British, and German governments invited the leading European aerospace firms to propose a plan for creating a single European champion, the European Aerospace and Defense Company (EADC). Sweden, Italy, and Spain joined this group in the summer of 1998. But as quickly as the vision of one European industry fortress had been created, it died when BAe decided at the end of 1998 that it would acquire the Marconi defense assets of GEC, its British competitor, creating BAE Systems. This merger created a large system-integrating firm in Britain, but also a potential competitor in the United States, where the merged company made 22 percent of its sales. The creation of BAE Systems, however, served as a major stimulus for the emergence of a second large European firm. DASA responded to the British move by out-bidding the British firm for control of the Spanish aerospace industry champion, CASA, and negotiated with Aerospatiale Matra for the creation of the European Aeronautic, Defense and Space Company (EADS) in October 1999. EADS, in turn, absorbed the Spanish firm and, in 2000, negotiated a joint military aircraft venture with the Alenia division of Finmeccanica.

These two large mergers, and the continuing integration of European aerospace and electronics, are rapidly changing the map of the European defense sector. There will be two major prime contractors in Europe with the assets and know-how to integrate advanced technology into European defense capabilities. Moreover, these decisions foreshadow other moves, still being considered, to consolidate other areas such as shipbuilding, land combat systems, and helicopters.

Given the flow of defense and dual-use technologies across the Atlantic, a natural next step would be for transatlantic industry ties to develop. Such ties would encourage a transfer of defense technology and know-how that could facilitate interoperability and efficiency among the allies. However, neither economic logic nor government decisions have led to closer relationships among major prime contractors across the Atlantic. Over the years, only British firms have entered the U.S. market to any extent, both with sales to the Defense Department and acquisitions in the private sector.[62] There are few cases of partnerships or acquisitions by continental European firms in the U.S. market, since Aerospatiale sold off its holding of Fairchild in the early 1990s and Thomson-CSF's bid to acquire Vought Aerospace was frustrated in 1992.

Nor has there been any significant acquisition of European defense assets by U.S. firms, despite much discussion of the interest of Lockheed Martin, Boeing, and Raytheon in penetrating the European aerospace market. The U.S. General Electric company does have a joint venture with the French firm SNECMA, marketing the CFM-56 engine. Boeing has purchased ownership of the Czech aircraft firm Aero Vodochody, in anticipation of expanding aircraft purchases by the new NATO members.

---

62. BAE Systems has long been active in the United States. GEC/Marconi acquired U.S. defense electronics firm Tracor in 1997 and, in 2000, the new BAE Systems agreed to buy Lockheed Martin's Sanders electronics unit, doubling its sales in the United States. See Greg Schneider, "Lockheed Agreement Tests U.S. Policy," *Washington Post*, July 14, 2000, p. E1. Rolls-Royce sells jet fighter engines for the two joint U.S./UK aircraft: the AV-8B Harrier and T-45 trainer. In 1996, Rolls acquired U.S. engine manufacturer Allison Engine, increasing its foothold in the U.S. market for aircraft and land equipment engines. British defense firm Lucas also merged into the U.S. market and is now part of TRW. "Britain Opts Out of Europe," *Economist*, January 23, 1999, p. 71; Charles Goldsmith, "Britain's GEC Agrees to Buy Tracor in a $1.1 Billion Deal," *Wall Street Journal*, April 22, 1998, p. 2.

Transatlantic discussions have begun to accelerate between companies that seek strategic partnerships: Raytheon with Thomson, Boeing with BAE Systems, Lockheed Martin with EADS and Airbus, and Northrop Grumman with DASA/EADS. A partnership has emerged between the first pair, with prospects of others on the horizon. In general, U.S. firms tend to have a program or product line orientation to their strategic thinking, not a goal of global market presence. There is some recognition in the U.S. industry that market presence in Europe may be of long-term corporate benefit in an era of globalizing defense businesses. A European presence would provide U.S. firms with the opportunity to influence common procurement and industrial policy rules in the European Union, ensuring that those rules do not create a wall around the European market that the U.S. firms cannot penetrate.

With the consolidation of the European industry, moreover, there is some recognition in Europe that partnerships with U.S. firms may now be created on a more equal footing. EADS, too, is discussing the prospect of further partnerships in the United States. The primary obstacle to taking advantage of transatlantic opportunities is politics. In Europe, the appeal of a separate European policy and military capability, sustained by a European "fortress" industry, remains potent. There is also significant political and bureaucratic resistance in the United States to integration in the transatlantic defense market. U.S. strategic and defense planning also emphasizes autonomy, reducing the likelihood that the military services will look to Europe for technological or industrial cooperation or defense capabilities.

There are sizable administrative obstacles facing European firms that seek to enter the U.S. market. U.S. Defense Department officials and advisory boards have recognized that the underlying globalization of technologies and the needs of coalition operations make greater transatlantic industrial cooperation a desirable objective. While there are plans to ease U.S. export controls and obstacles to investment, the dismantling of "fortress America" is unlikely to proceed quickly, given the political and bureaucratic issues at stake. The Defense Department made it clear to U.S. and European defense executives in October 1999 that joint ventures and partnerships among the major system integrators would be encouraged, but mergers among the large firms were unlikely in the near future.[63]

Moreover, major new joint transatlantic defense programs are scarce. Funding for the joint U.S.-British land vehicle, known as Tracer in the

63. Robert Wall, "New Strategy Emerging for Transatlantic Linkups," *Aviation Week and Space Technology*, November 1, 1999, p. 27; and author's interviews.

UK, was reduced in the FY 2001 U.S. Army budget request. The British decision to buy the European Meteor missile for its Eurofighter aircraft was a setback for Raytheon's effort to enter the European missile market.[64] The European decision on air transport leading to the selection of a military version of the Airbus is likely to discourage sales of the Boeing C-17 to European allies.[65] A gain for a homegrown European transport capability would be a loss for interoperability in the Alliance. The pending NATO decision on future airborne ground surveillance architecture pits a U.S.-led group including Belgium, Canada, Denmark and Norway against a Franco-German-Italian-Dutch group. The ultimate choice will send a signal about whether the technology will be solely European or transatlantic.

The United States faces a key decision with respect to the future Joint Strike Fighter, intended to succeed the Air Force's F-16, the Navy's F/A-18, and the Marine Corps AV-8B Harrier, as well as British fighters. BAE Systems is an associate partner in the program, creating an initial transatlantic link that could eventually spread to the continent as the European allies look for a successor to Eurofighter, Gripen, and Rafale. The program is not yet truly transatlantic, but a U.S. decision to delay it could create an incentive for the Europeans to look to their own industry to meet next-generation fighter requirements.[66]

All told, trends in the defense industry, defense exports, and cooperative programs are not encouraging for greater transatlantic cooperation. It may be some time before the European industrial consolidations are digested and the new firms can turn in a transatlantic direction. U.S. export control and investment policies are unlikely to change quickly. An expansion of the transatlantic agenda for cooperative programs seems unlikely as well. None of these trends suggest a positive environment in which the United States can safely rely on European defense capabilities.

---

64. See Douglas Barrie, "Program Choices to Define UK Arms Path," *Defense News,* November 1, 1999.

65. Seven European governments are discussing the A400M option (Belgium, Britain, France, Italy, Germany, Spain, and Turkey), for a potential buy of 288 aircraft. However, the plane could not be delivered before 2006, while the British requirement comes two years earlier and the French a year earlier. Michael J. Witt, "Airbus Military Sees Bright Future for A400M Transport," *Defense News,* November 8, 1999, p. 22.

66. The Air Force has hinted that they may sacrifice JSF funding to secure adequate resources for the more advanced, stealthy F-22, a decision that would set back the transatlantic character of the program. See Elizabeth Becker, "Air Force Willing to Abandon Joint Fighter to Save the F22," *New York Times,* October 23, 1999, p. A-10.

A "European Dividend" Would be Small

The purpose of this book is to explore alternative ways in which the United States can fulfill its military requirements within limited defense resources. This chapter has explored the degree to which a stronger European defense capability might enable the Europeans to take over defense missions, operating together with the United States or supplementing its capabilities, in ways which allow the United States to forgo some forces and expenditures. Given the state of play in European defense, however, U.S. defense planners should not count on reaping a large burden-sharing dividend in the near term as a consequence of the European Union's decision to take on a defense role. The realities of European defense planning are sufficiently complex that such a dividend, should it appear, will only do so well down the road from the planning horizon in this volume.

The broadest recommendation one can make, given this fundamental reality, is that it is in the long-term interests of the United States to do what it can to encourage the emergence of a European Security and Defense Policy and military capability that is transparent and cooperative with U.S. defense planning and integrated as far as possible into the NATO alliance. By early in the next decade, such an entity or at least the British and French parts of it, might serve as a multiplier for U.S. forces.

What are some of the steps the United States might take to encourage an evolution in this direction, and what might be their budgetary implications? First, the difference in strategic perspectives matters. The United States is unlikely to forgo the long-range strike forces, logistics, transportation, sustainment, and intelligence it requires to operate globally. Europe is unlikely to include a global dimension in its defense planning in the near term. Only the British and the French have projected developing expeditionary capabilities that could supplement U.S. assets. Operating out of region, the British are likely to provide a small amount of air power, and potentially a few brigades of ground forces that could inter-operate with the United States. Further downstream, the French could provide supplementary air power and precision-guided munitions, building on the capabilities deployed for the Kosovo air campaign. While these would be useful additions to U.S. capabilities, they do not change substantially the amount of air power and precision munitions the United States projects buying in the future.

It is exceedingly unlikely that the Germans will be major contributors to out-of-area expeditionary or high-intensity operations in the near term.

In the Gulf War, $54 billion of the $61 billion in U.S. costs were reimbursed by allies who benefited from the U.S. prosecution of the war but were reluctant or unable to provide forces, including the Germans. It is difficult to imagine the Germans being willing today or in the future to substitute funding support for capability in this way, given both financial constraints and political reluctance to repeat the experience of the Gulf War funding.

Second, if the primary European strategic commitment will be the security of Europe, there may be some potential nearer-term savings, achieved gradually, from the development of the "headline goal" force decided on in Cologne and Helsinki. This force would be designed to carry out humanitarian, rescue, peacekeeping, and other Petersberg tasks, less high-intensity or technologically demanding than expeditionary missions or the high-intensity combat capability that dominates U.S. defense planning.[67] A force of 50,000–60,000, including significant German land force capabilities, could play a growing role in the kind of peace stabilization mission NATO is performing in Kosovo and Bosnia. Europe is already in a position to provide 20,000–30,000 soldiers to such a peace stabilization force and rotate it over time. This has permitted the United States to play a smaller role in the land force mission than it did in the Kosovo air war.

This could give the United States the near-term option of reducing two active duty U.S. Army divisions, which would have been used for peace stabilization operations in Europe. Congressional Budget Office (CBO) data suggests such a reduction could produce annual savings of $2.6 billion by the end of the decade.[68] Acquisition plans for heavy armored equipment might be modified over the long-term as well, reflecting greater European assumption of the peace stabilization mission in Europe, but it is difficult to estimate the possible savings.

Over the next decade, however, the United States will have to continue to provide the logistics, sustainment, transportation, communications, and intelligence needed to support European forces engaged in such missions. It is unlikely that the EU's "headline goal" rapid deployment forces planned will achieve autonomy along these dimensions by

---

67.   The Center for Strategic and Budgetary Assessment has proposed that the European allies take responsibility for "low end, manpower intensive operations like peacekeeping and urban control and eviction operations." Andrew Krepinevich, *Transforming America's Alliances* (Washington, D.C.: Center for Strategic and Budgetary Assessment, February 2000), pp. 44–45.

68.   Congressional Budget Office, *Structuring the Active and Reserve Army for the 21st Century* (Washington, D.C.: CBO, December 1997).

2003. However, to the extent the Europeans acquire dedicated sealift and airlift, the U.S. requirement for such assets dedicated to the European theater could also decline. The United States could rely on European transportation assets for intra-European deployments, especially if this involved European acquisition of U.S. C-17 aircraft. The CBO has also identified a proxy that could fit this option: the development of a common NATO air fleet of twenty C-17 aircraft, for which the United States and Europe could share the cost. According to the CBO option, five-year savings would amount to $3.1 billion; ten-year savings could come to $4.0 billion, with annual savings reaching perhaps $200 million.[69] The Europeans would, however, face a difficult fiscal and political decision with this option, since it would mean either forgoing acquisition of a military version of the A400 Airbus or spending significantly more on airlift than currently planned.

A third near-term option would be for the United States to cede responsibility to the Europeans for naval coverage in the North Atlantic and the Mediterranean, leaving U.S. naval forces free to cover the Pacific and Indian Oceans.[70] However, it is difficult to imagine the United States relying entirely on the Europeans for naval protection, nor is it clear that such an option would produce any savings, if the objective is to leave the United States free to use the Navy's twelve carriers to provide 100 percent naval coverage in the South Asian and Asian theater. If, however, as part of such an option the Navy reduced the fleet by two carrier battle groups (leaving ten carriers including a reserve carrier), annual operating savings could reach roughly $2.4 billion by the end of the decade, with procurement savings (carriers, aircraft, surface combatants, and submarines) of $1.8 billion.[71]

These are the only European theater options that could produce near-term savings for the United States while assuring that military requirements were reliably met by European forces. The other options in the transatlantic arena would deliver savings or capabilities only over a longer period, not easily measurable in terms of budgetary savings.

If the United States wishes to encourage the Europeans to accept more global responsibilities over time, it would make sense for the defense reviews on both sides of the Atlantic to be more closely integrated. Discussions of strategy, doctrine, and forces within the NATO framework only go part way toward this objective. The Europeans have generally

---

69. Ibid., pp. 46–47.

70. See Krepinevich, *Transforming America's Military*, p. 52.

71. CBO, *Budget Options for National Defense*, pp. 15–16.

not been included in the strategy discussions that are part of the U.S. Quadrennial Defense Reviews, but they could be, starting with the 2001 exercise. Regular meetings and briefings could provide useful European input to shaping the U.S. strategic vision, while conveying to the Europeans the capabilities and operational doctrine the United States would like to see develop on the European side.

The ability of the United States to rely on European capabilities, either for peace stabilization or high-intensity operations, will depend significantly on the degree to which the Europeans meet the goals of the Defense Capabilities Initiative in NATO. As long as there is not a direct dialogue between this effort and EU force planning, mistrust and unpredictability will stand in the way of achieving synergies, compatibility, and interoperability. Progress on the DCI, especially in developing stronger European logistics and stockpiles for sustainability, would strengthen both the ESDP and NATO interoperability. Ultimately, the U.S. burden in logistics and sustainability in Europe could be relieved. The United States should insist on an open channel of communications between the two exercises.

Technology could well become the Achilles' heel of transatlantic defense interoperability. The Europeans have declared the intention of investing in technology that will close the gap in information, communications, intelligence, all weather, day-night air operations, and precision guidance exposed by the Kosovo air campaign. On top of creating the force to carry out the Petersberg tasks, however, this is an ambitious agenda; European budgets will not be adequate to cover it in the near term. The United States needs to continue to urge the Europeans to make greater investments in defense technology to attain this goal. Moreover, as politically difficult as it is, the Defense Department needs to revisit regularly options for buying European defense technology, to help stimulate European investment in compatible advanced defense technologies. The Europeans and Americans should aim to do better at defining joint requirements and carrying out joint procurements to meet those requirements in such areas as all-weather, day-night aircraft, precision-guided munitions, and communications equipment. Resulting improvements in interoperability and increased volume of orders would point the way to greater efficiencies and procurement savings.

The United States should continue to urge the Europeans either to increase defense budgets or to reallocate defense resources toward meeting the dual requirement of advanced technology and the equipment to deploy and sustain expeditionary forces. Budget increases are likely to come slowly in Europe, given the political pressures; U.S. diplomacy could help provide the explanation for why they are necessary.

The United States needs to make a major effort to overcome internal resistance to greater technology transfer and investment flows across the Atlantic. Neither Europe nor the United States will reap the full advantages of dual-use technologies, adequate market size, a healthy stream of investment, or increased competition in the defense market unless barriers are lowered with countries that provide credible controls against transfer of sensitive technologies to third countries.[72] While the payoff from license-free or less restrictive trade regimes will not emerge at once, it can only be beneficial to both sides over the next decade, leading to savings downstream.

If U.S. savings through enhanced European defense capabilities are to emerge, they will only do so slowly, and with considerable effort on both sides of the Atlantic. Strategy convergence needs to be achieved, and both sides need to agree on a different distribution of missions. European defense budgets will need to grow and the Europeans will need to invest, in particular, in research, development, and production of more advanced defense technologies. Finally, the transatlantic defense market will need to evolve toward greater transparency, openness, and flexibility. These are all tall orders, though not impossible. They will demand both hard work and good will over the next decade.

---

72. The U.S. government announced 17 reforms to existing U.S. export control rules in May 2000, including a proposal to extend a license exempt regime to countries that agree to upgrade their security regimes to U.S. standards. This proposal should go some way to facilitating greater flexibility in transatlantic industry trade and business relationships. See Robert Wall, "U.S. Issues New Export Regulations," *Aviation Week and Space Technology*, May 29, 2000, pp. 38–39.

Chapter 5

The Hunt for Small Potatoes: Savings in Nuclear Deterrence Forces

David Mosher

Throughout much of the last decade, the United States has been able to turn to its nuclear forces and missile defense programs for savings. The end of the Cold War has allowed it to reduce its nuclear forces and modernization programs, and change how the forces are operated, through a series of formal arms control agreements and unilateral measures. The United States has also been able to reduce the size and pace of activity of its nuclear weapons complex and to trim the scope of its national missile defense effort. Those cuts have allowed the country to reap sizable savings. From 1990 to 2000, the United States cut its total nuclear deterrence budget by forty percent, after accounting for inflation—from $59 billion to $35 billion (see Table 5.1).[1] That reduction is one and a half times greater than the 25 percent cut in total spending for national defense over the same period.

But those days may be over. Future nuclear arms control agreements may improve U.S. security, but they will not produce large savings. The peace dividend has largely been realized for deterrent forces, unless the United States significantly changes its deterrence doctrine or its approach

---

1. A comprehensive analysis of historical spending on nuclear deterrence can be found in Stephen I. Schwartz, ed., *Atomic Audit: The Costs and Consequences of U.S. Nuclear Weapons Since 1940* (Washington, D.C.: Brookings Institution Press, 1998). By its accounting, the United States averaged nearly $100 billion a year on nuclear weapons and related activities during the Cold War, indicating that the magnitude of the drawdown, which began in the late 1980s, is even greater than indicated in this chapter. The *Atomic Audit* estimates that the United States spent about $36 billion in 1998 (expressed in 2000 dollars), which is very similar to the estimate in Table 5.1 of $35.3 billion in 2000.

Table 5.1.   U.S. nuclear budgets, 1990 and 2000 (in billions of 2000 dollars of budget authority).

	1990	2000
Department of Defense		
Offensive Forces	26.9	9.0
Missile Defenses		
NMD	2.1	1.5
TMD	0.1	2.1
Other	2.4	1.4
Subtotal, Missile Defense	**4.6**	**5.0**
C3I	11.9	6.2
Arms Control Compliance and Other	0.2	2.1
Total, DoD	**43.7**	**22.3**
Department of Energy	7.3	4.5
Weapons Actvities	2.7	5.8
Waste Management	0.0	0.2
Fissile Materials Disposition	5.3	1.5
Other	**15.3**	**12.0**
Total, DoE		
Reduce Proliferation Threats from Former Soviet Union		
Cooperative Threat Reduction (DoD)	0.0	0.5
Non-Proliferation (DoE)	0.0	0.2
Reduce Brain Drain and Export		
Controls (State)	0.0	0.2
HEU and Pu Disposition	0.0	0.2
Total, Threat Reduction	**0.0**	**1.1**
Grand Total	**58.9**	**35.3**

Sources: Author's estimates based on data from the Department of Defense; the Department of Energy; the Ballistic Missile Defense Organization; Congressional Budget Office, *The START Treaty and Beyond* (Washington, D.C.: CBO, October, 1991); Stephen I. Schwartz, ed., *Atomic Audit: The Costs and Consequences of U.S. Nuclear Weapons Since 1940* (Washington, D.C.: Brookings, 1998); and William Hoehn, *Russsian Nuclear Security and the Clinton Administration's Fiscal Year 2000 Expanded Threat Reduction Initiative: A Summary of Congressional Action* (Princeton, N.J.: Russian-American Nuclear Security Advisory Council, February 2000).

Note: Numbers may not add to totals due to rounding.

for maintaining the weapons stockpile. The United States has cut its nuclear forces and nuclear weapons programs far enough that what remains is mostly the large fixed cost of doing business; further cuts will result in increasingly small savings.

Not only are future arms reductions likely to produce small savings, but several factors will continue to place upward pressure on costs. Missile defenses will be the most likely cause of budget growth. Spending will increase sharply over the next decade as the United States accelerates development of a national missile defense system, deploys it, and begins to operate it. Pressures will also continue to mount for more spending on theater missile defenses to protect U.S. troops and allies from growing arsenals of short- and intermediate-range ballistic and cruise missiles. Given the variety of theater defenses and the number that must be purchased and operated to protect troops and allies, spending for those systems could exceed the costs of national missile defense.

Second, future arms control measures may actually increase costs, depending on how they are implemented. At best, savings from further cuts are likely to be minimal. The number of platforms will already be quite low under START II in both relative and absolute terms: fourteen submarines and 500 ICBMs.[2] The number of warheads may be reduced in the future, but further shrinkage in the number of platforms is likely to be very small, if it happens at all. In addition, inspection regimes are likely to become increasingly intrusive and costly as forces are cut below START II levels. For example, the framework for START III that Presidents Clinton and Yeltsin signed in Helsinki in 1997 calls for verifiable warhead dismantlement, a potentially expensive proposition. Disposition of surplus fissile materials will also require new expenditures for several decades.

Third, the United States may find it necessary to increase its assistance to Russia over the next decade to lock up, consolidate, and convert its nuclear materials, and keep its weapons experts from selling their skills abroad. Finally, by the end of this decade, the United States will have to start investing in replacements for its Trident missiles, and by early in the next decade must begin developing a replacement for its Trident submarines and ICBMs. Those programs will add several billion dollars to the budget each year. Costs might be even higher if a U.S. decision to deploy a national missile defense causes Russia to scrap the

---

2. Any reductions of nuclear-capable bombers and dual-role fighter aircraft by future arms control agreements will not reduce costs, because the size of those forces is determined largely by requirements for conventional (non-nuclear) missions.

START II treaty and the United States responds by keeping its forces at today's levels.

In short, although the United States may be able to squeeze a few billion dollars a year out of the budget by cutting its ICBMs and ballistic missile submarines, those savings are likely to be overwhelmed by spending on national and theater missile defense. Savings may also be offset somewhat if assistance to Russia is increased to reduce nuclear threats, and more intrusive verification accompanies deeper reductions in nuclear weapons. There are many important reasons to reduce nuclear threats further by pursuing new arms control agreements, reducing forces, dismantling warheads, and securing and disposing of fissile materials; significant savings is just not one of them anymore.

This chapter focuses on U.S. deterrent forces, which include three central components: nuclear weapons, delivery systems, and theater and national ballistic missile defenses.[3] They are treated together here because they are, or in the case of missile defenses will become, part of the nation's ability to deter the use of nuclear, biological, and chemical weapons against the United States, its forces, and its allies, or cope with their use if deterrence fails. Arms control is also an important factor because it establishes the parameters around which the U.S. and Russian deterrents are shaped. Nuclear threat reduction efforts with the former Soviet Union are also included here because they can help to limit the emergence of future nuclear weapons states. The chapter begins with a review of the nuclear downsizing that began even before the Cold War ended. With that context, it examines how much further nuclear budgets can be cut. Finally, it outlines several sources of pressure that may drive budgets up in future years.

The 1990s: Realizing the Peace Dividend

The 1990s were a decade of steep decline for deterrent forces. Not only were forces reduced by the START I treaty, but modernization programs were slashed and bombers and command and control platforms were taken off alert through a series of unilateral measures that reflected the thawing of the Cold War and the demise of the Soviet Union. Strategic

---

3. It could be argued that theater missile defenses do not belong in a discussion of deterrent forces. After all, they will be deployed with conventional forces to regional conflicts. But the real pressure to build such systems has always been to protect forces against missiles carrying chemical, biological, or nuclear weapons, even if many of the missiles that the defenses ultimately encounter will probably carry conventional warheads.

missile defense programs were also scaled back considerably from the ambitious plans of the Reagan era. The nuclear weapons production complex was shrunk significantly to support a much smaller nuclear stockpile.

THE BUSH YEARS: UNILATERAL CUTS AND THE START TREATIES

When George Bush became president in January 1989, the United States had robust plans to continue the nuclear buildup started under President Carter and greatly expanded under President Reagan. Although the Bush administration originally intended to continue those programs, the rapidly changing world made it difficult to justify all of them. Within three years of assuming office, the Bush administration made a number of significant cuts to nuclear forces, modernization plans, and alert rates, sometimes on its own initiative and sometimes with prodding from Congress (see Table 5.2).

In one of the boldest reductions of the Cold War, on September 27, 1991, President Bush ordered unilateral cuts in battlefield nuclear weapons and removed all nuclear weapons from surface ships. He also changed the alert rates of several elements of the force, removing bombers and Minuteman II intercontinental ballistic missiles from 24-hour alert status, and halting round-the-clock flights of nuclear command and control aircraft. President Gorbachev responded eight days later with similar actions. The Bush administration also negotiated and signed both the START I and START II treaties, which would reduce U.S. and Russian strategic nuclear forces to 6,000 and 3,500 accountable warheads, respectively.[4] Neither treaty would limit short-range nuclear forces or the number of nuclear weapons that each side keeps in its stockpile. After securing the ratification of START I, the Bush administration began the process of reducing forces to meet its limits.

Perhaps the most significant impact that the Bush administration had on the budget for the nuclear deterrent was to terminate most of the high-profile, expensive modernization programs, including the road-mobile Small ICBM, the rail-mobile Peacekeeper (MX) ICBM, the SRAM-II and SRAM-T short-range attack missiles, and the Follow-On To Lance short-range surface-to-surface missile. The administration also capped

---

4. The START I counting rules allow for the United States to deploy several thousand more strategic warheads than 6,000. This is because the treaty heavily discounts bomber warheads: it counts as one warhead bombers that do not carry cruise missiles, even though they can carry 16 to 24 nuclear bombs. It also counts bombers that carry cruise missiles as carrying only 10 warheads, even though U.S. B-52 bombers can carry up to 20 cruise missiles. By contrast, START II counts the actual number of warheads each bomber can carry.

Table 5.2. Changes in U.S. Nuclear Forces, 1990 to 2000.

	Plans, Circa 1990		
	Status	Goal	Status, 2000
Modernization Programs			
Small ICBM	In development	N/A	Canceled
Rail-based Peace-keeper ICBM (MX)	50 deployed in silos, rail-basing under development	100 on trains	50 in silos
B-2A Stealth Bomber	In development	132	21
Advanced Cruise Missile	In development	1,000	~400
Follow-On To Lance	In development	N/A	Canceled
SRAM-II	In development	N/A	Canceled
SRAM-T	In development	N/A	Canceled
Trident Submarine	In production	At least 21	18, but 14 after 2005
W-88 warhead	In production	1,000 or more	~400
National Missile Defense	Phase I of large, space-based defense under development	Highly effective shield against thousands of Soviet missiles	Limited defense against a few tens of warheads; under development
Operations			
Minuteman II ICBMs	450 operational	Eventual retirement	Taken off alert in 1991, eliminated by 1998
Bombers	One third of force ready to launch within minutes	No change	Taken off alert in 1991
Command and Control Aircraft			
TACAMO	In flight 24 hours a day	No change	Less frequent patrols
NEACP	In flight 24 hours a day	No change	Grounded
Tactical Forces			
Cruise missile on submarines	Deployed	No change	Removed in 1991, kept in U.S.
Weapons on surface ships	Deployed	Modernization	Removed in 1991, dismantled
Battlefield (Army) weapons	Deployed	Modernization	Removed in 1991, dismantled
Air delivered bombs	Deployed	Modernization	Deployed, numbers reduced

Sources: Department of Defense, *Annual Report to the President,* January 1989–1993, March 2000; Congressional Budget Office, *The START Treaty and Beyond* (Washington D.C.: CBO, October 1991); NRDC Nuclear Notebook, "U.S. Strategic Nuclear Forces, End of 1998," *Bulletin of the Atomic Scientists,* January/February 1999.

Notes: ICBM = Intercontinental Ballistic Missile; N/A = not available; SRAM = Short Range Attack Missile; SRAM-T = Tactical SRAM; TACAMO = Take Charge and Move Out aircraft for communications with submarines; NEACP = National Emergency Airborne Command Post.

the production of Trident submarines at 18 (down from a goal of 21 or more). The Congress forced the administration to reduce the scope of several other programs, including the B-2 bomber (capped at 20 rather than 132) and the advanced cruise missile (capped at 217 down from 1,000). In addition, the Bush administration reduced the scope of the Strategic Defense Initiative, redirecting it from a program based on President Reagan's vision of an impenetrable shield against a large Soviet attack to one that would defend against an accidental or unauthorized Soviet attack of some 200 warheads. Although that change did not reduce annual budgets significantly at the time, it sharply reduced future funding requirements. Finally, responding to the prodding of a bipartisan effort in Congress led by Senator Sam Nunn and Senator Richard Lugar, the Bush administration began to implement a program aimed at helping Russia and other states of the former Soviet Union eliminate excess missiles and bombers and secure its nuclear warheads.

The Bush administration also made two significant changes in the nuclear weapons program of the Department of Energy (DoE): it began to reduce the size of the production complex and started the process of cleaning up the complex. In addition, the Bush administration discontinued making the powerful W-88 warhead for the D-5 missile after production was halted for safety reasons. President Bush also began the U.S. moratorium on underground testing by signing (reluctantly) a bipartisan amendment to the Energy and Water Appropriations Bill for Fiscal Year 1994. The U.S. moratorium continues to this day, even though the nuclear tests by India and Pakistan in May of 1998 vitiated the Congressional ban, which was to remain in force until another country tested a nuclear weapon.

THE CLINTON YEARS: MODEST CUTS AND NEW DEMANDS
The Clinton administration came to power hoping to cut spending on nuclear forces significantly, put an end to efforts to deploy national missile defenses, and increase theater missile defense programs. The administration's legacy, however, has been one of caution. It has cut forces and modernization very modestly beyond what the Bush administration had planned, and it is poised to start deploying a national missile defense, albeit a much smaller system than the Bush administration had wanted.

THE FIRST CLINTON TERM. The first Clinton term was marked by cuts to national missile defense and the continued drawdown of forces to meet START limits. The administration's most significant action was to reduce plans for spending on missile defenses sharply by demoting the Bush administration's program to deploy a national missile capable of defending against two hundred Soviet warheads to a "technology development program." Annual budgets fell from a projected $5–7 billion a year to $450 million. But the administration increased funding for theater missile defenses significantly, from $1.1 billion in 1993 to over $2 billion in 2000, to reflect the growing threat posed by short and intermediate-range missiles that was exposed during the 1991 Persian Gulf War.

The Clinton administration also continued to reduce forces to comply with START I by removing all 450 Minuteman II missiles, 77 B-52G bombers, and 22 Poseidon submarines from service. To save money, the administration completed those reductions several years ahead of schedule. Although the Clinton administration did not terminate the few nuclear modernization programs that it had inherited, it trimmed them. During the 1994 Nuclear Posture Review, the Pentagon determined that the United States could live with fourteen rather than eighteen Trident submarines under START II. That decision would avoid spending more than $4 billion to replace the aging C-4 missiles on the fifteenth through eighteenth boats with more capable D-5 missiles. The Nuclear Posture Review also reconfirmed the 1992 Bush administration decision to cap the B-2 stealth bomber fleet at 20 aircraft, and reduced the requirement for venerable, 1960s vintage B-52H bombers from 94 to 66.[5]

Since that review, the Republican-dominated Congress has opposed most of those proposed reductions, arguing that Russia must ratify the START II treaty first. Congress has prohibited the administration from taking steps to retire Trident submarines or B-52H bombers in advance of Russia's ratification. But the Congress finally relented in 2000, when it faced the prospect of having to spend several hundred million dollars to keep all eighteen Tridents in service. Nevertheless, the Congressional prohibition on reducing the B-52H force remains in effect, in part because the cost of keeping those bombers in the force is small. Meanwhile, the Clinton administration has been gradually increasing the number of B-52s it wants to keep, from 66 in 1995 to 71 in 1998, and most recently to 74 in 2000.

Perhaps the Clinton administration's most significant accomplishment during its first term was securing Senate ratification of the START II treaty in 1996. The treaty limits each side to 3,500 deployed warheads and will eliminate all multiple-warhead ICBMs. Russia's lower house of parliament, the Duma, ratified the treaty on April 14, 2000, but before the treaty enters into force, the U.S. Senate must ratify the protocol that de-

---

5.   One year later, however, in the middle of a tough reelection campaign, President Clinton decided to expand the B-2 fleet to 21 aircraft by converting a test vehicle to an operational bomber. He made the announcement at a visit to the B-2 plant in California.

lays final implementation of the treaty until the end of 2007. The Duma also attached a non-binding amendment to the enabling legislation for the treaty stating that Russia will abandon the treaty if the United States deploys missile defenses.

One of the Clinton administration's most aggressive efforts to reduce costs during its first term was aimed at the Department of Energy's nuclear weapons program. It accelerated the consolidation, started by the Bush administration, of the weapons complex to support a smaller START II–sized stockpile. It also cut the budget for designing and testing nuclear weapons from $5 billion a year to $3.5 billion a year in anticipation of a permanent moratorium on underground nuclear testing. Those reductions were partially offset, however, by the rising cost of the DoE's effort to consolidate and clean up the weapons complex.

Another flagship effort of the Clinton administration during its first term was to boost efforts to help control the nuclear threats from a disintegrating Soviet Union. It expanded the Nunn-Lugar program to help Russia eliminate nuclear launchers and secure its nuclear weapons. It created several programs to help secure the nuclear materials in Russia and former Soviet states suddenly left without protection by the collapse of the Soviet internal security apparatus and the social upheaval that came with the disintegration of the Soviet Union. The administration also created several programs to reduce the incentives for nuclear weapons scientists to sell their skills abroad.

THE SECOND CLINTON TERM. For a variety of reasons, the United States has made little progress toward reducing the cost of deterrent forces during the Clinton administration's second term. It has not made any further agreements with Russia to cut nuclear forces, and its newfound interest in national missile defense has led it to reverse many of the cuts it had made to such programs during its first term.

In addition to Congressional opposition to reducing forces, an important impediment to further nuclear reductions has been the administration's insistence that, despite Russia's strong wishes to do so, it will not negotiate deeper cuts with Russia until the Duma ratifies START II. The Duma ratified the treaty on April 14, 2000, but only after seven years' delay. During that time, the Clinton administration took several steps to prod the Duma to act on START II. For example, Presidents Clinton and Yeltsin agreed to a new framework for a START III treaty at their March 1997 summit meeting in Helsinki. The treaty would cut the number of deployed warheads to roughly 1,000 less than START II limits; each side would be allowed to deploy 2,000 to 2,500 warheads. Negotiations were to begin as soon as the Duma ratified START II. The agreement also set a new precedent for the destruction of warheads. It called for "measures relating to the transparency of strategic nuclear warhead inventories and the destruction of strategic nuclear warheads and any other jointly agreed technical and organizational measures, to promote the irreversibility of deep reductions including prevention of a rapid increase in the number of warheads." All previous agreements have focused on delivery platforms (missiles, bombers, and submarines) or the number of warheads deployed on each platform; here, for the first time, the agreement covered the number of warheads in the stockpile. The details of how transparent reductions would be accomplished have yet to be established.

During its second term, the Clinton administration also increased funding somewhat for programs to reduce the nuclear threats from Russia, although its support for those programs has not been as strong as some critics would like. For example, President Clinton has never given a major speech to drum up support for the programs within a reluctant Congress. The administration has also increased spending on the Department of Energy's stockpile stewardship and management program: its program for preserving the reliability and safety of the stockpile under a comprehensive test ban. In 1996, the administration projected future spending of about $4 billion a year; by 1999, the projections had risen to $4.5 billion. The administration has, however, succeeded in trimming the cleanup program slightly. It has managed to hold the line at $5.8 billion in 2000, or about $300 million below the peak in 1996, in inflation-adjusted terms.

The most significant change regarding spending on deterrent forces during the Clinton administration's second term was its decision to put the national missile defense program on an accelerated path for possible deployment by the end of 2005. This defense would initially consist of one hundred interceptors based in Alaska. It would also include a new X-band tracking radar based on Shemya island in Alaska, and five existing early-warning radars upgraded for the missile defense mission. Called Expanded Capability-1, the system is intended to protect all fifty states of the United States against an attack of twenty or so warheads from a "rogue" state such as North Korea. Because of its location in Alaska, the system would be able to protect against only a few warheads from the Middle East.[6] The system will be designed to handle only simple countermeasures. The administration expected to decide as soon as

6.   See Testimony of the Honorable Walter B. Slocombe to the House Armed Services Committee Hearing on National Missile Defense, October 13, 1999; and John M. Donnelly, "U.S. Told Russians About Classified Antimissile Capabilities," *Defense Week*, May 1, 2000.

the fall of 2000 to begin construction on the radar in Alaska, but on September 1, President Clinton opted to leave the decision to his successor.

An improved version of the system with better capability against countermeasures would be deployed as early as 2010. Called Capability-2, this system would include three more X-band radars, software upgrades, and a constellation of 24 satellites capable of tracking cold warheads and decoys in space with infrared sensors. The administration also has plans to roughly double the size of the system a few years after 2010 by deploying another 25 interceptors in Alaska, 125 interceptors at a site in North Dakota, adding five new X-band radars, and constructing a new early-warning radar in Hawaii. The resulting 250-interceptor Capability-3 system is intended to intercept 20 or so warheads that are launched from Asia or the Middle East, even if accompanied by complex countermeasures.

Estimates for the cost of the three systems are not yet well defined. As of this writing, the most recent estimate from the administration pegs the cost of deploying the Capability-1 system at $25.6 billion through 2015, including $18.6 billion to deploy the system and $7 billion for the first ten years of operations. The total costs over the twenty-year life of the system are expected to be $32 billion. That total includes about $5 billion that was spent to develop the system from 1996 to 2000. The administration has not released recent estimates for the cost of the Capability-2 or Capability-3 systems.

Overall, spending for all types of ballistic missile defense has risen to more than $5.2 billion in 2000 from the low point of $2.8 billion in 1994 and 1995 in the first years of the Clinton administration.

How Much Lower Can We Go?

At the close of the Clinton administration, the United States is left with forces and a nuclear weapons complex that look very much like those that were projected at the end of the Bush administration. Further reductions are possible, but likely only if the recent Duma ratification of START II leads to its entry into force and to a START III treaty.[7] Even then, sav-

---

7. The Duma's ratification of START II on April 14, 2000, does not guarantee that the treaty will enter into force. The version it ratified includes the Helsinki protocol extending the treaty's entry into force until the end of 2007. That protocol has not been submitted to the Senate for ratification and its passage has become hostage in a dispute about the Anti–Ballistic Missile (ABM) treaty between the Clinton administration and hardliners in the Senate. Furthermore, the enabling legislation for START II passed by the Duma ties Russia's adherence to the treaty to the continued adherence to the ABM treaty by the United States.

ings are likely to be relatively small. For example, if a START III treaty that reduces nuclear forces to between 2,000 and 2,500 warheads is negotiated and ratified, costs are not likely to fall by more than roughly a billion a year, on average, over the next fifteen years.[8]

Future savings are likely to be modest because the United States has cut its long- and short-range nuclear forces so steeply over the past decade that the cost of having nuclear weapons and delivery platforms has become dominated by the high fixed cost of staying in the nuclear business. A simple example will illustrate this problem: suppose that the United States were to change its deterrence doctrine significantly and reduce its force to six Trident submarines, eliminate its ICBM force, and convert its heavy bombers to conventional roles. Suppose it also reduced its stockpile stewardship program by closing (mostly) one of its two nuclear weapons design labs and shutting down all testing and readiness activities at the Nevada Test Site. Together, those changes would save roughly $3 billion a year in the long run, including more than $1 billion in average annual replacement costs. If the budget for nuclear command, control, communications, and intelligence were cut by one third to reflect the smaller nuclear force, this approach would save a total of roughly $5 billion a year in the long run.

Although those savings are not inconsequential, the deep cuts in this example (a nearly 60-percent reduction in submarines and complete elimination of the other two legs of the triad) would reduce spending for deterrent forces by only 14 percent; annual spending would still top $30 billion a year. Moreover, such a significant change in nuclear forces and doctrine is unlikely for a number of reasons discussed below. Short of getting out of the nuclear business altogether and abandoning efforts to develop missile defenses, it will be difficult for the United States to cut deterrence budgets significantly. The rest of this section examines possible cuts to nuclear forces and the nuclear weapons complex.

CUTTING FORCES

There are not many forces left to cut, particularly after START II enters into force. After 2005, the Navy will have only fourteen Trident submarines, down from thirty-one in 1990. If START II enters into force, the Air Force will eliminate its fifty Peacekeeper missiles and retain only five hundred ICBMs, each armed with one warhead (see Table 5.3). Future arms control agreements may make sharp reductions in the number of deployed warheads, but they will probably require only marginal

---

8. See CBO, "Letter to the Honorable Thomas A. Daschle regarding the estimated budgetary impacts of alternative levels of strategic forces," March 18, 1998.

Table 5.3. U.S. Strategic Nuclear Forces, Past, Present, and Future (numbers in parentheses are the total warheads deployed on each type of platform).

	1990	2000	START I (Dec. 5, 2001)	START II (Dec. 31, 2007)	START III (Dec. 31, 2007)
Minuteman II	450 (450)	0	0	0	0
Minuteman III	5000 (1500)	500 (1500)	500 (1500)	500 (500)	0–500 (0–500)
Peacekeeper (MX)	50 (500)	50 (500)	50 (500)	0	0
Total, ICBMs	**1,000 (2,450)**	**550 (2,000)**	**550 (2,000)**	**500 (500)**	**0–500 (0–500)**
Poseidon C3	11 (1760)	0	0	0	0
Poseidon C4	12 (1536)	0	0	0	0
Trident C4	8 (1536)	8 (1536)	8 (1536)	0	0
Trident D5	2 (384)	10 (1920)	10 (1920)	14 (1680)	10–14 (1,000–1,700)
Total, SLBMs	**31 (5,216)**	**18 (3,456)**	**18 (3,456)[b]**	**14 (1,680)**	**10–14 (1,000–1,700)**
B-52G	77	0	0	0	0
B-52H	95	92	74	74	0–74
B-1B	97	93[a]	93[a]	0[a]	0[a]
B-2A	0	21	21	21	21
Total, Bombers	**269 (4,300)**	**206 (1,750)**	**188 (1,750)[c]**	**95 (1,320)[d]**	**95**
Grand Total, Warheads	**12,000**	**7,200**	**7,200[e]**	**3,500**	**2,500**

Sources: Department of Defense, *Annual Report to the President,* March 2000; and Congressional Budget Office, *The START Treaty and Beyond* (Washington, D.C.: CBO, October 1991); NRDC Nuclear Notebook, "U.S. Strategic Nuclear Forces, End of 1990," *Bulletin of the Atomic Scientists,* January/February 1991; and NRDC Nuclear Notebook, "U.S. Strategic Nuclear Forces, End of 1998," *Bulletin of the Atomic Scientists,* January/February 1999.

Notes: Totals exclude tactical nuclear weapons. The United States deployed roughly 10,000 in 1990, has about 1,500, and probably will keep that number under START I and II, although neither treaty limits the number of tactical nuclear weapons. The number of tactical weapons could be lower under the START III framework.

a. 93 B-1Bs have been given new roles as conventional bombers, but they are still accountable under START I.

b. Ultimately, the United States intends to keep 14 Tridents under START I, which would be counted as carrying a total of 2,688 warheads. But it will not reach that level at least until 2005, when it will retire the last of its four oldest Trident submarines. Originally, the United States planned to deploy 3,456 SLBM warheads under START I, or 18 Trident submarines with their full declared loading of 8 warheads on each of their 24 missiles.

c. Under START I counting rules, the United States would be counted as having only 1,594 weapons on bombers because each B-1B and B-2A is counted as carrying only one warhead. The B-52H is counted as carrying 20.

d. This is the total number of bomber warheads that would be allowed to stay within the 3,500 warhead limit. The actual number deployed could be lower.

e. Under START I rules, the United States would be counted as having only 6,000 weapons.

changes to the number of platforms. The reason is simple: in the interest of ensuring the survivability of its forces, the United States will insist that it be able to spread its warheads over as many missiles and submarines as possible.

As a result of U.S. and possibly Russian concerns about survivability, future treaties will probably reduce the number of warheads carried on submarines, but not require significant cuts to the Trident force. Even in the case of deep cuts, the United States will likely insist on retaining at least ten submarines in order to ensure—for survivability and targeting reasons—that it can keep at least three or four submarines at sea all the time, with at least one in each ocean. If the Trident force is cut to ten, savings would amount to less than $500 million a year because the cost of operating the force is driven by the infrastructure necessary to support the submarines and the weapon system: it is relatively insensitive to the number of submarines in the force. If all 500 ICBMs are eliminated, savings would not be much more than $1 billion a year through 2020. Reducing the number of nuclear-capable bombers will not save any money because the size of the bomber force after the Cold War is driven by the increasing demand for bombers in conventional (non-nuclear) conflicts.

CUTTING THE NUCLEAR WEAPONS COMPLEX
Fixed costs are even higher in the DoE's nuclear weapons complex. Actions taken by the Bush and Clinton administrations to consolidate the production complex have reduced the costs for producing and maintaining weapons considerably. The complex has now been consolidated from ten sites to four—Savannah River, Kansas City, Pantex, and Los Alamos—and has been retooled to support a stockpile of START II proportions with the ability to expand to support a START I stockpile, if necessary. Further cuts in the stockpile are unlikely to reduce costs much further. One reason is that only about one-tenth of the $2-billion-plus annual budget for production is directly related to the size of the stockpile. The lion's share of the production budget funds activities such as security and infrastructure that are quite insensitive to production rates. Savings will also be difficult to achieve because production rates are so low today that overhead costs—the cost of just maintaining the physical infrastructure and skilled employees to produce all the different types of components needed for the weapons in the stockpile—are a huge fraction of production costs. Efforts to increase efficiency and reduce fixed costs should be strongly encouraged, but cannot be expected to alter the budget story for the DoE significantly.

The DoE's three weapons design laboratories have survived the end of the Cold War largely intact, at least in a budgetary sense. Although they experienced cuts and layoffs early in the Clinton administration, those lean times were short-lived. The laboratories have roared into the new century with bigger budgets and renewed vigor, although they have lost some of their experienced cadres of weapons designers and testers. Budgets are at or above the average levels during the Cold War. The science-based stewardship program that the Clinton administration has adopted to preserve the reliability of the stockpile without explosive testing, as well as the price that the laboratories have requested for their continued support of the Comprehensive Test Ban Treaty (CTBT), has all but guaranteed that budgets at the laboratories will be well protected from future cuts. Thus, the level of effort expended at the labs is almost completely independent of the number of weapons that remain in the stockpile.

Critics have proposed three ways to reduce the costs of the stewardship program. First, the United States could at least partially consolidate the two weapons laboratories at one location. Savings from such a policy might reach $300 million to $400 million a year.[9] But the politics of the CTBT make such an outcome unlikely. Any such move would be met with howls of protest from the laboratories about the effects that it would have on preserving the reliability of the stockpile. Supporters of the test ban in Congress would probably oppose consolidating the laboratories to avoid jeopardizing the chances for ratifying the treaty. Indeed, President Clinton explicitly made preserving both laboratories one of his "safeguards" to make the CTBT acceptable to the laboratories and the Congress.[10] The second way to reduce costs would be to cancel some of the fancy new testing and simulation facilities that the laboratories plan to build. But many of those have been completed or nearly so, and in any case, only a few percent of the laboratories' budgets each year will be dedicated to those projects. A third path to savings would be for the United States to adopt a production-based, rather than a science-based, program to maintain the reliability and safety of the arsenal, as some have suggested.[11] But while this strategy of replacing aging weapon components with identical parts might allow the laboratories to shrink some-

9. For example, see CBO, *Budget Options for National Defense*, March 2000.

10. Another of the safeguards that President Clinton established is to keep the Nevada test site open and ready to resume explosive testing of nuclear weapons underground within three years of a presidential decision to do so.

11. See, for example, Tom Zamora Collina and Ray E. Kidder, "Shopping Spree Softens Test-Ban Sorrows," *Bulletin of the Atomic Scientists* (July–August 1994), pp. 23–29; and Greg Mello, *No Serious Problems: Reliability Issues and Stockpile Management*, Tri-Valley CARES (Livermore, Calif.: Citizens Against a Radioactive Environment, February 6, 1995).

what, it would probably require that the production of components be increased, particularly nuclear components. That, in turn, could require building a new, much larger facility to produce plutonium "pits," the core of the fission trigger in modern thermonuclear weapons. It is unclear at this time how much a production-based stewardship program would cost or save.

As a result, there are few easy ways to cut the $4.5 billion weapons activities budget at the DoE. The possibilities that exist for cuts would garner modest savings and would be politically difficult to achieve without endangering crucial laboratory support for the current testing moratorium and the CTBT. Furthermore, some unpaid bills lurk in the shadows. DoE may have to build a larger pit production facility, modernize its plant for producing secondaries—the fusion part of a thermonuclear weapon—and upgrade infrastructure throughout the complex, parts of which are 40–50 years old. In addition, the laboratories plan to build some expensive new experimental facilities within the next decade or so. The $5.8 billion waste-management and cleanup budget will also be difficult to cut: most of it is spent just managing the wastes that remain in the complex, and cleanup of most wastes will come much later. Although some efficiencies might be possible, those efforts are likely to continue at the same pace and with the same budgets for the foreseeable future, to complete a process that the DoE has estimated will cost at least $200 billion and others have estimated will cost up to $400 billion.[12] Pressure from environmental groups and local communities to accelerate the cleanup could boost budgets, at least in the short run.

In short, as long as the United States continues to be a nuclear power, keep submarine-launched ballistic missiles at sea, maintain a robust early-warning network and command and control system, and pursue a science-based stockpile stewardship program, the price tag for nuclear forces will not fall much below where it is today, even if forces were slashed to 1,000 weapons. Moreover, several pressures looming on the horizon are likely to push costs higher.

Future Sources of Cost Pressure

Ballistic missile defenses will be the most potent source of cost pressure over the next few decades. The simple fact is that missile defense is tough

---

12. U.S. Department of Energy, Office of Environmental Management, *The 1995 Baseline Environmental Management Report*, DOE/EM-0290, Executive Summary (Washington, D.C.: U.S. Government Printing Office [U.S. GPO], June 1996), p. xxiii; and Schwartz, *Atomic Audit*, pp. 383–389.

to do, and it will take a large commitment of resources and time to have a shot at solving the problem, if it can be done at all. Moreover, deploying and operating missile defenses will create an entirely new category of spending. The United States could deploy six or seven new systems over the next decade or two. Those budget pressures would be compounded if the increasing threat of cruise missiles forces the United States to develop defenses to protect troops, allies, or even the United States.

NATIONAL MISSILE DEFENSE

National missile defense (NMD) will be the primary source of budget growth. Like it or not, national missile defenses are probably here to stay in some form or another. The combination of the proliferation of weapons of mass destruction and ballistic missiles and the growing U.S. penchant for intervention has created a powerful tide of support for NMD within the U.S. defense establishment and the Congress. Momentum to deploy an NMD system has grown over the past two years to the point that few in Congress are willing to vote against legislation calling for deployment. The Clinton administration's current plan may be delayed, changed, or even scrapped for a new approach, but budgets for NMD will continue to wax, or at least hold steady.

The administration's plan to deploy a simple NMD system will consume at least $2.6 billion in 2002, up from $1.5 billion in 2000, for a total price tag of $25.6 billion through 2015, according to administration figures. Yet those estimates are certainly optimistic. The administration acknowledges that its program is very high risk and the schedule is very compressed. In fact, the ink was barely dry on its 2001 budget request when the head of the Ballistic Missile Defense Organization (BMDO), Lieutenant General Ronald T. Kadish, told Congress that he needed an additional $300 million in 2001 alone, an increase of nearly 20 percent.[13]

The Congressional Budget Office (CBO) recently released a less optimistic estimate for the NMD system.[14] The independent agency placed the cost of deploying the Expanded Capability-1 system and operating it for 10 years at $29.5 billion: $3.9 billion higher than the administration's number (see Table 5.4 for details). According to the CBO, the administration's plan to deploy and operate the Capability-2 system to counter more sophisticated countermeasures would increase costs by at least another $16.7 billion through 2015, for a total of $46.2 billion. That estimate

13. See Michael C. Sirak, "BMDO Says Extra $1 Billion Would Reduce Risk, Speed Missile Purchases," *Inside Missile Defense*, Vol. 6, No. 5 (March 8, 2000), p. 1.

14. Congressional Budget Office, *Budgetary and Technical Implications of the Administration's Plan for National Missile Defense*, April 2000.

Table 5.4. CBO Estimates of Total Costs for the Clinton Administration's National Missile Defense, 1996–2015 (in billions of dollars).

Category	Administration's Estimate — Expanded Capability-1	CBO's Estimates — Expanded Capability-1	Capability-2	Capability-3
Design, Procurement and Construction				
Interceptors	6.1	7.1	9.5	12.7
X-band radars	1.1	1.2	2.5	4.6
Early-warning radars	1.2	1.3	1.3	1.7
Command, control and communications facilities	2.0	2.2	2.2	3.6
Test and evaluation	2.2	2.2	2.8	2.8
System integration	5.4	5.4	5.4	5.4
Construction	0.5	1.5	1.8	4.0
Subtotal, design, procurement and construction	18.6	20.9	25.6	35.0
Operations				
Operational Tests	2.7	4.2	5.2	5.2
Day-to-day tests	1.9	1.9	2.4	3.4
Operational integration	2.4	2.4	2.4	5.3
Subtotal, operations	7.0	8.5	10.0	13.9
SBIRS-Low				
Research and development	0	0	4.2	4.2
Procurement	0	0	2.7	2.7
Operations	0	0	1.1	1.1
Replacing satellites	0	0	2.7	2.7
Subtotal, SBIRS-Low	0	0	10.6	10.6
Total, NMD w/o SBIRS	25.6	29.5	35.6	48.8
Total, NMD w SBIRS	25.6	29.5	46.2	59.4
Annual Operating Costs After 2015				
Ground-based defense	0.6	0.6	0.7	1.1
SBIRS-Low	0	0	0.5	0.5
Total, Annual Operating Costs after 2015	0.6	0.6	1.2	1.6

Source: Congressional Budget Office, *Budgetary and Technical Implications of the Administration's Plan for National Missile Defense* (Washington, D.C.: CBO, April 2000), p. 10.

Notes: SBIRS = Space-Based Infrared System. Numbers may not add to totals due to rounding. Estimates show the costs that would be required through fiscal year 2015. They cover different periods of time based on when each system becomes operational. The estimate for Expanded Capability-1 covers fiscal years 2005 through 2015; Capability-2, 2010 through 2015; and Capability-3, 2011 through 2015.

includes $7 billion to deploy SBIRS-Low infrared tracking satellites that will be essential for discriminating warheads from decoys. (SBIRS stands for space-based infrared system.) It also includes $3.8 billion to operate the satellites through 2015, or about $475 million a year. Expanding the system to the administration's objectives—a Capability-3 system with 125 interceptors at two sites and five additional ground-based radars—would bring the total to $59.4 billion through 2015, according to the CBO. The system would cost about $1.6 billion to operate each year thereafter. If the United States decides to deploy the Capability-3 system, annual spending on NMD would average $3.6 billion from 2001 through 2015, or $2 billion more than the Pentagon plans to spend on NMD in 2000. This means that if defense budgets do not rise in real terms, a commitment to deploy NMD will eat into the budgets of other programs by at least $2 billion a year. This will occur at a time when the Army, Navy, and Air Force will be expecting large increases in their procurement budgets to modernize their forces. During the peak procurement years of 2007 and 2008, the NMD budget would exceed $6 billion a year.

Even the CBO's estimates may be optimistic. For example, its report acknowledged that using a more traditional approach to building the system would increase costs relative to its estimate for the current fast-paced program. Naturally, that raises the question of how a crash program to develop an extremely complex, never-before-tried system that must meet stringent performance and reliability standards could cost less than one that would reduce risk by taking more time to test the system on the ground and in space. Nor did the CBO's estimate include the cost of the research and development that must continually be done both to keep the system ahead of opponents' attempts to undermine it with counter-measures and to develop the next-generation defense. Such an effort would cost at least several hundred million dollars annually. Costs will also rise significantly if the United States decides it must deploy defenses to protect itself against cruise missiles or short-range ballistic missiles that can be launched from ships—threats that some analysts, including the U.S. intelligence community and some of its critics, believe are real and should be taken more seriously.[15]

THEATER MISSILE DEFENSE

Cost pressure is also likely to come from theater missile defense programs. Given the difficult nature of missile defense and the complexity of

---

15.   See National Intelligence Council, *Foreign Missile Developments and the Ballistic Missile Threat to the United States Through 2015*, September 1999; and the Gates Commission, *NIE 95–19: Independent Panel Review of "Emerging Missile Threats to North*

the systems, the costs of theater missile defense programs will certainly rise above the administration's current estimates. If the theater ballistic missile threat continues to grow and mature, the Pentagon may need to buy even more missile defense batteries, aircraft, and ships than it currently plans. It may also have to develop new types of defenses. Furthermore, there is not nearly enough money in the budget to fund all the programs that are in the pipeline, even if prices do not rise above current estimates. At least two programs under development have not been fully funded: the Navy's Theater-Wide Defense and the Army's Medium-altitude Extended Area Defense System (MEADS). Those programs have strong support in some quarters, which means that they will be hard to kill, particularly if the threat grows. Finally, the Pentagon will have to continue a robust research and development effort to stay ahead of the changing threat. For all those reasons, it is reasonable to expect the cost of theater missile defense to rise by at least $1 billion a year or more.

REDUCING NUCLEAR THREATS, TREATY VERIFICATION, AND FORCE MODERNIZATION

Budgets could also rise if the United States opts to do more to address nuclear threats from Russia and other former Soviet states, as some analysts have advocated.[16] Those threats could become much more significant and real for the United States than anything that North Korea, Iran, or Iraq could do on their own. Increases could come from expanding the nonproliferation programs at the DoE, the Defense Department, and the State Department. Increases could also come from new programs, such as those proposed to help Russia improve its decaying early-warning system.[17] The costs of disposing of excess fissile materials in the United States will also start to rise over the next decade as the country begins to

---

America During the Next 15 Years," December 23, 1996, <www.fas.org/irp/threat/missile/oca961908.htm>.

16. For example, see David E. Mosher, Oleg Bukharin, and Todd E. Perry, "Minding Russia's Nuclear Store," *IEEE Spectrum*, March 2000; Matthew Bunn, *The Next Wave: Urgently Needed New Steps to Control Warheads and Fissile Material*, Carnegie Non-Proliferation Project and the Harvard Project on Managing the Atom, March 2000; and Congressional Budget Office, *Cooperative Approaches to Halt Russian Nuclear Proliferation and Improve the Openness of Nuclear Disarmament*, May 1999.

17. See Geoff Forden, Theodore Postol, and Paul Podvig, "False Alarm, Nuclear Danger," *IEEE Spectrum*, March 2000; CBO, "Letter to the Honorable Tom Daschle regarding improving Russia's access to early-warning information," September 3, 1998; and CBO, "Letter to the Honorable Tom Daschle regarding the analysis of additional options that would improve Russia's access to early-warning information," August 24, 1999.

build and operate plants to produce mixed-oxide (MOX) fuel and to vitrify materials that cannot be used in MOX. Additional resources may be needed if the United States decides to help Russia dispose of its excess fissile materials, too.

Deep cuts in nuclear forces may also apply some upward pressure on budgets. This may seem counterintuitive. But it stems from the increased demands that parties to any deep-cut agreement would place on monitoring and verification systems and on-site inspections. Some proposals envision extensive new sensor networks and frequent, intrusive on-site inspections. In some cases, verification regimes may require infrastructure changes that could be quite expensive. For example, if the parties demand high confidence that warheads are being dismantled, the United States might have to make changes to its Pantex plant to prevent inspectors from learning sensitive information about U.S. warheads; or it may need to move monitored activities to the Device Assembly Facility at the Nevada Test Site, a proposition that would be quite expensive.[18]

Finally, costs could rise over the next decade or so as the Defense Department begins the process of replacing its aging nuclear forces. Because the Navy's oldest D-5 missiles will approach the end of their service lives by 2015, the Navy must start to develop a replacement by around 2005. The Air Force must also start developing a replacement for its Minuteman III a few years later. Together, replacing those systems could increase budgets by $1 billion to $2 billion a year some time in the next decade. If the START II treaty does not enter into force, the Air Force may have to come up with a solution to preserve or replace its Peacekeeper force, which could run out of test missiles soon after 2010. Restarting the production line or developing a new missile would cost at least $4 billion, according to the CBO.[19]

Cutting Deterrent Forces Will Not Solve the Problem

Unfortunately, deterrent forces offer no real fixes to the Defense Department's long-term budget woes, because the nuclear peace dividend has largely been spent and there is pressure to increase funding for missile defense. The total budget for deterrent forces has already fallen from $59 billion in 1990 to around $35 billion in 2000 after accounting for inflation,

---

18.   Department of Energy, Office of Arms Control and Nonproliferation, "Transparency and Verification Options: An Initial Analysis of Approaches for Monitoring Warhead Dismantlement," May 19, 1997.

19.   CBO, "050–03: Remove Peacekeeper Missiles ahead of Start II Ratification," in *Maintaining Budget Discipline: Spending and Revenue Options*, April 1999.

a reduction of 40 percent, or more than one and a half times the reduction that the budget for national defense has experienced over the same period. Potential savings remain, but will not be easy to achieve. There are plenty of good reasons to consider deep cuts in nuclear weapons, but big savings is no longer one of them.

Nor does the future look promising for those who would be happy to hold the line on spending for deterrent forces and invest in other defense accounts instead. The administration's push for national and theater missile defenses will probably drive budgets upward by at least $3 billion dollars a year over the next two decades, and perhaps significantly higher if the threat from ballistic and cruise missiles grows. Nor is this trend likely to abate with a change in administrations: Al Gore has given no indication that he would deviate from the Clinton administration's current plan, and George W. Bush has endorsed spending even more on missile defense if he becomes president. Budgets could also rise if efforts to reduce the nuclear risks from Russia are expanded or strict verification measures are required for future arms control agreements. In short, defense planners will have to look elsewhere for solutions to their budget problems; the nuclear cash cow of the 1990s has largely been milked dry.

Chapter 6

Buying ". . . From the Sea": A Defense Budget for a Maritime Strategy

Owen R. Cote, Jr.

Geopolitical and technological changes to the external security environment of the United States, and a post–Cold War domestic political economy dominated by an aging baby boom generation, may create demand for a more disciplined approach to defense spending. One such approach would use military strategy as a means of making choices among different military forces and capabilities. Since the early 1960s, U.S. political leaders have used military strategy as a means of identifying all the military options they wished to preserve. In the future, they may once again have to use strategy as a means of eliminating options rather than preserving them, much as Eisenhower's Massive Retaliation strategy did in the 1950s before the arrival of Flexible Response.

This chapter describes a defense budget for a military strategy that makes two basic assumptions: that the U.S. military should not plan on having access to a developed local base structure in advance of the contingencies it is likely to face in the future, and that it should plan on facing opponents able to threaten the viability of its traditional methods of rapid power projection. Because access will be constrained, I argue that the U.S. military will need to rely relatively more on its naval forces for rapid power projection, and that those forces will need to produce more leverage over events ashore than has been possible from the sea in the past. I also suggest ways that the Army and the Air Force can innovate in order to reduce their reliance on overseas bases and remain relevant in an access-constrained security environment.

The first section of this chapter discusses the rationales for these two basic assumptions, and of the strategy of maritime leverage that they suggest. The second section is a review of the relevance of each of the four military services to this military strategy. The third section identifies those Department of Defense (DoD) force structure and procurement programs that are least pertinent to the proposed military strategy, and suggests a series of force and program reductions that collectively result in annual cutbacks, relative to current plans, worth $28 billion by the year 2010. Combined with a package of infrastructure reforms saving $10 billion over today's plans (described in Chapter 3), these program cutbacks would hold the defense budget at roughly its current level for a decade. The last section describes some defense program additions, totaling $3 billion annually by 2010, that would fund several innovative programs that would be particularly useful to the proposed military strategy, but that are likely to remain underdeveloped and underfunded in the current defense program.

Strategic Assumptions

The strategic assumptions underlying the maritime strategy address geopolitical and technical trends in both the near and the far term. The dominant geopolitical change in the new security environment has been the virtual elimination, for military planning purposes, of the U.S. continental commitment to the security of Western Europe from attack by the Warsaw Pact. The dominant technical change in the new security environment has been the continued and even accelerating advance in the performance of sensors, weapons, and communication links, all broadly driven by the underlying exponential advance in the speed and processing power of microelectronic information processors. These and other subsidiary changes in the external security environment mutually interact in many ways, but with two general consequences, one of which the United States is already experiencing today, and one that it is likely to face in the coming decades.

The near-term consequence is that the U.S. military will find itself fighting in conflicts where the political stakes for the United States are dramatically lower than those of its adversaries, and where pre-arranged military alliances are either absent or not directly relevant. In these conflicts, the opponent will be unable to contest U.S. military superiority in direct, force-on-force engagements, but will seek instead to attack the political will of its leaders by deploying its more limited military capabilities against those points where it will be most able to cause U.S. military casualties.

In general, these points of vulnerability will vary according to the degree to which U.S. military forces present the opponent with large, fixed, surface targets such as air bases or ports close to the theater of battle; the degree to which U.S. forces must penetrate ground, sea, and air bat-tlefields protected by modern defensive weapons with non-stealthy, manned platforms; and the degree to which the opponent is able to focus its more limited exploitation of modern military technology at those points of maximum U.S. weakness or exposure. Under no circumstances will the resulting vulnerabilities be decisive in a traditional military sense: the goal for an opponent will be to use these vulnerabilities to drive up the political costs of an engagement, ideally in such a fashion as to deter the engagement altogether.

In the more distant term, the battlefields for which the U.S. military needs to prepare are, of course, less well defined, but a longer-term per-spective does force consideration of the potential reemergence of one or even several "peer competitors," that is, the reemergence of a bipolar or multipolar balance of power to replace what some are already calling today's unipolar moment.[1] Should such a power or powers emerge, the issue of preserving a Eurasian balance of power would return as the main focus of U.S. military planning, and this focus is more likely to be on political fault lines with a maritime rather than a continental aspect. This is because the collapse of the former Soviet Union and the reunification of Germany have fundamentally altered the balance of power along Eurasia's major land boundaries, making it unlikely in the extreme that a renewed continental commitment of U.S. ground and air forces on the scale which obtained during the Cold War will be necessary.[2]

Instead, strategically significant imbalances in the Eurasian balance of power are most likely should China continue to grow in power and ambition, intensifying the existing triangular competition for security and prestige between China, Japan, and India, and threatening the many wealthy medium powers in the long littoral extending between Korea

---

1. See, for example, Michael Mastanduno, "Preserving the Unipolar Moment," *International Security*, Vol. 21, No. 4 (Spring 1997), pp. 49–89; and Mark S. Sheetz, "Correspondence: Debating the Unipolar Moment," *International Security*, Vol. 22, No. 3 (Winter 1997/1998), pp. 168–175. See also Samuel P. Huntington, "The Lonely Superpower," *Foreign Affairs*, Vol. 78, No. 2 (March–April 1999), pp. 35–50.

2. This is not to say that there will be peace along these borders or that the United States will not have interests at stake should conflict occur along them, just that it will be unnecessary for the United States to provide the main source of balance on the ground among the competing powers in the form of a large, forward-deployed Army. For a strong statement of this view regarding Germany and Russia, see John J. Mearsheimer, "Back to the Future: Instability in Europe After the Cold War," *International Security*, Vol. 15, No. 1 (Summer 1990). I make the same assumption here regarding China and Russia for similar reasons.

and the Persian Gulf. Should an imbalance of power threaten to result, the United States might once again need to commit a major element of its military forces to restore the balance. That commitment would be conditioned by two factors: the borders in need of protection will bisect seas rather than rolling plains, and the opponent will be sufficiently advanced to exploit modern military technology much more widely and deeply than opponents like Iraq or North Korea, for example. This will result in a return to more traditional military planning, in which both sides have the highest national interests at stake and are willing to suffer substantial military losses in their pursuit, and in which victory will be determined by the result of relatively unlimited force-on-force struggles for control of the sea and the land alongside it, between opponents wielding the most advanced weapons available.

STRATEGY AND THE NEAR-TERM SECURITY ENVIRONMENT

In the near term, U.S. military strategy needs to account for the political asymmetries between the United States and its potential opponents, the military asymmetries, and the changed nature of U.S. alliance relationships. Taking these factors into account in anticipating likely conflicts makes clear the importance of minimizing casualties, helps identify where casualties are most likely to be incurred, and demonstrates why allies will be more likely to withhold or limit access to local bases.

POLITICAL LEADERS OF STRONG POWERS FIGHTING WEAK POWERS OVER LESS THAN VITAL INTERESTS WILL CONSTRAIN THEIR MILITARY FORCES IN ORDER TO AVOID CASUALTIES. The U.S. aversion to casualties in post–Cold War conflicts has been much discussed. Fear of casualties measured in the thousands or even tens of thousands dominated the debate over whether to launch a ground war during Desert Storm, a conflict in which U.S. stakes were as high as they are likely to be in any future conflict. In the event, casualties of Desert Storm were orders of magnitude lower than expected, leaving the question of U.S. tolerance for casualties open for debate.[3] But then the events of early October 1993 in Mogadishu, Somalia, seemed to resolve the debate.[4] The death of a small number of Rangers and Delta Force troopers led the United States to abandon that operation abruptly. A growing consensus developed that the United

---

3. For a summary of this debate, see Harvey M. Sapolsky and Jeremy Shapiro, "Casualties, Technology, and America's Future Wars," *Parameters*, Vol. 26, No. 2 (Summer 1996), pp. 119–127.

4. The best account of those events is Mark Bowden's masterful *Black Hawk Down: A Story of Modern War* (New York: Atlantic Monthly Press, 1999).

States could be stopped in its tracks by the deaths of a few of its soldiers, leading some to question the viability of its enormous but seemingly unusable military power.

The recent experience in Kosovo does not provide evidence that the United States is not casualty-averse. NATO air crews were ordered to remain above 15,000–20,000 feet throughout the entire conflict because it was only at that altitude that they remained immune from Serbian air defenses, while of course ground forces were foresworn from the outset. This reduced nearly to nil NATO's ability to stop or limit the ethnic cleansing being conducted by Serbian army and police units in Kosovo, and drove NATO political and military leaders to adopt a gradual strategic bombing campaign designed to coerce Serbian compliance, which took months to succeed.

The evidence supporting the proposition that the United States has become casualty-averse is overwhelming, but the explanation for this aversion has more to do with the strength of the U.S. position in the world, rather than the weakness of its leaders or its people. As Stephen Walt has argued, the United States is the most secure country the world has ever seen:

[Which] leads to something of a paradox: Although solving many global problems requires active U.S. involvement, Americans do not see them as vital to their own interests and they are unwilling to expend much effort addressing them. . . . Americans would like to coerce others to do what they want, but they aren't willing to risk much blood or treasure to make sure they do.[5]

In this view, the U.S. aversion to casualties, and the degree to which political leaders will constrain how the military fights in order to reduce their exposure, will depend on the stakes the United States has in the conflict. Because of the great overhang of U.S. power in today's security environment, and because of its basic security, few if any conflicts are likely to engage its vital interests, and many conflicts, like Kosovo, will be fought over much lesser interests.

This basic structural paradox sets the bar very high for the U.S. military, because it must win while keeping its exposure to losses extremely low by historical standards. Certainly, the degree of acceptable exposure will vary somewhat, depending on whether a conflict is a major contingency on the Korean peninsula or in the Persian Gulf, or instead a humanitarian intervention in Latin America or Central Africa. Yet because

---

5. Stephen Walt, "Muscle-bound: The Limits of U.S. Power," *Bulletin of Atomic Scientists*, Vol. 55, No. 2 (March–April 1999), p. 44.

there is little prospect of war with a great power, there is little prospect that the U.S. military will be allowed or ordered to fight as great powers have traditionally fought their wars in the twentieth century.

The main military consequence of this increasingly apparent reality will be a growing demand for weapons that can stand off at a distance from enemy defenses and avoid direct fire engagements with their targets at short ranges. In many cases, such as attacks from the air against high-profile, fixed targets on the ground, precision weapons have solved this problem. In other cases, such as in attacks from the air against mobile or hidden targets, the problem of combining effectiveness with essential immunity from attack is far from solved, but it is at least imaginable how to get there. However, there are still other cases, such as urban counter-insurgency operations by a regular army against local guerillas, where it is difficult even to imagine a low-casualty, standoff solution in cases where the opponent is highly motivated and its attacker is not.

The push to provide standoff solutions to battlefield problems will not address all military problems, but it will be ubiquitous as long as asymmetric advantages in new military technology give U.S. forces the ability to stand off, and as long as asymmetric political stakes favor the weaker power in a contest of wills. And just as powerful structural reasons for the asymmetry of political will between the United States and its likely opponents in future conflicts are likely to endure, a powerful asymmetry in the ability to exploit modern military technology favoring the United States is also likely to endure.

COMPARED TO THE UNITED STATES, LESSER POWERS MUST FOCUS THEIR INVESTMENTS IN MODERN MILITARY TECHNOLOGY IN ONLY A FEW MISSION AREAS. Because they spend so little on defense compared to the United States, lesser powers must focus their military investments more narrowly, and the U.S. military must not let its pursuit of a much broader set of capabilities blind it to the threats it will face where that focus occurs.

Desert Storm was a major contingency in which important U.S. interests were clearly at stake. On its eve, the U.S. Senate voted narrowly to support a ground invasion to liberate Kuwait in which thousands of U.S. casualties were expected. Yet the opponent in this case—Iraq—had a defense budget that was less than 5 percent the size of the U.S. defense budget. In the near term, it is extremely difficult to imagine the United States getting into a future conflict with a state whose military capability would even match Iraq's 1991 capabilities.

A defense budget of $10–15 billion a year, which is as much as any so called "rogue state" spends on defense, can by definition buy only a small portion of the capabilities provided by a budget of some $300 billion a year. Public descriptions of the threat posed by these rogue states often mask this reality. This is especially apparent when one looks at the air forces and navies of these states, which cede enormous sanctuaries of control to their opponents compared to the efforts, say, of the former Soviet Union. Thus, the U.S. Navy faces almost no threat to its deep-water operations, because smaller states cannot even begin to afford long-range sea-denial assets such as nuclear attack submarines. Likewise, the U.S. Air Force is able to gain total control of the airspace over friendly forces quickly, and to penetrate hostile airspace, because very few states can afford even to attempt to defend their own airspace fully. Such a defense would not only require a modern tactical air force, but equally important and even more expensive, supporting assets such as sophisticated Airborne Warning and Control System (AWACS) aircraft. Only when a country can afford such assets in their requisite numbers, and when it has the skill to operate them effectively, can it aspire to secure its own airspace and launch offensive operations from within it. U.S. air and naval forces encounter serious threats only when they close with the enemy and attack, because most states can afford to defend their coastlines and airspace only with much shorter range, defensive weapons such as anti-ship cruise missiles and surface-to-air missiles.

Yet within their engagement envelopes, both the capability and availability of these weapons are growing faster than are the capabilities of U.S. forces that must suppress them. It is within the engagement envelopes of such weapons that the most expensive U.S. instruments of rapid power projection, such as manned bombers and aircraft carriers, face their most serious threats. For example, take the case of penetrating ground-based air defense networks based on mobile SAM systems. In reference to the experience in Kosovo, where Serbian air defenses were based on mobile SAMs dating from the early 1970s, the Air Force has acknowledged that it "needs to find and kill non-cooperative defensive systems much more effectively than it can today."[6] In describing a scenario in which more modern mobile SAMs had been introduced into the conflict, General John Jumper, then Commander of Allied Air Forces in Europe has acknowledged that the Air Force "would have had to fight [its] way in with brute force because we don't have the techniques to adequately defend ourselves against SAM-10s and 12s."[7]

---

6. Prepared Statement of Lt. General Marvin Esmond, DCS, USAF, House Armed Services Committee, October 19, 1999, p. 1.

7. General John Jumper, Commander of U.S. Air Forces in Europe during Allied Force, in David Fulghum, "Security Leaks and the Unknown Bedeviled Kosovo Commanders," *Aviation Week and Space Technology*, November 1, 1999, p. 33.

The first quotation is an acknowledgment that while current defense suppression techniques are designed to destroy a "cooperative" target, they can only hope to suppress a target that is "non-cooperative." A cooperative target is one that seeks to complete a SAM engagement against a package of strike aircraft, and in doing so creates a continuous radar signal that defense suppression escorts can locate within hundreds or thousands of feet; the escorts can then jam the signal to reduce its range and attack it with a short-range, high-speed antiradiation missile (HARM). If the SAM operator stays on the air in an effort to complete the engagement, the HARM has a good chance to destroy the engagement radar before the engagement is completed and the SAM missile loses its guidance, or in the military vernacular, "goes silly." If, on the other hand, the SAM operator shuts down, i.e., if it is non-cooperative, both the SAM missile and the HARM go silly, and both the SAM radar and the aircraft it is shooting at survive. In the first case, the defense system is destroyed; in the second it is only suppressed.

Iraqi SAM operators during the early days of Desert Storm were, by and large, cooperative, meaning that early in the war their engagement radars were essentially destroyed, and after that allied air operated freely at medium altitude without need for close SAM-suppression escorts. In contrast, during Allied Force, Serbian SAM operators were non-cooperative, meaning that every Allied strike package needed the full panoply of SAM-suppression escorts. Because those escorts have become so-called high demand/low density (HD/LD) assets, this put an upper bound on the rate at which the campaign could be prosecuted.

The Serbian air defense system was based on the SAM-6, the first Soviet mobile radar-guided SAM, which first saw action in the 1973 Yom Kippur war. The Jumper quotation above indicates that the more modern mobile SAM-10s and SAM-12s first deployed in the 1980s, which the United States has yet to encounter, can defeat current U.S. defense suppression assets. This is because their phased-array engagement radar and 80–100-mile range missiles (versus 25 miles for the SAM-6) can complete an engagement well before HARM-carrying aircraft would come into range to launch their missiles.

Note that there are doctrinal problems here as well. First, SAM suppression assets are HD/LD because the U.S. Air Force is focused on the air-to-air aspect of defense suppression. For example, after Desert Storm, it retired both of its dedicated SAM-suppression platforms—the F-4G HARM missile shooter and the EF-111 jammer—to help pay for the development of a new air superiority fighter, the F-22. Yet Iraqi radar-guided SAMs shot down or damaged at least thirteen allied aircraft during Desert Storm, whereas its fighter aircraft shot down one allied aircraft at most.[8]

Second, the Air Force also appears to remain committed to defense suppression techniques that rely on autonomous, HARM-shooting aircraft to locate and attack SAM engagement radars. For example, there are already indications that the Air Force's answer to the SAM-10 problem will be to replace today's HARM shooter, the F-16CJ, with an F-22 variant, and to develop a faster, longer-legged HARM.[9] In other words, it would choose to replace a $50 million platform with a $150 million platform, and a $250K weapon with one that will edge closer to the cost of standoff weapons like the $500K Tactical Tomahawk, which obviate the need for any defense suppression assets at all. However, this approach would still be dependent on a cooperative target, and would therefore still not prevent a non-cooperative, mobile target from surviving to fight again another day.

Alternative approaches to the defense suppression mission that would be effective against non-cooperative opponents will depend on networks of standoff sensors that can instantaneously locate a SAM radar with precision sufficient to target it with a GPS-guided standoff weapon. Such an approach separates the sensor that finds the target from the shooter that launches a weapon against it, and therefore eliminates the need for these two functions to be combined in a manned combat aircraft such as the F-22.[10]

Therefore, future opponents are likely to focus their efforts on the purchase and operational exploitation of weapons like the Russian SAM-10 air defense system or the submarine-launched, SS-N-23 anti-ship

---

8. As in most recent conflicts, short-range, heat-seeking SAMs and anti-aircraft artillery (AAA) were the main killers of U.S. aircraft in Desert Storm, accounting for 71 percent of the 38 aircraft lost and 48 that were damaged. Radar-guided SAMs were responsible for 16 percent of the aircraft lost or damaged. These losses generally occurred when allied aircraft pressed their attacks against Iraqi ground forces at altitudes of less than 15,000 feet. The remaining 13 percent of aircraft losses are classified as having unknown causes, but only one of those losses is thought to have been caused by an Iraqi fighter. Thomas A. Keaney and Eliot A. Cohen, *Gulf War Air Power Survey Summary Report* (Washington, D.C.: U.S. Government Printing Office, 1993), p. 61.

9. See, for example, David A. Fulghum, "JSF and F-22 Refocused On Electronic Warfare," *Aviation Week and Space Technology,* July 3, 2000, pp. 35–36.

10. For more on the defense suppression problem and alternative approaches to solving it, see Owen Cote, *Mobile Targets From Under the Sea,* MIT Security Studies Conference Series, December 1999, pp. 25–31 at <http://web.mit.edu/ssp/>.

missile.[11] Higher profile but inherently more expensive prestige weapon purchases, such as a squadron or wing of modern tactical fighters or several major naval surface combatants, buy only a "shopfront" capability that can be quickly destroyed or rendered irrelevant at the outset of a conflict, as was, for example, the Serbian Air Force in Allied Force.

U.S. military strategy must adapt itself to this reality. Many of the most important tactical and operational challenges that dominated Cold War military planning and procurement will not exist on future battlefields, while others will remain, in some cases in more advanced form. A continued focus on the former, especially in a time of more restrained defense spending, will come at the expense of the latter, and this would be dangerous because it is in the latter area where U.S. opponents will be seeking victory.

U.S. ALLIANCE RELATIONSHIPS AND ACCESS TO OVERSEAS BASES WILL BE LESS FORMAL AND MORE UNPREDICTABLE THAN THOSE THAT OBTAINED DURING THE COLD WAR. The main Cold War alliance relationships between the United States, NATO, and Japan benefited from basic agreement among the parties to each alliance on the threats that justified it, the tools needed to oppose those threats, and the essential equality of national interests and thermonuclear risks at stake for all its members. Although the United States dominated each alliance, it also committed itself to the most binding of security guarantees: the promise to use U.S. nuclear weapons, if necessary, to defend allied territory from attack, whether conventional or nuclear. In return for this commitment, U.S. allies granted unprecedented access to bases within their territory and allowed the United States to station hundreds of thousands of troops. The rights of access and operational activity granted by each host nation were codified in formal status-of-forces agreements and were therefore predictable and reliable enough to be assumed as a given in Cold War military planning.

Both alliances were a response to the Soviet threat, and both continue after its demise, but neither, with the important exceptions of Japan in a Korean war and Turkey in Iraq, provides the United States access to local bases near or along the long littoral from the Red Sea to the China Sea. There, a better model for the alliance relationships that will provide such access, when it is granted, is the U.S.-Saudi relationship.

---

11. On the antisubmarine warfare challenges posed by modern non-nuclear submarines and antiship guided missiles, see Owen Cote, *Antisubmarine Warfare After the Cold War*, MIT Security Studies Conference Series, June 1997, <http://web.mit.edu/ssp/>.

Originally formed early in the Cold War, the relationship grew in importance to both the United States and Saudi Arabia after the fall of the Shah appeared to eliminate Iran as a buffer between the Soviet Union and Persian Gulf oil. Yet the United States gained only limited access to Saudi bases in support of its Rapid Deployment Force (RDF), mostly in the form of port visits and pre-positioning of ammunition and other supplies. Iraq's invasion of Kuwait resulted in a decision by the Saudi monarchy to allow U.S. forces unlimited access, but that decision was not made until four days after the invasion began, when Iraqi forces were already poised on the Saudi border.[12] After the war, the Saudis allowed U.S. combat aircraft to remain deployed, but refused U.S. requests to pre-position a brigade set of heavy armor.[13] Those deployed air forces are not always available for use in a crisis, as during Operation Desert Fox in December 1998, when the Saudis refused permission for strike aircraft to fly from their bases.[14]

Many factors explain this Saudi reluctance. The Saudi regime is a Sunni feudal monarchy that sits on a peninsula surrounded by Shia fundamentalism; it is an Arab state enjoying good relations with Israel's largest supporter; it is wealthy state with a small population that abuts several poorer states with large and growing populations. For all these and other reasons, the United States can solve only some of the Saudis' security problems, and in fact creates or exacerbates others. For example, there is no question that the Saudi regime's greatest domestic threat comes from fundamentalist Islamists, and the U.S. military presence serves as a lightning rod for their claims that the current regime has failed to protect the holy cities of Mecca and Medina from the infidel.

Both the December 1997 *Report of the National Defense Panel* and the more recent Hart-Rudman Commission report *New World Coming* have discussed other reasons why access to local bases in future conflicts will remain uncertain. For example, the latter noted that:

In dealing with security crises, the 21st century will be characterized more by episodic "posses of the willing" than the traditional World War II–style alli-

---

12.   *Conduct of the Persian Gulf War* (Washington, D.C.: U.S. Department of Defense, April 1992), p. 35.

13.   Peter Grier, "Pentagon Speeds Forces to Hot Spots, " *Christian Science Monitor,* October 18, 1994, p. 1.

14.   Douglas Jehl, "Saudis Admit Restricting U.S. Warplanes in Iraq," *New York Times,* March 22, 1999, p. 6.

ance systems. The United States will increasingly find itself wishing to form coalitions but increasingly unable to find partners willing and able to carry out combined military operations.[15]

When the alliances that produce base access are episodic and temporary, the access they produce will be as well.

Finally, and perhaps most importantly, those like the Saudis who today grant access to U.S. forces do so without the security guarantees that the United States gave its important Cold War allies. This makes it harder for them to determine whether giving U.S. forces access will increase or decrease their long-term security. For example, as the National Defense Panel argued, this might lead to limits on access for U.S. forces when potential allies face regional rivals armed with weapons of mass destruction.[16] During the Cold War, the United States made commitments to its major allies that use of such weapons against their territory would be met by retaliation in kind by the United States, but such guarantees are absent in alliance relationships with countries such as Saudi Arabia.

This is not to argue that U.S. forces will gain no access to bases abroad. When faced with clear threats to their sovereignty, many smaller states will ask for help, and when it is in the interests of the United States to respond, its forces will be given access. But this access will often come late, after a conflict has already begun; it will often be austere, in that few preparations will have been made in advance; and it will often be withdrawn or sharply limited after the particular conflict that caused it is resolved.

STRATEGY AND THE LONGER-TERM SECURITY ENVIRONMENT

The longer-term security environment is inherently less predictable than the near term, and it is therefore more difficult to make specific assumptions about its likely characteristics. But two assumptions seem credible: first, it is unlikely that the United States will have to make a major continental commitment in order to preserve a balance of power in Eurasia; and second, the battlefields on the Indo-Pacific littoral where the United States will need to make military commitments will be much more lethal than today, because its likely opponents will be able to exploit the most modern military technology.

---

15. The U.S. Commission on National Security, *New World Coming* (Washington, D.C., August 1999), p. 7, <http://www.nssg.gov/Reports/>.

16. *Report of the National Defense Panel*, December 1997, pp. 12-13, <www.dtic.mil/ndp/>.

MAJOR CONTINENTAL COMMITMENTS ON THE EURASIAN LAND MASS WILL NOT BE NECESSARY. The unification of Germany and the collapse of the Soviet Union made Germany and Russia much more equal in basic power potential, and also established a number of medium-size buffer states between them. Today, Germany's non-nuclear status is compensated by continuing NATO nuclear guarantees, and NATO also serves to enmesh Germany in a series of multilateral relationships that limit the potential for insecurity among other powers like France and Poland. Both of these NATO functions can endure without the need for a major U.S. commitment of ground forces.[17]

The land border separating Russia and China has also acquired buffer states such as Kazakhstan and Mongolia, so that the two larger countries abut only briefly between those two newly independent states in China's upper Xinjiang province, and more extensively along the border between Manchuria and the Russian maritime provinces. Both these borders could become future sources of instability, but those instabilities should be constrained both by the fact that China and Russia are likely to remain major nuclear powers, and by the fact that the vulnerabilities along their land borders are mutual. That is, China is vulnerable to separatism in Xinjiang province, which is near the base of Russian land power, and Russia is vulnerable to separatism in its maritime provinces, which are near the base of Chinese land power.

Finally, India is also likely to become and remain at least a medium nuclear power, and its geography gives it a powerful buffer against invasion along the entire Indo-Chinese land border. Central Asia and the Indian subcontinent are likely to be enormous sources of future instability, but geography and nuclear weapons make it unlikely that that instability will provoke a major ground war between India and China.

The most likely venue of future major great power competition and even war will, instead, have a more maritime focus. China and Japan is one obvious potential dyad, and China and India is another. A complicated triangular competition among these powers over control of the energy flows from the Middle East and Central Asia is also possible, if not likely. The medium powers that sit astride the same sea routes, such as Singapore, Malaysia, Indonesia, the Philippines, Korea, and of course, Taiwan, will all have stakes in the outcome, and will all face competing pressures to balance or bandwagon against different perceived threats to their own interests.

---

17. Current U.S. ground force deployments in Europe do have the additional benefit of being partially subsidized by their host nations; as long as these subsidies continue, these deployments may make sense for budgetary rather than strategic reasons.

The United States will be the balancer of last resort in these competitions, and the power that will determine the balance in these competitions will be seaborne.[18] This will put a premium on forces that can independently survive in and gain control over contested sea and littoral battle spaces against all comers, and when necessary, can project power rapidly ashore. The requirements for power projection ashore will stop short of an independent ability to wrest control of significant land areas from another great power, and will be focused instead on two capabilities: the ability to deploy long-range fires rapidly as an equalizer in land conflicts between medium powers and larger powers, and the ability to deploy both long-range fires and ground forces rapidly to a weak power threatened by a medium power in those rare instances when the former's survival and autonomy are an important U.S. interest.

The latter type of conflict has been relatively ubiquitous in the immediate post–Cold War era, and were today's "unipolar" moment to last forever, it would likely remain the only type of conflict for which the U.S. military needed to prepare. But the unipolar moment is likely to be replaced by a more multipolar world in which the United States will face the prospect of conflict with great powers that spend $150 billion rather than $15 billion on defense.

Thus, the United States should plan on dominating other great powers at sea without allied assistance, but it should only plan on fighting other great powers on land with the assistance of another medium power. In both cases, the battlefields of the longer-term security environment will be much more lethal because the asymmetry in wealth and technological prowess that favors the United States today will be gone or significantly reduced.

BATTLES BETWEEN GREAT POWERS FOR CONTROL OF THE SEA AND LAND WILL BE DECIDED IN PRIOR BATTLES FOR CONTROL OF THE UNDERSEA AND SPACE. Technology has already made fixed land targets essentially indefensible from conventional attack by U.S. forces, and both the fiscal and human costs of mounting such attacks should drop even further should U.S. forces fully embrace standoff weapons with guidance that integrates signals from Global Positioning System (GPS) satellites and miniaturized

---

18. On the United States being an offshore balancer of last resort, see Christopher Layne, "From Preponderance to Offshore Balancing: America's Future Grand Strategy," *International Security*, Vol. 22, No. 1 (Summer 1997), pp. 112–123. I predict that the United States will adopt that broad role for reasons quite different from those proposed by Layne, but his description of how such strategy might work in practice is useful. On Britain's historic role as an offshore balancer in Europe, see Daniel A. Baugh, "British Strategy during the First World War in the Context of Four Centuries: Blue-Water versus Continental Commitment," in Daniel Masterson, ed., *Naval History:*

inertial navigation systems (INS).[19] Technology will also soon greatly increase, from today's low level, the ability of U.S. forces to attack a variety of moving or mobile targets such as SAM radars, tactical ballistic missiles (TBMs), and armored vehicles, using long-range fires.[20] These long-range fires will be cued by wide-area sensors which will initially be air-based, but which will eventually migrate to space-based platforms in earth orbit. This growing arsenal of capability to use long-range fires to attack fixed and mobile land targets takes advantage of the enormous asymmetries in technological prowess that now favor the United States over its likely opponents.

Capabilities analogous to this were developed much earlier by the U.S. Navy in its Cold War struggle with the Soviet Navy, and particularly with the Soviet submarine force. The latter posed the greatest conventional threat to allied sea lines of communication, and as early as the late 1950s, the Navy was using undersea-based acoustic sensors to detect and track Soviet submarines on an ocean-wide basis, and to cue long-range anti-submarine warfare (ASW) platforms to prosecute them. This capability was also based on an asymmetry in technological prowess, in this case the ability to understand the significance of and exploit narrow-band low-frequency acoustic signal processing, but that asymmetry was eventually eliminated by the Soviet Union, albeit too late to influence the course of the Cold War.

Major asymmetries in technological prowess are rare in great power conflicts, and usually evanescent when they do occur. The dominant technological characteristic of the longer-term security environment is that the U.S. advantage over the rest of the world would be eliminated or greatly reduced if one or several new great powers arise in Eurasia. In prospective battles with such a power, the United States will once again have to assume the golden rule of war between equals: that which it can do unto others, they are likely to be able to do unto it.

The Sixth Symposium of the U.S. Naval Academy (Wilmington, Del.: Scholarly Resources Inc., 1987), pp. 85–110.

19. The most comprehensive treatment of the technology underlying this statement is Naval Studies Board, National Research Council, *Technology for the United States Navy and Marine Corps, 2000–2035*, Vol. 5: *Weapons* (Washington, D.C.: National Academy Press, 1997), especially pp. 106–120.

20. For an excellent analysis of the prospects for using long-range fires to halt an armored/mechanized force attack, see David A. Ochmanek, Edward R. Harshberger, David E. Thaler, and Glenn A. Kent, *To Find and Not to Yield: How Advances in Information and Firepower Can Transform Theater Warfare*, Project Air Force, The RAND Corporation, Santa Monica, Calif., 1988.

This will have many unpredictable consequences for U.S. military planning. For example, the military value of space-based sensors is likely to transform space into the same type of warfare medium that the air became during and after World War I. It may also lead to a growing dependence on undersea platforms as a base for long-range fires, because submarines may be the only weapon launchers able to approach an enemy coast early in a major conflict. In both cases, U.S. military planners faced with an increasingly lethal environment on or near the surface along the Eurasian littoral are likely to seek sanctuaries from which they can more safely obtain information and project power. But in a competition with a peer, no operating medium will remain a sanctuary for long, and battles for control of those mediums will be much more intense than they would be in today's security environment.

U.S. military planners are likely to be driven to seek sanctuaries in space and under the sea surface because the surface and near-surface environment in areas contested by great power militaries will be extremely lethal. Fixed targets on the surface will be indefensible if within range of an opponent's likely arsenal of precision TBMs and cruise missiles, for as long as the supply of those weapons lasts. Even mobile targets will be at much greater risk of prompt destruction if the opponent retains access to wide-area battlefield surveillance assets. The fact that the latter will eventually need to be deployed in space is the main reason space will become a battleground in the long term.

One main conclusion that should inform current defense planning concerns the issue of access to overseas bases. Where such access is uncertain and episodic in the near-term security environment for essentially political reasons, it is likely to remain problematic in the longer term for purely military reasons. Even if available, such bases are unlikely to be viable, because like all large fixed locations within a certain radius of the opponent, they are likely to be indefensible as long as the opponent has a supply of standoff weapons to attack them. Forces that nevertheless must operate on the surface and close with the enemy will be able to do so only if they operate in such a way as not to present large, predictable, fixed targets to the opponent, and if the opponent's battlefield surveillance capabilities against mobile targets are degraded or destroyed.

THE SERVICES AND THE NEW SECURITY ENVIRONMENT

A U.S. decision to adopt a maritime strategy would primarily affect the Army and the Air Force. Both the Army and the Air Force have force structures and doctrine for their use that assume relatively unrestricted access to airfields and ports within a theater of conflict. In an access-constrained environment, these forces will have difficulty projecting power. The Navy and the Marine Corps face a different challenge, which is to build on the relatively unrestricted access already provided by their forward-deployed forces, and give those forces added leverage over events ashore through improved power-projection capabilities. In short, the Army and the Air Force need to restructure their forces in order to make them less dependent on fixed bases ashore, while the Navy and the Marine Corps need to expand their reach ashore from the sea.

In the near term, the Navy and Marine Corps face fewer obstacles in expanding their reach ashore than the other services face in getting ashore. Put another way, more radical innovation in doctrine and force structure will be necessary in the Army and the Air Force to integrate them better with the demands of the new security environment. In the next three sections, I outline the main changes in doctrine and force structure that would be necessary for each service.

A LONGER-LEGGED AIR FORCE MORE FOCUSED ON EXPLOITING RATHER THAN GAINING AIR SUPERIORITY

With the end of the Cold War, and after the Gulf War, the Air Force chose to emphasize its fighter force over its bomber force, stealth over non-stealth, air-to-air over air-to-ground, and fixed ground targets over mobile targets. In each of these four areas, the new security environment demands that the Air Force reassess its priorities.

BOMBERS VERSUS FIGHTERS. The main issue concerns the balance between the bomber and fighter forces. Both rely on overseas bases in order to project power, but the fighter force does so much more intensively; bombers only need bases enroute to the theater of operations from which tankers can operate to refuel them. There will be many circumstances in which a state may allow U.S. tankers to fly from its bases but not allow U.S. combat aircraft to do so, because the former activity has a lower political threshold than the latter. Thus, bombers will often get access that might be denied fighters because they allow an allied nation to maintain the fiction that it is not directly supporting U.S. combat operations.

This access comes at a cost, in that bombers are individually more expensive, and fly fewer sorties because of the greater distances they must fly, but this cost is reduced relative to fighter aircraft when the latter face limits, in both time and space, on their access to local bases. In the longer term, these political limits on access will be joined by military ones when opponents are able to deploy submunition-dispensing, GPS/INS-guided ballistic and cruise missiles. Within a radius of 500 to 1000 kilometers, such missiles will limit the use of any airfield, and particularly airfields lacking the expensive hardened aircraft shelters and maintenance facilities that the U.S. Air Force built during the Cold War in Western Europe and Northeast Asia, but which are rare elsewhere.[21] These military constraints on access will further reduce the comparative advantages of tactical fighters versus bombers.

STEALTHY VERSUS NON-STEALTHY. The balance between stealthy and non-stealthy aircraft may also need to be rethought. Stealth aircraft are much more expensive than non-stealthy aircraft, but after the Gulf War, the Air Force decided never to buy another non-stealthy aircraft because it argued that the cost of stealth was more than compensated by the cost savings represented by active and passive defense suppression assets rendered unnecessary by stealth. But the assumption that stealth would provide this major cost avoidance is already proving difficult to sustain. For example, both B-2s and F-117s were provided direct jamming support by EA-6Bs in Allied Force, a form of support that the Air Force claimed that the F-117 did not need in its strikes against downtown Baghdad in Desert Storm. There is also evidence that the Serbians were able to use low-frequency radars to track F-117s and B-2s during Allied Force, which may have played a role in the F-117 shootdown. The point is that passive and, in the future, active defense suppression measures will likely remain necessary to assure penetration of any manned strike asset.

This means in turn that the Air Force's post–Gulf War decision to divest or reduce its defense suppression assets in anticipation of an all-stealth force structure has unbalanced the current force, especially because that force remains predominantly non-stealthy, and is therefore limited in its ability to operate against modern air defense assets by the size of the defense suppression force that supports it. This has led to the concept of a "high demand, low density" asset, meaning an asset that is a major determinant of success in combat, but which is underrepresented in the force structure. Prime among such HD/LD assets are Air Force defense suppression assets.

FOCUSING ON THE AIR-TO-AIR MISSION AS THE KEY TO AIR SUPERIORITY. Alongside the Air Force's focus on fighters and stealth is a focus on air-to-air combat as the key to air superiority, and a desire therefore to maximize air-to-air capabilities, treating various air-to-ground capabilities as a lesser included case. This focus is manifest in the F-22 program, both in terms of how the aircraft is designed, and in terms of the portion of the Air Force's overall investment in the future that it consumes. But there is considerable evidence that this focus will prove misguided, both

---

21. For an excellent discussion of this issue, see John Stillion and David T. Orletsky, *Airbase Vulnerability to Conventional Cruise-Missile and Ballistic-Missile Atacks: Technology, Scenarios, and U.S. Air Force Responses* (Santa Monica, Calif.: Project Air Force, RAND, 1999).

in the near and the far-term security environment. In the near term, opponents are likely to build their air defense systems around ground-based defenses, because such defenses provide a better entry-level capability for smaller powers when they are fighting against a major power like the United States. In the distant term, in the event that a peer competitor emerges, it is likely that strike operations on both sides will be dominated by unmanned ballistic and cruise missiles, which will not need fighter escorts to penetrate defenses, and against which manned fighter interceptors will be relatively ineffective.

Instead, the key to gaining air superiority in the future is likely to be the ability to destroy quickly rather than merely suppress ground-based air defenses. The distinction between suppression and destruction turns on the ability of an air defense system to force its opponent to devote resources to counter it over time. When defenses are merely suppressed, they survive to create the demand for more suppression the next day, and they also limit both the pace and scope of the attacker's operations. When defenses are destroyed, they no longer impose these costs on the attacker, who is then free to devote all its assets to exploiting the air superiority it has gained, and is also free to use tactics that maximize the effects of those assets. Finally, the mission of destroying enemy air defenses, rather than merely suppressing them, will probably become one of the first areas where an interlinked network of sensors and stand-off shooters will fully replace traditional manned aircraft operating autonomously over future battlefields. Thus, in the near term, relative to defense suppression assets like the EA-6B and the F-16CJ, Air Force fighters like the F-15C have become, in effect, "high density, low demand" assets, and in the more distant term, the same fate is likely to befall the F-22.

EXPLOITING AIR SUPERIORITY. The Air Force is devoted to the premise that, once gained, air superiority can be exploited in a way that assures rapid, relatively cost-free victories to the side that gains it. Today, it focuses its exploitation efforts on attacking fixed targets that affect the opposing leadership's will to fight, with the goal being the coercion of that leadership into giving up its gains. The historical basis for this focus is undeniably related to the maxim that when all you have is a hammer, everything looks like a nail. Because fixed targets have generally been easier to attack than mobile ones, the Air Force needed a theory of how attacking such targets would lead to victory, even though most of an opponent's military forces are generally mobile. In the aftermath of the Gulf War, with the operational introduction of stealth platforms armed with precision weapons, the Air Force argued that its capabilities had finally caught up with its doctrine, and that rapid, wide-reaching attacks against fixed strategic targets would constitute the best means of exploiting the fruits of air superiority in future wars.[22]

Allied Force will be used both as a confirmation of this view, and as an example of the dangers in having an air force that has adopted it. That is because Allied Force also demonstrated how relatively ill-prepared the U.S Air Force is to attack mobile targets effectively. The evidence for this was the Serbian Army's ability to conduct its months-long ethnic cleansing operations without any appreciable interdiction by allied air forces, and its survival of the war without suffering significant damage to its own forces, all despite the fact that more than 2000 air attacks using more than 8400 weapons were allocated against Serbian ground forces, about a third of the total air effort.

Faced with evidence of its inability to attack mobile targets effectively, Air Force leaders have tended to argue one of two things. One argument is that these operations, though not very effective, were still effective enough to produce some damage to Serbian forces, and that the eventual Serbian retreat suggests that this damage was sufficient to contribute to victory. Another argument is that mobile targets are simply not important compared to fixed strategic targets, and that politically motivated decisions to divert air forces toward mobile targets are a misuse of air power.

Neither argument is tenable in the long term, particularly for an organization whose essence is the operation of expensive manned combat aircraft. If mobile targets are important, as most would agree, then it will not be acceptable for the Air Force to be no more effective against them in future attacks as it was in attacks against fixed targets during the strategic bombing campaigns of World War II. In addition, even assuming that attacks against strategic targets constitute an alternative in some cases, such attacks against fixed targets will increasingly be conducted by unmanned, GPS/INS-guided weapons. Therefore, against a finite set of well-defended, fixed targets, such weapons will increasingly be delivered by standoff ballistic or cruise missiles launched from platforms that do not need to penetrate enemy defenses, rather than manned combat aircraft like the B-2, F-117, or a strike variant of the F-22 dropping short-range gravity or glide bombs.

---

22.   The best example of this focus on attacking fixed, strategic targets for the purpose of coercion is John A. Warden III, "Employing Air Power in the Twenty-first Century," Richard A. Shultz Jr. and Robert L. Pfaltzgraff, Jr., eds., *The Future of Air Power in the Aftermath of the Gulf War* (Maxwell Air Force Base, Ala.: Air University Press, 1992), pp. 57–82. For a critique of this doctrine, see Robert A. Pape, *Bombing To Win: Air Power and Coercion in War* (Ithaca, N.Y.: Cornell University Press, 1996).

AN ARMY THAT CAN GET THERE FASTER WITH MORE

Almost every major post–Cold War military conflict in which the United States has been involved has highlighted a curious fact about the U.S. Army's force structure. It has very light forces that can deploy quickly by air, and it has very heavy forces that must deploy more slowly by sea, rail, or on well-developed roads. The problem is that its light forces, consisting of foot-mobile infantry, lack tactical mobility and are easily overmatched in terms of combat power, while its heavy forces, which can overmatch any foe, pay for their combat power with deployment timelines often measured in months rather than weeks or days.

This force structure remains essentially unchanged from the immediate post-Vietnam years, when the Army's heavy forces were focused on defending the inner German border, where they could rely on extensive forward deployments in peacetime, and when it had just finished a jungle war in which both the terrain and the enemy's tactics dictated the use of foot infantry in most combat. But since the end of the Cold War, in both major contingencies such as Desert Shield and lesser contingencies such as Bosnia or Kosovo, the Army has had to deploy rapidly to theaters where it lacks forward deployed forces, and where neither terrain nor the capabilities of opposing forces make it wise to send very light forces.

PRE-POSITIONING IS NOT THE ANSWER. The Army has not ignored this problem. For example, since the Gulf War it has pre-positioned five heavy brigade sets of equipment, one each ashore in Kuwait, Qatar, Italy, and South Korea, and one afloat. Pre-positioning has both strengths and weaknesses. Its main strength is that it allows the deployment of heavy forces at the rate that airlift can deliver their personnel. Pre-positioning ashore provides the cheapest means of rapidly reinforcing a specific theater where the United States has close allies that face a well-defined nearby threat, as in Kuwait and South Korea. Pre-positioning at sea provides a more flexible but also more expensive means of accomplishing this task when the location of a contingency cannot be predicted in advance, or when peacetime bases ashore are not available for political reasons.

However, pre-positioning in both its forms requires that duplicate sets of unit equipment be bought for the U.S.-based units that will use this method of rapid deployment, adding to its expense. Maritime pre-positioning, which provides the most flexibility, adds the constraint that units may only deploy to locations where a large airport is collocated with a deep-water port. Thus, even in well-developed regions, maritime pre-positioning does not provide a means of rapidly deploying heavy forces inland, and in less developed regions, limitations in the available transportation infrastructure ashore can severely constrain the movement of equipment at every stage of the sequence, from its unloading at the port of debarkation, its marriage with personnel flown in from the United States, and once formed, the overland movement of units to the scene of battle.

The Army's experiences in both Bosnia and Kosovo illustrate the resulting dilemma. In both cases, light forces were considered inadequate in terms of both firepower and protection, but it took the Army three months to move an armored division by rail from Germany to Bosnia. The challenges of deploying heavy divisions into Kosovo would have resulted in equal or even longer deployment times.

AIR-DEPLOYABLE MEDIUM-WEIGHT COMBAT TEAMS. In the aftermath of Allied Force, the Army decided to pursue a more radically innovative approach to this problem. At the heart of this approach is the concept of air-deployable motorized brigades.[23] These brigades will be built upon vehicles weighing no more than 20 tons, or a little more than a quarter of what a main battle tank weighs, with substantially more firepower and protection than the thin-skinned jeeps and trucks that light forces use for their tactical mobility. These vehicles will also fit within the cargo cube of a C-130 tactical airlifter, and as many as six or more of them will fit in strategic airlifters that can now carry only one main battle tank at a time. The Army's new initiative is designed to provide combat units that are as air-deployable as today's light forces, but that possess sufficient firepower and protection for those increasingly common contingencies where the threat does not demand the overwhelming combat power of a heavy armored force, but does foreclose the use of light forces.

In the longer term, an air-deployable force is going to be important because there is no better example of the type of fixed target that will be rendered terminally vulnerable than a large seaport. For example, major ports of the type now necessary for the rapid debarkation of heavy Army equipment pre-positioned at sea are not ubiquitous, even in the industrialized world. Even in major contingencies in developed areas, there are usually only a few available. Furthermore, they are in use continuously at the outset of a conflict because large pre-positioning ships, which arrive at the rate of several a day, take at least 48 hours to unload. Major airfields of the type required by large military and commercial airlift aircraft will also be vulnerable for the same reasons.

---

23. The best summary of this concept remains John Gordon IV and Peter A. Wilson, "The Case For Army XXI 'Medium Weight' Aero-Motorized Divisions: A Pathway to the Army of 2020," Strategic Studies Institute, U.S. Army War College, May 27, 1998, pp. 1–24, available at <http://carlisle-www.army.mil/usassi/ssipubs/stdyprog.htm.>

Air-deployable motorized brigades force will enable the Army to pursue alternative methods of rapidly deploying and sustaining its early-entry forces. In the near term, an interim force will allow the Army to deploy Brigade Combat Teams (BCTs) directly into relatively ubiquitous small airfields using existing short takeoff and landing (STOL) C-130s and C-17s, the rationale being the rapid inland delivery of ground forces into relatively permissive but austere environments, usually in support of lesser regional contingencies or as the leading edge of a deployment to a major contingency. In and of itself, this capability reduces the Army's vulnerabilities to attack against fixed targets because STOL airlift provides access to many more bases, each of which can therefore be used less intensively, making the timing of an effective attack against them more difficult for an opponent to predict. As technology evolves, the Army envisions a more advanced "Objective Force" for the longer term, and air and sealift technology that will allow it to be deployed and sustained by air with even less dependence on fixed airfields will need to be developed.

SELF DEPLOYING, C-130–SIZE, VTOL AIRLIFT. The vision of the future recommended here centers on new vertical takeoff or landing (VTOL) or near-VTOL tactical airlift aircraft and new sea-based pre-positioning assets designed so that they can be unloaded at sea by those aircraft. Such capabilities would greatly expand the strategic and operational mobility of motorized brigades by speeding their deployment into austere airfields using existing strategic and tactical airlift capabilities, and by allowing a portion of those forces to be sustained directly from the sea without need for a port once they are deployed.[24] More ambitiously, in concert with the Army's objective force, unit equipment and supplies could be pre-positioned on large Mobile Offshore Bases (MOBs) to which personnel could be flown using traditional airlift, and from which complete units could deploy and be sustained by tactical airlift aircraft which combined VTOL with some degree of stealth.

In the near term, this might involve a C-130–size, tilt-rotor aircraft based on the Marine Corps' V-22, and a modification to current pre-positioning ships that would allow the transfer of fuel and cargo to their flight decks. A more ambitious concept might depend on developing large mobile offshore bases and ways of making large VTOL airlifters more stealthy, which might require a jet-powered, tailless, tilt-wing aircraft.

---

24. Here, the concept is similar to the Marine Corps' Hunter Warrior experiment, albeit on a brigade-size rather than a battalion-size scale.

In both the near and more distant term concepts, the key is to combine the attributes of the Air Force's C-130 fleet and the Army's heavy lift helicopter fleet to produce an aircraft that has the speed and range to self-deploy across oceans, and the VTOL capability to gain independence from airfields and provide direct ship-to-foxhole delivery.

When combined with the motorized brigades, such an aircraft would eliminate two obstacles that would limit use of those brigades if they were supported by traditional air and sealift assets alone. First, the Army's lift helicopters now constitute one of the single largest consumers of strategic airlift. Eliminating that demand would free up airlift for more brigade unit equipment. Second, once deployed, the fuel consumed by the turbine engines in both the Army's helicopter and main battle tank fleets are its single largest sustainment requirement. The latter would be eliminated if the Army's VTOL lift aircraft could be sustained from ships at sea, and of course the former is eliminated by the motorized brigades.

IT'S THE LIGHT FORCES, STUPID. The main difference between this argument for the motorized brigades and the one currently used by the Army is that I argue that, at least in the near term, the Army is too light, not too heavy.[25] It is the Army's light forces that lack credible scenarios for their use, not its heavy forces, which remain relevant in all major regional contingencies on land. This difference is reflected in the cuts proposed for the Army force structure in the next section, which focus on its light forces rather than its heavy forces.

A NAVY WITH MORE LEVERAGE ASHORE

The Navy's current force structure, blessed by the 1997 Quadrennial Defense Review, consists of a total of about 300 combatants and support vessels, including 12 carriers, 12 amphibious ready groups, 50 attack submarines (SSNs), 14 ballistic missile submarines (SSBNs), and 116 surface combatants.[26] Because it is a relatively young fleet, this 300-ship Navy can be maintained at current rates of investment in new ship construction past the year 2010. Beyond that point, and particularly beyond 2020, either bloc obsolescence will cause a rapid fall in the size of the fleet, and create the demand for rapid increases in funding, or ship lives will need to be extended beyond their currently projected lifetimes.

If the Navy were to begin now trying to reduce this bow wave of future spending requirements to maintain a 300-ship Navy, it would need

---

25. I am indebted to Colonel Brian Zahn, USA, for this formulation.

26. Statement of Ronald O'Rourke Before the Senate Armed Services Committee, Subcommittee on Seapower, March 2, 2000, p. 2, cited hereafter as O'Rourke testimony.

to add about $2.0 billion to its annual ship-building budget.[27] This addition to current budgets would cause only a small improvement to the Navy's near-term ability to project power from the sea because it would cause only a small increase in its forward-deployed force structure in the years before bloc obsolescence sets in.

A 350-SHIP NAVY OR A MORE INNOVATIVE 300-SHIP NAVY? One way to increase more dramatically the Navy's ability to project power from the sea would be to expand it well beyond its current size. Indeed, four specific proposals for such an expansion appear likely from the Navy: increase the SSN force structure to 55–68 by 2015;[28] increase the surface combatant force to 138;[29] add two amphibious ready groups for a total of 14; and add three carrier battle groups for a total of 15 carriers.[30] Collectively, these increases would result in a roughly 350-ship Navy, and would immediately demand much larger increases in ship construction funding beyond that needed simply to sustain the 300-ship force.

I propose instead that the Navy increase its ability to project power from the sea through innovation. Both the sea control and power-projection capabilities of the current, forward-deployed, 300-ship Navy can be improved by changes in doctrine, rather than an expansion in force structure. In many cases, these changes in doctrine can be accomplished through changes in the division of labor among the Navy's existing platforms, and the following sections give such an example. Furthermore, this approach also eschews major additional funding in the near term toward paying the currently projected bill for sustaining a 300-ship force beyond 2020. If the Army and the Air Force adopt measures like those suggested here, they will by 2010 be able to reclaim some of the relative burden they will give up to the Navy during the coming decade, and the Navy's fleet size can be reduced accordingly. If they do not, additional funds will be drawn from Army and Air Force accounts after 2010 in order to preserve a 300-ship Navy.

SUBMARINES AND LONG-RANGE PRECISION WEAPONS. One major opportunity for naval innovation lies in more fully exploiting the capability of existing submarine assets as launch platforms for existing or already

---

27. O'Rourke testimony, p. 11.

28. Hunter Keeter, "Danzig: Importance of Submarines Likely to Rise," *Defense Daily*, February 24, 2000, p. 1; and Robert Hamilton, "Support Growing For More Submarines," *New London Day*, March 7, 2000.

29. Robert Holzer, "U.S. Navy Hopes To Expand Fleet," *Defense Week*, January 31, 2000, p. 1.

30. O'Rourke testimony, pp. 2–3.

planned standoff precision weapons. Long-range precision weapons can dramatically reduce the mass that must be projected from the sea in order to produce a given effect ashore, while at the same time expanding the mass that can be projected by a given naval force. They reduce the requirements for mass by making target destruction possible with one or two precision weapons rather than 10 or 100 iron bombs. By allowing long standoff ranges from the target, they increase the number of platforms that can serve as precision weapon launchers. This means that both surface ships and submarines can join aircraft carriers to form a triad of naval strike warfare assets, and it also means that each weapon launcher is capable of achieving much greater and more precise effects. Future improvements in long-range precision weapons will occur at the steep rate characteristic of technologies still in their infancy.

The security environment the Navy faces is one where U.S. access to overseas bases is greatly reduced and where the proliferation of relatively low-cost and easy-to-use access-denial weapons such as modern diesel-electric submarines, anti-ship and land attack missiles, and naval mines continues to grow. This is a world in which the Navy will have to provide a larger portion of national power-projection capabilities, while also placing much more emphasis on sea control than it does now. This is the security environment the United States is already beginning to face along the long arc of the Indian and Pacific ocean littorals. In it, the U.S. Navy's relevance is likely to exceed its currently projected capabilities by a wide margin.

Long-range precision weapons such as the Tomahawk cruise missile allow the Navy to involve all of its combatant platforms in strike warfare; but in addition, their deployment in larger numbers by the submarine force would free up additional surface and aviation assets for countering opposing sea-denial efforts, whether in air and missile defense, mine warfare, or for the ASW effort against very quiet modern submarines. ASW in particular is a mission that demands a coordinated all-arms approach that includes surface ships, submarines, fixed and rotary-wing air assets, and the integrated undersea surveillance community.

CONVERT EIGHT TRIDENT SSBNS TO SSGNS. The specific utility of the submarine force will grow most dramatically if the added launcher capacity available in Trident SSBNs made surplus by the end of the Cold War is exploited. Under current plans, arms control reductions will soon liberate four SSBNs from their nuclear deterrence mission. SSBNs converted to carry conventional guided missiles instead of nuclear ballistic missiles (SSGNs instead of SSBNs) could well prove to be the dominant platforms for precision strike from the sea, especially early in a contingency when the air and sea control battles are still being contested and the multi-mission pull on attack submarines, surface combatants, and carriers will be highest. Historically, in comparison to smaller attack submarines, surface platforms have had many more vertical launchers and have therefore been able to deploy more strike weapons, even considering the fact that these weapons had to compete for space with air-defense and ASW weapons in the surface ship's magazine. This basic comparative advantage disappears when the submarine half of the comparison is a converted Trident SSGN. An SSGN would combine all of the traditional capabilities of an attack submarine, along with almost three times as much vertical launcher volume in its converted missile tubes as is available on an Aegis cruiser.

The Navy should convert a total of eight Trident SSBNs to SSGNs, rather than the four conversions contemplated in current planning. This can be done while also preserving the same number of SLBM warheads called for by the 1996 Nuclear Posture Review.[31]

Cuts in Defense Programs and Activities

This section offers an alternative procurement and force structure program that would save $28 billion a year by 2010 and bring U.S. military planning more in line with the strategic assumptions described in the previous section.

SAVINGS FROM CUTS IN PROCUREMENT

By 2010, reductions in planned procurement programs can save approximately $12.6 billion a year and at the same time help shape future military forces better for the future they face. The alternative cancels procurement now for the F-22, Comanche, Crusader, C-130J, Trident D-5 SLBM, and the Advanced Amphibious Assault Vehicle (AAAV); cuts back on procurement for the Apache Longbow helicopter; and delays the Joint Strike Fighter.

CANCEL F-22. The F-22 is an extremely expensive (and capable) platform optimized for air-to-air combat, as discussed above. But prowess in air-to-air combat will not be the key to gaining and exploiting air supremacy in the future security environment. Rather, the main challenge to gaining air supremacy will be networks of advanced surface-to-air missile (SAM) networks based on systems like the Russian SAM-10.

---

31. The nuclear posture review called for an SLBM force of about 1750 warheads. Reducing the number of Trident SSBNs from fourteen to ten would simply require that each SLBM carry seven rather than five warheads if a total force of 1750 warheads were to be preserved.

These systems will pose serious challenges to current defense suppression tactics that require manned aircraft to locate and attack them autonomously, even if the aircraft involved are F-22s. This is because a single aircraft cannot locate a radar with both the precision and speed needed to attack it with a GPS/INS weapon before the SAM missile strikes home, meaning that anti-radiation missiles like HARM will still be required to attack the SAM engagement radar. But the phased-array engagement radars of systems like the SAM-10 provide detection ranges that require even the stealthiest manned aircraft to use weapons that can be launched from significantly greater range than today's 15-mile–range HARM. A further problem is that today's HARM is the largest weapon that can be carried in an F-22's internal weapon bay, which is optimized for carriage of smaller air-to-air weapons. In order to carry longer-range weapons, an F-22 would have to carry them externally, making it no more stealthy than the aircraft it was designed to replace.

These challenges will likely drive military planners to an approach that destroys radar-guided air defense systems from a distance as soon as they turn on their engagement radars. This will depend on networks of offboard sensors in which at least three separate but interlinked antennas use time-difference-of-arrival techniques to locate even the shortest pulses of radar energy immediately, and with the precision necessary to target GPS/INS weapons. Initially, these networks will use existing sensor platforms such as the Global Hawk high-endurance Unmanned Aerial Vehicle (UAV) or the U-2, and in the longer run they will use constellations of satellites in low earth orbit. The existence of such a network of offboard sensors will enable non-stealthy platforms launching air, ground, or sea-launched tactical ballistic missiles (TBMs) of at least 100-mile range to attack the SAM radars from well outside their engagement envelope.

Another suggested alternative role for the F-22 is as a fighter-bomber, able to deliver air-to-ground weapons as well as air-to-air weapons. Indeed, there is a long and largely successful history of converting fighters purpose-designed for the air superiority mission into highly effective fighter-bombers: witness the F-15E and the F-4.[32] But again, stealth changes this equation because stealth requires internal weapons carriage, and the F-22's air-to-air orientation led its designers to provide only enough internal volume for the equivalent of two 1000-pound bombs. By comparison, the Navy version of the Joint Strike Fighter (JSF), which will be designed as a fighter-bomber from the start, will be able to carry the

---

32. Richard P. Hallion, "A Troubling Past: Air Force Fighter Acquisition since 1945," *Airpower Journal*, Winter 1990, pp. 2–23.

equivalent of two 2000-pound bombs internally. Cutting the F-22 saves $4.35 billion.

CANCEL COMANCHE. The rationale for cutting Comanche, for a savings of $1.6 billion, is twofold. First, the doctrinal niche that Comanche occupies is unnecessary in the near term and probably not viable in the longer term. Second, as with all rotary-wing aircraft, the Comanche is a voracious consumer of strategic airlift. Below, I suggest that most or all rotary-wing aircraft in the Army's inventory be replaced with VSTOL platforms that can self-deploy over long distances, so I will focus here on the first rationale for canceling Comanche: its doctrinal irrelevance.

As a scout helicopter, Comanche is replacing the OH-58 in the role of finding and identifying targets for attack helicopters like the Cobra and the Apache. But the Army has already removed all the OH-58s from the active inventory and is now using Apaches in both the scout and the attack role, because Comanche will not deploy for almost a decade. Apache is effective under most circumstances today as its own scout, though it lacks some of the sensor capabilities of its predecessor.

Furthermore, in high threat environments, or under circumstances in which casualties must be kept to a minimum, it is going to be very difficult if not impossible to rely on a manned platform for the scout mission. This was reflected in the recent Apache deployment to Kosovo, which caused the Army to pull its Hunter Unmanned Aerial Vehicles out of storage for use as scouts for the Apaches. In this concept of operation, the Apache and the UAV are connected by line-of-sight data links that allow the Apache to control the UAV, and the UAV is given a laser designator along with optical and infrared sensors so that it can find and mark targets that the Apaches can attack without exposing itself.[33] In the long run, a more advanced implementation of this concept will be both superior and much cheaper than the currently planned Comanche-Apache combination.

CANCEL CRUSADER. In this budget, the size and composition of the Army's current heavy-division force structure are held constant, and continuing modernization of its existing platforms is funded, because these forces are necessary for major contingencies that may arise in the near term security environment in places such as Korea and the Persian Gulf. But in the longer-term security environment, there is much less rationale for developing and procuring new systems to outfit traditional heavy division formations, and cutting Crusader saves $1.2 billion. Crusader is the only truly new ground system currently being developed for the

33. On the Apache-UAV concept, see Hunter Keeter, "Hunter Likely Shot Down by a Missile," *Defense Daily*, April 9, 1999, p. 6.

Army's heavy divisions, and it is unnecessary in the near- to mid-term because the currently funded Paladin, Multiple Launch Rocket System (MLRS), and Army Tactical Missile System (ATACMS) will be more than sufficient. This is especially so because guided rocket artillery such as MLRS and ATACMS is increasingly taking the place of tube artillery like Paladin and Crusader in many fire-support missions. For example, though some foreign tube artillery available for export outranges Paladin, MLRS will be responsible for most counter-battery fire, as it was during Desert Storm.

Furthermore, the Army has already acknowledged that Crusader is not a natural fit with its future, by slowing its development in order to develop a lighter, wheeled ammunition resupply vehicle for the tracked gun system. Though this might result in a marginal increase in strategic mobility, it will reduce Crusader's tactical mobility, thereby vitiating another rationale for Crusader, which was its increased tactical mobility over Paladin.

CANCEL C-130J. In the near term, the youthfulness and large, congressionally inflated size of the current C-130 fleet will provide more than sufficient tactical airlift to U.S. forces for some time. In the longer term, beyond 2010, the development and eventual procurement of a C-130–size tilt rotor or other advanced tactical airlifter will produce a more appropriate lift platform for a security environment in which traditional air fields will be more vulnerable. Cutting the C-130J will save $110 million.

The C-130J is a modest improvement on current C-130 models, but its development costs were born internally by Lockheed rather than the Air Force because the latter never made them a requirement. Part of the logic behind its internal development by Lockheed lay in the belief that it would be attractive in the export market, and that the Air Force would eventually be forced by Congress to buy it anyway. The U.S. Air Force requirement for the C-130J has never been strong, and there is no need to replace the existing tactical airlift fleet with a new aircraft.

REDUCE LONGBOW BUY BY SIX BRIGADE EQUIVALENTS. The Army currently has fourteen attack aviation brigades, one for each division, and one for each Corps headquarters. The alternative saves $800 million by preserving eight brigades' worth of Longbow conversions in order to support six divisions and two Corps headquarters, leaving two divisions and one Corps headquarters without organic attack helicopter support. This reflects the fact that in the near term, the Army is likely to face many contingencies without the tank-heavy, target-rich threat environment for which heavy attack helicopters are most appropriate. It also reflects the fact that in the longer term, the Army's organic air attack assets should have a self-deployment capability.

STOP TRIDENT D-5 SLBM PRODUCTION. Cancellation of Trident D-5 production (saving $200 million) reflects a recommendation to concentrate the roughly 1700 RV SLBM force allowed under START on ten SSBNs rather than fourteen. This allows for eight rather than four SSGN conversions, and eliminates the need for buying D-5s to outfit SSBNs eleven through fourteen, now deployed in the Pacific and carrying older C-4 missiles.

CANCEL AAAV. AAAV is an amphibious infantry fighting vehicle designed to replace the Marine Corps' aging AAV-7s. AAAV's main advantage is its in-water speed: roughly 25 knots, versus eight for the AAV-7. Marine doctrine for beach assaults sets an hour as the upper limit for the run in to the beach by its assault vehicles, and AAAV's enhanced speed will therefore allow the amphibious ships which launch it to stand off up to 25 miles from the beach, triple the current capability. This difference is significant because a ship 25 miles from a coast is just over the visual horizon from that coast, whereas a ship that must deploy closer will be clearly silhouetted against the horizon. Thus, AAAV's main effect will be to increase the survivability of Marine amphibious vessels in traditional beach assaults.

The problem with AAAV is that such traditional beach assaults, like airborne assaults, have become obsolete. In a direct-fire engagement against prepared defenses, modern man-portable weapons make such assaults suicidal. The future of the Marine Corps amphibious, forced-entry capabilities lies in its commitment to vertical envelopments of hostile beaches, using platforms like the V-22. Canceling the AAAV would save $400 million.

SAVINGS FROM CUTS IN FORCE STRUCTURE

The alternative proposed in this chapter calls for phased reductions of some of the Army and Air Force forces by 2010. It eliminates two active light divisions (82nd Airborne, 101st Air Assault), the XVIII Airborne Corps headquarters, all eight Guard divisions, twelve Guard field artillery brigades, six apache brigades, two Army lift brigades (CH-47), and two active and one Guard F-16 wings. Combined savings relative to current plans come to about $15.4 billion annually by 2010.

ELIMINATE 82ND AIRBORNE AND 101ST AIR ASSAULT. Light Army divisions, and the airborne and air assault divisions in particular, make no sense in either the near or the longer term security environment, and their elimination saves $3.2 billion. They are completely unsuited to high-intensity conflict, and their organic vehicles do not provide enough armored protection to their infantry in more limited conflicts and peacekeeping operations. Certain cultural roles played by these units within the Army's overall infantry community, and the very limited demand for airborne and air assault type operations, can both be met by the Army's Ranger regiment. Conversion of the other two active light divisions into motorized infantry or cavalry regiments is discussed below.

ELIMINATE XVIII AIRBORNE CORPS HEADQUARTERS. An active Army of eight division equivalents does not need four Corps headquarters. Savings in personnel and O&M from the elimination of one active Corps headquarters would be roughly equal to the savings that result from eliminating an active division, at $1.6 billion.

ELIMINATE ALL EIGHT GUARD DIVISIONS. The Army's Guard divisions are essentially undeployable under any but the most extreme, and therefore unlikely, scenarios of all-out mobilization for traditional World War II–style infantry and armored combat on a continental scale. Even with this large cut in Guard force structure, which saves $3.2 billion, fifteen enhanced-readiness brigades of somewhat greater deployability remain available for possible use in peacekeeping operations, and as mobilization assets in support of a second major regional contingency.

ELIMINATE TWELVE GUARD FIELD ARTILLERY BRIGADES. Guard field artillery brigades are marginally more deployable than their armored and mechanized cousins, at least from the perspective of their consumers in the active Army, as was demonstrated in Desert Shield, when guard artillery brigades were deployed but armored and mechanized roundout brigades were not. But from a doctrinal perspective, classic tube artillery firing unguided shells will be less important on future battlefields, and this $1.2 billion cut still leaves five artillery brigades in the Guard force structure to support the active force.

ELIMINATE SIX ACTIVE APACHE BRIGADES. Most of the rationale for eliminating six active Apache brigades (saving $3.0 billion) was discussed above in the section on cutting Longbow procurement. This cut leaves the Army with eight active Apache brigade equivalents.

ELIMINATE ALL CH-47S IN THE ARMY INVENTORY. The Army's two rotary-wing lift brigades, and other smaller CH-47 units, exist largely to support the airborne and air assault units eliminated above. The estimated $1.1 billion savings from eliminating all CH-47s in the Army inventory include the additional $100 million in annual savings in procurement achieved by forgoing CH-47 modernization.

ELIMINATE TWO ACTIVE AND ONE GUARD F-16 WINGS. F-16s assigned national air defense missions, or unable to use either the HARM targeting system (HTS) or LANTIRN in air-to-ground operations are the least useful, and therefore the least-used combat aircraft in the Air Force's inventory; their elimination would save $1.1 billion. The aircraft that fall in this category are used mostly to shoot Maverick anti-tank weapons whose utility on future battlefields is diminishing. These aircraft should be replaced by high-payload aircraft such as the B-1 that will drop GPS-guided weapon dispensers from high altitude that deploy submunitions such as sensor-fuzed weapon. An additional rationale behind the proposed reduction in F-16 Maverick shooters is that a long-range platform like the B-1 will be more useful than F-16s in early, halt-phase operations when local base access is uncertain.

ELIMINATE ONE OIL-FIRED AIRCRAFT CARRIER AND ITS ASSOCIATED AIR WING. The recommendation for elimination of one oil-fired aircraft carrier and its associated air wing assumes the establishment of a new homeport for a CVBG in the eastern Mediterranean, discussed below. Savings of $1.0 billion are for operations and support only and would not affect future carrier or aircraft production.

Additions in Defense Programs and Activities

The defense budget option proposed in this chapter also makes seven additions to current defense programs and activities. These additions would cost a total of $3 billion annually and are designed to support innovations that increase the ability of U.S. forces to project power in an access-constrained security environment.

REPLACE SIX ACTIVE ARMY LIGHT INFANTRY BRIGADES AND TWO ARMORED CAVALRY REGIMENTS WITH EIGHT ACTIVE INTERIM BRIGADE COMBAT TEAMS

Six active Army light-infantry brigades and two armored cavalry regiments should be replaced with eight active Interim Brigade Combat Teams (IBCTs). These brigades would be based on off-the-shelf variants of vehicles such as the Light Armored Vehicle (LAV) now used by the Marine Corps, or the Army's Armored Gun System (AGS). In addition to a standard infantry fighting vehicle (IFV), these brigades would probably also employ variants that carried a 105mm gun, a 120mm mortar, and an anti-tank guided missile (ATGM) like TOW, Hellfire, EFOG-M, or LOSAT. The conversions would cost $700 million a year for the next ten years beyond what the Army has already budgeted for this purpose.

Five of the brigades might be motorized infantry, emphasizing the IFV version of the LAV, and three might be cavalry, emphasizing the gun, mortar, and anti-tank missile variants. Both would be more useful adjuncts to the Army's heavy divisions in major regional contingencies than the light infantry formations they replace, while each might also develop a special mission focus relevant to the new security environment. For example, a motorized infantry brigade would be the ideal unit for many types of peacekeeping operations where traditional light infantry units are not lethal enough, and where a primitive logistics infrastructure makes heavy armored and mechanized units slow to deploy.

For similar reasons, a motorized cavalry brigade that combined both direct and indirect fires in a brigade-size, wheeled unit would be far more lethal than an airborne, air-assault, or normal light infantry brigade, but would not be any more difficult to deploy by strategic airlift as the leading edge of a deployment to a major regional contingency. This was the traditional role of the ready brigade of the 82nd Airborne, a role it played in Desert Shield, but for which it is ill-suited. The Army recognized this during Vigilant Warrior in 1994, when the presence of an armored brigade set of equipment pre-positioned in Kuwait eliminated the need for deploying paratroopers. In those future cases when the United States must rapidly deploy ground forces to protect an ally from an attack by armored or mechanized forces without the advantage of prior pre-positioning, a motorized cavalry brigade would provide much more combat power and require no more airlift than a light infantry brigade.

MAKE ARMY IBCTS FULLY AIR-MOBILE

There is no better example of the type of fixed target that will become increasingly vulnerable in the longer term than a large seaport. In the near term, even in the industrialized world, such ports are often scarce enough as to delay the deployment of ground forces early in a conflict. Motorized brigades will enable the Army to pursue alternative methods of rapidly deploying and sustaining its early entry forces that rely less on large seaports. In the near term, IBCTs will already allow the Army to deploy brigade-size units directly into small but relatively ubiquitous airfields using existing short takeoff and landing (STOL) C-130s and C-17s.

New VTOL tactical airlift aircraft and new sea-based pre-positioned assets designed so that they can be unloaded at sea by those aircraft might enable the Army to sustain motorized brigades by air from the sea. This would provide the Army with the ability, early in a conflict, to engage in both strategic and operational maneuver in austere environments over intercontinental ranges without need for a major port or overland transportation infrastructure.

A non-developmental approach to obtaining this capability would involve a C-130–size, tilt-rotor, airlifter based on the Marine Corps' V-22 (Quad Tilt Rotor or QTR), and a modification to current pre-positioning ships that would allow them to transfer fuel and cargo to these aircraft from their flight decks. The key to this option is the QTR, which comes close to combining the attributes of the Air Force's C-130 fleet and the Army's heavy lift helicopter fleet to produce an aircraft that has the speed and range to self deploy across oceans, and the VTOL capability to gain independence from airfields, allowing direct ship-to-foxhole delivery. When combined with the IBCT concept, such an aircraft would eliminate two obstacles that would limit use of IBCTs if they were supported by traditional air and sealift assets alone. First, the Army's lift helicopters now constitute one of the single largest consumers of strategic airlift. Eliminating that demand would free up airlift for more IBCT unit equipment. Second, once deployed, the fuel consumed by the turbine engines in both the Army's helicopter and main battle tank fleets are its single largest sustainment requirement. The former would be eliminated if the Army's VTOL lift aircraft could be sustained from ships at sea, and of course the latter is eliminated by the IBCTs. This option allocates $1.0 billion a year toward this objective.

REPLACE ARMY AND MARINE SCOUT AND ATTACK HELICOPTERS WITH
CANARD ROTOR/WING AIRCRAFT (CRW)

The Army and Marine scout and attack helicopters should be replaced with Canard Rotor/Wing aircraft (CRW). Like tilt rotors, CRW aircraft combine attributes of fixed and rotary wing aircraft. The difference from tilt rotors is that CRWs lift less payload in the VTOL mode, but are faster and longer-legged during normal flight. In addition, unlike both rotary wing and tilt rotor aircraft, CRW aircraft are inherently more amenable to radar stealth treatment because they have no rotating lifting surfaces during normal flight. Thus, CRWs are ideal platforms, whether manned or unmanned, for future organic Army and Marine attack and scout aviation assets. Like tactical fighters, they could self-deploy to a conflict, eliminating another major Army strategic airlift requirement, and once there, they could also exploit in-theater maritime pre-positioned assets for fuel and simple maintenance, like the QTR described above. This budget puts $700 million a year for ten years toward development of both manned and unmanned CRW aircraft.

CONVERT EIGHT TRIDENT SSBNS TO SSGNS

Four of the eighteen Trident SSBNs will become surplus to the nuclear deterrence mission if and when START II goes into effect. The Navy's budget already contains the money needed to operate fourteen SSBNs, refuel them as necessary, and arm the oldest of the remaining four with new Trident II SLBMs. It also already contains about $1.0 billion for the submarine force to use either for preserving SSNs or converting surplus SSBNs to SSGNs. The cost to finish procuring Trident II SLBMs is about $2.0 billion over the next ten years. The Clinton administration's Nuclear Posture Review called for a force of fourteen SSBNs under START II primarily because of concerns that a Trident force smaller than fourteen might lead to the closure of one of its two bases, one in the Atlantic and one in the Pacific. Preserving a two-ocean Trident force is important, both because it eliminates targeting restraints that might otherwise arise from the need to avoid overflying one country in order to target another, and because it forces an opponent that might seek to trail U.S. SSBNs to have a two-ocean SSN force. These decisions about the minimum size of the SSBN force were made prior to the emergence of the option to convert SSBNs to SSGNs.

The option to keep a force of ten SSBNs and eight SSGNs takes advantage of the fact that such a force would ensure a two-ocean Trident force, and therefore allow the submarine force to concentrate the 1750 warheads allowed it under START II on ten SSBNs without compromising either their survivability or flexibility. This would free up a total of $3.0 billion to devote to converting eight SSBNs to SSGNs, about $2.0 billion to refuel and convert four boats, and about $1.0 billion to convert four boats whose refuelings are already funded under current plans. In the net, this option would cost $200 million a year.

ACCELERATE AND EXPAND THE NAVY'S ADVANCED LAND ATTACK MISSILE (ALAM) PROGRAM

The Navy's Advanced Land Attack Missile (ALAM) program should be accelerated and expanded. ALAM is a long-term Navy program to develop a more advanced ship and submarine-launched, tactical ballistic missile than the interim Land Attack Standard Missile (LASM). Current ALAM requirements are for the most lethal TBM of a range greater than 200 miles that will fit within existing surface and submarine vertical launchers of 20 feet by 21 inches. This option adds $400 million a year to the ALAM account and adds requirements for also developing the smallest possible single-stage TBM with a 250-pound payload that can exceed a 200-mile range.

The logic behind this addition to the program is to use projected advances in the accuracy of INS/GPS-guided weapons to fill existing vertical launcher tubes with more weapons, rather than simply to maximize the lethality of a single weapon that fills those tubes. This would be accomplished by exploiting the fact that the payload required to achieve a given effect can be reduced by placing it closer to its target.

Because currently projected increases in INS/GPS accuracy produce disproportionately greater reductions in required payload, and because payload is far and away the main determinant of missile size and volume, a virtuous rather than a vicious circle is created from an engineering perspective. A 200-mile range TBM with a 250-pound payload can be designed using off-the-shelf technology to be small enough so that six can fit in the space that one LASM or Tomahawk occupies today. This would mean, for example, that over 2000 such weapons could be carried in a Trident SSGN if all its launcher volume were used. ALAM would also be designed in modular fashion such that two first-stage motors could be combined to create a 600-mile, two-stage missile, and so that both unitary and sub-munition payloads could be deployed.[34]

OBTAIN AN ADDITIONAL OVERSEAS HOMEPORT FOR ONE CVBG

An eleven-carrier force with two overseas homeports would provide substantially more forward presence than today's twelve-carrier force supported by one such homeport. Roughly speaking, today's force provides 2.5 CVGBs forward at any time, while the option described here would provide between 3.5 and 4 forward at any time.

REPLACE F-16S, F-15ES, AND F-117S WITH THE NAVY OR MARINE VERSION OF JSF

The Air Force's F-16s, F-15Es, and F-117s should be replaced with the Navy or Marine version of JSF. By killing the Air Force version of the JSF, this option would allow the Air Force to embrace short takeoff and vertical landing operations, or in the case of the Navy variant, something like the Marine Corp's current concept for building an expeditionary airfield for its F-18s using roads, aluminum matting, and arresting gear. In either case, or should the Air Force choose a mix of the two, the effect would be a dramatic reduction in the dependence of the Air Combat Command's tactical aircraft on local bases. Should the Air Force choose a mix of both versions, it would also benefit from the much longer range (900 versus 700 miles) and internal weapon payload (4000 versus 2000 pounds) of the Navy version over the Air Force version.

In the near term, this would make it easier to support truly expeditionary air operations in regions where large bases are not available. Probably more important is the longer-term reduction in vulnerability created by such a move, as it makes it much more difficult for an opponent to attack and shut down tactical air operations by attacking a few central bases. Instead, it would allow and encourage both the Air Force and the Marine Corps to explore more fully operational concepts for tactical aircraft basing like those adopted by the Swedish Air Force, which

---

34. For a fuller discussion of what I am suggesting here, see Naval Studies Board, *Technology for the United States Navy and Marine Corps*, Vol. 5, pp. 106–120 and 260–261.

use roads for runways, and which rely on motorized "base battalions" to fuel, arm, maintain, and provide air traffic control for dispersed aircraft squadrons.[35]

Why Not Buy "... From the Sea?"

The basis for a maritime strategy can probably best be summarized by describing why other chapters in this volume reject it. The main difference between the maritime strategy and the Air Force–centered flexible power projection strategy proposed by Karl Mueller in Chapter 8 revolves around the issue of access to regional air bases, and the main difference with the strategy proposed by James Quinlivan in Chapter 7 concerns the metric that should be used to size the Army.

In the near term, air base access will revolve around the political calculations made by U.S. alliance partners. In the longer term, it will become a military issue, where access will depend on whether an opponent has deployed GPS/INS-guided, submunition-dispensing cruise and ballistic missiles, and whether U.S. allies have built substantial extra hardened basing capacity into their infrastructure. This last issue is probably the most important. Only bases with individual hardened aircraft shelters and protected working and living areas will be able to support high-tempo tactical air operations in the future security environment. For those who believe that such bases will be ubiquitous, that the U.S. Air Force will be able to pre-position ammunition and other supplies at those bases, and that it will be given immediate, unrestricted access to those bases as soon as a conflict erupts, there would be little reason to be concerned with increasing the leverage of sea-based strike assets ashore.

Regarding the Army, there appear to be two key force-sizing issues: the required size and timing of its response to a second major regional contingency, and the extent to which provision is made in the force structure for lesser regional contingencies and peacekeeping deployments. In broad terms, the maritime strategy preserves today's armored and mechanized force and modernizes it, which means that it preserves as much MRC-capability as is proposed by James Quinlivan in Chapter 7. Where the maritime strategy differs is in its approach to sizing the force for peacekeeping; the eight-division force proposed in this chapter will be more limited than the force proposed in Chapter 7.

Like the Army proposed in Chapter 7, the maritime strategy does call for developing medium-weight forces that are better suited to lesser re-

---

35. See, for example, John D. Morrocco, "Saab Pursues Additional Export Orders for Gripen," *Aviation Week and Space Techology*, May 24, 1999, pp. 74–75.

gional contingencies and peacekeeping missions, but unlike that force, it does not embrace a force structure big enough to maintain both a ready, two-MRC heavy force and a large commitment to peacekeeping operations. Instead, it embraces a force structure that will force political leaders to use heavy units earmarked for a second MRC if it wishes to maintain or expand the Army's current peacekeeping burden.

The most important assumption underlying the maritime strategy concerns access to regional bases. Given the likely constraints on access to such bases, it is important to focus investment on better utilizing bases where access is more secure, whether those bases are on land at a greater distance from the theater of conflict, or at sea. This will require an Army that can deploy from the United States faster with more, an Air Force with longer legs and more focused on exploiting air superiority, and a Navy that exerts more leverage ashore from a secure sea base.

Chapter 7

Flexible Ground Forces

James T. Quinlivan

This chapter builds a future U.S. force structure that is balanced to deal with a range of likely future environments. At the core of this force structure is a potent Army, modernized to exploit technological opportunities and balanced to carry out a broad range of missions that might be demanded in the near future. In developing the plan for the future, this chapter prescribes force structures for the active and reserve components of the Army and the other services consistent with a particular view of the future and the capabilities of the different services. As pointed out in Cindy Williams's introduction, the challenge of this period is to design future forces in an era that lacks a defining threat while responding to the onerous demands of a succession of smaller contingencies.

The Army should be the centerpiece of the force structure for the future world, because the future world does not yet have a "center." This force is built around certain premises. First, when U.S. interests must be staked out, this is best accomplished through alliances that closely reflect the interests of their members. Active U.S. participation in the military structures of an alliance is essential to transforming a paper alliance into a militarily feasible proposition. The strongest form of U.S. commitment

The author is grateful to the other chapter authors for comments and discussions—particularly Owen Cote and Karl Mueller. In addition, Michael Brown, Leland Joe, Steve Kosiak, Thomas McNaugher, Barry Posen, and Thomas Szayna provided helpful comments on earlier versions of this chapter. An anonymous reviewer provided helpful, and tactful, suggestions toward the final version. The opinions expressed in this chapter are solely those of the author and do not represent the opinions of RAND or any of its sponsors.

to an alliance and allies will continue to be the presence of U.S. ground forces.

Second, in whatever regional wars the United States must engage, and particularly in the situations of the Persian Gulf and Korea, the ultimate U.S. threat is that any conflict involving the United States might become a ground war fought to a decisive conclusion. However rarely executed, the ultimate threat of "our flag over their capital" is a tool that must be available to U.S. leaders.

Third, the succession of smaller-scale contingencies, some unilateral and some multilateral, will not end. Forces must be designed to carry out such tasks without wearing them out and destroying their capabilities for major theater wars.

This chapter builds a flexible Army using a variety of forces and technologies to meet the urgent demands of the present while investing in technologies that may change the nature of ground warfare profoundly by the end of the decade. The chapter starts with a brief discussion of a future security environment, gives a general idea of how the force structure for this environment should be developed, and offers a detailed program and its budget implications for the Army and the other services.

Visualizing a Future Defense Environment

Key elements of the future security environment are U.S. alliances, especially in Europe; and the possibility of both major theater wars (MTWs) and smaller-scale contingencies (SSCs).

Careful selection of alliances and careful cultivation of their military mechanisms are the best way to protect many of the key vital interests of the United States, which are known now and will endure for some time. Europe is important to the United States, and will continue to be important. Within Europe, the United States has chosen NATO as the vehicle through which to approach security issues in the region of Europe and on its fringe. The United States will have strong reasons to work for the continued success of this alliance within its European setting, whether or not the alliance develops a reach to other regions of U.S. interest.

The utility of a U.S. presence in NATO for the future of Europe is largely taken for granted in political terms, but the precise terms of what this means for military presence and participation is more complicated. As pointed out by Gordon Adams in Chapter 4, the Europeans currently do not have high-technology military capabilities in the numbers or at the level of the United States, nor do they have much ability to project what power they do have rapidly to other regions of U.S. interest. To become peers of the United States in the application of high-technology weapons, the Europeans will need time and lots of investment in technology. Even more demanding may be the time and effort needed to reshape European militaries as social institutions. Despite changes in uniform and weapons, the patterns of European armies have been much the same for more than a century: dominated by the cycle of training each successive year's class of conscripts. Until recently, only Britain and Luxembourg among the Europeans did not rely on conscription to fill the ranks of their militaries. Now, however, the vast European conscript armies of the Cold War are shrinking away. Moving to a new system of professional militaries means that all of the European militaries will be profoundly different. This difference will, of course, be most dramatic in the former communist states. In forming their new national armies on democratic bases with professional militaries, the involvement of the United States in NATO and the U.S. forces in NATO has been critical as a role model and a source of training.

In the next few years, all of the armies of Europe will be new, even armies with which the United States has worked for decades. In order for U.S. forces to work with this new NATO as well as it did with the old, the practical requirement is a continued presence on the ground that jointly trains the new armies as the United States and NATO jointly develop the welter of agreements and procedures that make working together a practical matter.

Commitment to NATO does not mean that the United States will be involved in all European disputes or peacekeeping efforts. In fact, in matters of solely European interest and scale, the Europeans have found ways to carry out operations outside of a NATO setting, as in the Italian-led international forces that carried out a stabilization operation in Albania. In other situations, however, where NATO's core interests, including those of the United States, are involved, shared values and also shared sensitivities to the financial costs and possible military casualties of smaller-scale contingencies are likely to require the United States to contribute a share to the ground force requirements of NATO undertakings. The recent operations in the former Yugoslavia have shown that a "coalition of the willing" can contribute substantially by providing individual detachments, companies, and battalions so long as a "coalition of the able"—that is, the Multinational Division Forces with British, French, and U.S. headquarters—provide the structure in which these smaller units can contribute.

Despite distinct limits on the ability of the Europeans to project force distant from their homebases, there are areas where alliance operations can reduce the requirements for continuous U.S. presence, particularly in the Mediterranean and along its African rim. With the Arab-Israeli conflict receding as a day-to-day priority for U.S. presence, the possibility exists that U.S. naval presence might usefully be reduced and covered by locally based NATO forces.

Outside Europe lies the world of the potential two major theater wars or "2 MTWs." As pointed out in Chapter 1, there is a real difference between the realistically assessed requirements of the situations of Korea and the Persian Gulf, and a generic "2 MTW capability." Nevertheless, as the United States moves to design future forces, the particular requirements of Korea and the Persian Gulf will influence—sometimes consciously and sometimes unconsciously—when features unique to these two theaters or unique to the Gulf War are taken as inherent properties of future wars.[1]

The role of U.S. ground forces in Korea and the Persian Gulf has changed over time. The capable Korean Army can now conduct a strong defense of South Korea. Unless the campaign goes badly wrong, U.S. ground forces would make their greatest contribution in a counter-offensive phase intended to decisively defeat the aggressor. In the Gulf, early-arriving U.S. ground forces falling in on pre-positioned equipment would conduct a joint defense with Saudi and Kuwaiti forces aided by very strong U.S. air and naval strike forces. The main U.S. ground forces would arrive to conduct a counter-offensive and follow-on operations. In either case, carrying on from the counter-offensive, ground forces would conduct operations until the war was won. Thus, rather than fighting desperate defensive battles against vastly superior numbers, the special contribution of ground forces in the particular setting of these two theaters will be moving more toward conducting offensive operations, possibly still against superior numbers but probably not against superior combat power.

One element that affects MTW force-sizing decisions is the question of what constitutes "winning" in a major theater war. An ability to wage a counter-offensive to regain any lost ground and restore the status quo ante constitutes one answer. However, the full political objectives of an operation might impose a requirement to extend a counter-offensive to a general offensive; this could add significantly to force requirements.[2]

---

1. The use of illustrative planning scenarios in the Defense Guidance both reflects and reinforces these tendencies.

2. As Alexander George noted of the Gulf War, a U.S. desire for the removal of Saddam Hussein from power added an objective characteristic of total war to a limited war. Alexander L. George, *Bridging the Gap: Theory and Practice in Foreign Policy* (Washington, D.C.: United States Institute of Peace Press, 1993), p. 91 and note 2, p. 157. In

Thus the operational definition of "victory" in a generalized MTW scenario needs to consider that the U.S. forces may be required not only to defeat the enemy's forces in some technical sense, but ultimately have the capability to "pursue . . . victory to the point where the balance is beyond all possible redress."[3] Raising the U.S. flag over an opponent's capital might seem an overly dramatic ending, perhaps too much a throwback to simpler times, but in the particular cases of Korea or the Persian Gulf, it is equally unimaginable that either a second Korean War or a second Gulf War would be permitted to end with the opposing regime still in power. The design of force structures for MTWs or regional wars must consider whether U.S. forces should forgo such capabilities.

The counterpoint to the major theater war is the smaller-scale contingency, which has its own influences on force structure decisions. The range of smaller-scale contingencies has broadened as the post–Cold War era has evolved. So far, it has included unilateral interventions (Panama and Haiti), many noncombatant evacuation operations (e.g., in Liberia), active participation including commitment of major ground force elements in peace enforcement operations (Bosnia and Kosovo), and logistics assistance to multilateral peace operations led by other nations (as in Rwanda or East Timor). Such operations might be termed "reluctant engagements," in which U.S. power and forces are only committed after other options have been ruled out or demonstrated as inadequate to the situation.[4]

Some of these operations have been well within the capabilities of the battalion-sized Marine Expeditionary Units (MEUs) that are carried by an Amphibious Ready Group (ARG). These smaller operations have largely

---

the aftermath of the Kosovo Conflict, U.S. policy again raised the removal of a foreign leader as a desired objective of what had been seen as a limited war. U.S. experience with attempting to remove Iraq's production capabilities for weapons of mass destruction, and Iraq's efforts to retain such capabilities, might also suggest that demanding such disarmament is closer to an objective of total war. Adopting a declaratory policy of prosecuting leaders who initiate the use of weapons of mass destruction would also add an objective characteristic of total war and make it contingent on behavior in what might have been initially thought to be a limited conflict.

3.   Clausewitz's phrase still represents a desirable capability. Carl von Clausewitz, *On War*, ed. and trans. Michael Howard and Peter Paret (Princeton, N.J.: Princeton University Press, 1976), p. 597.

4.   This expression draws on the suggestive image of the title of Richard Haass, *The Reluctant Sheriff: The United States after the Cold War* (New York: Council on Foreign Relations Press, 1997). See also Haass, *Intervention: The Use of American Military Force in the Post–Cold War World*, rev. ed. (Washington, D.C.: Brookings Institution Press, 1999).

fallen within the general practice of "a battalion or less and lasting a month or less."[5] Others have been large and protracted and have drawn on the Army for sustained operations stretching over many years. The steady demand for forces for such operations and their special situations have required frequent rotations and drawn down the readiness of participating units for operations in MTWs.[6]

In the 1993 Bottom-Up Review, a class of operations distinct from the Major Regional Contingencies was set up to capture "contingencies that are less demanding than an MRC but still require significant combat forces and capabilities. Such operations may range from multilateral peace enforcement to unilateral intervention." The generic answer to such problems was one air assault or airborne division, one light infantry division, one mechanized infantry division, one Marine Expeditionary Brigade, one to two carrier battle groups, one to two composite air wings, plus special operations forces, civil affairs units, airlift and sealift forces, combat support and service support units, with a total of 50,000 combat and support personnel.[7] Whatever the precision of this statement, however, it was lost in the practical application that forces derived from the two-MRC requirement were presumed available for these missions and were simultaneously presumed available for commitment to MRCs.

Since the time of the Bottom-Up Review, we have had a number of opportunities to learn that the requirements of such operations might be quite different than those of major operations and not lesser-included cases of a force structure designed exclusively for major contingencies. One category of smaller-scale contingency that suggests force structuring criteria is a protracted engagement such as that in Bosnia or Kosovo. Although the United States will not seek out such opportunities, some situations may be important to the United States or to alliances of which the United States is a part, leading to U.S. involvement. While Bosnia and Kosovo are far from home and far from possible MTWs, they are not unlike the situation that could arise in places closer to home and for which

---

5.   Mark Cancian, "Still the Nation's 9–1–1 Force?" *Marine Corps Gazette*, April 2000, pp. 28–31.

6.   R.E. Sortor, *Army Forces for Operations Other than War*, RAND Arroyo Center, MR-852-A, 1997; J.M. Taw et al., *Meeting Peace Operations Requirements while Maintaining MTW Readiness*, RAND Arroyo Center, MR-921-A, 1998; Congressional Budget Office, *Making Peace while Staying Ready for War: The Challenges of U.S. Military Participation in Peace Operations*, December 1999.

7.   Les Aspin, *Report on the Bottom-Up Review*, Section III, "Forces to Implement the Defense Strategy," October 1993. The list of Army forces required coincided exactly with the divisions of the XVIII Airborne Corps.

the United States might have to be solely responsible. In such situations the military provides a stabilizing force that permits the establishment of order and resumption of normal civil government.

When external powers such as the United States act as "the world's policeman," a good way to think about the force requirement is roughly similar to the way that one would think about providing policemen in a civil society: The basic problem is not the destruction of an enemy, but providing security (and control) of a population so that they have confidence that they can support a government authority of their own. The number of "world policemen" required is proportional to the size of the population.

If the "number of policemen required" looks like the result of a constant multiplied by the size of the population, what is the constant? How many troops per thousand of population would you need? The United States has a bit more than two sworn police officers per thousand of population. For cases drastic enough to require outside intervention, the number is much higher. In the case of Northern Ireland, for example, the British maintained a security force (consisting of military and Royal Ulster Constabulary) of about 20 per thousand of population. In its initial entry into Bosnia-Herzegovina, the Implementation Force (IFOR) brought in multinational forces corresponding to more than 20 soldiers per thousand of population. After five years, its successor Stabilization Force (SFOR) finally fell below 10 per thousand. Operations in Kosovo during 2000 show the same pattern; forces are now sized at something above 20 per thousand (given a very rough estimate of population).[8]

Numerically, most of the troops required for such operations are not specialized, but rather are infantry and their supporting arms and services. While specialized skills are used, such as civil affairs, special forces, psychological operations, and military police—and may be required out of proportion to their numbers in the active force—the bulk of the force is drawn from the general purpose forces, and additional skills unique to the situation are acquired in special training. The specialized forces may provide the key elements of a solution to the underlying problem, but they work inside the secure environment provided by the larger force.

In any future peacekeeping operation that involves U.S. troops or its NATO allies, the force will have very strong capabilities to protect itself and to intimidate opponents. Debacles experienced by peacekeepers in situations that suddenly degenerated into conflict—the Indians in Sri Lanka, Americans and Pakistanis in Somalia, and most recently the Afri-

---

8. James T. Quinlivan, "Force Requirements for Stability Operations," *Parameters*, Winter 1995–1996, pp. 59–69.

can peacekeepers in Sierra Leone—have provided convincing evidence that such cautions are entirely proper.

This rough calculation suggests the size of the forces that would be required in such settings. There are a number of implications that flow from this. Even small countries or portions of countries could require large forces. In regions where the United States would be part of a larger security organization and its partners have large and competent forces, multinational forces can share the burden, but even the U.S. share of the total force might be sizable. Moreover, as demonstrated in the former Yugoslavia, when multilateral forces are brought together, providing an overarching command and control structure for many small contributions becomes a critical issue. Finally, simply providing these forces does not guarantee a solution to the problem. The forces only buy time for a government to win local allegiances and establish its own authority, but the emergence of such a government is not guaranteed.

Besides requiring large numbers, stability operations have required these numbers over long periods. The British forces in Northern Ireland operated with a large force for more than two decades. The operation in Bosnia has already gone on for five years. Experience has led to a practice of limiting the tour of duty for troops in such environments to about six months. The first U.S. rotation into Bosnia was to have been a year, and a recent call-up of reservists (from the 49th Armored Division of the Texas National Guard) was to have been longer, but the general practice seems to be pressing toward the six-month standard, like the standard sea tour. The effect of such rotating deployments, even seemingly small ones, causes complications across the force, affecting the readiness of non-deploying units and the ability to offer stabilized subsequent tours to individuals.[9]

In order to have an estimate of the total forces necessary to provide a rotation base adequate to the total task it would be nice to have a standard force-sizing. Some people argue for a rule that says that it takes three units to have one deployed, based on the notion that for each unit deployed, another is getting ready to deploy and one is just recovering from having been deployed. With the six-month deployment period, such a "rule of three" would have units returning to deployment as soon as twelve months after their previous deployment. British practice based on experience in Ulster has been that the minimum desirable period away from deployment is more like twenty-four months. This suggests, instead, a "rule of five": five units in the force structure for each one de-

---

9. J. Michael Polich et al., *Small Deployments, Big Problems*, RAND Arroyo Center Issue Paper, 2000.

ployed. This may produce a daunting number. Rather than thinking of it as a multiplier to obtain the number of units required, it can be thought of as a "force divider," to calculate the number of units that might be sustained over time with twenty-four months between deployments. This "rule of five" is used as a rough metric to gauge how many units a force structure might maintain over time in a SSC while undergoing about the same rate of exposure to the SSC environment as the British endured in Ulster. This is about the upper limit of deployment to combat-like SSCs that might be considered sustainable.

HOW THEATER BALLISTIC MISSILE DEFENSE, WEAPONS OF MASS DESTRUCTION, AND POSSIBLE NEW RESPONSIBILITIES MAY AFFECT FORCE REQUIREMENTS

There are reasons to be cautiously optimistic about the ability of U.S. field forces to operate in difficult environments, including exposure to chemical or biological weapons, once deployed. The real questions have to do with whether certain classes of threats can keep large forces from deploying into theater. At the theater level, an opponent's ability to threaten the use of weapons of mass destruction as part of an "anti-access" strategy interacts strongly with the U.S. ability to provide theater ballistic missile defenses, both to cover its own forces and to protect allies.

If a regional opponent can plausibly threaten missile-delivered weapons of mass destruction on an ally's territory as a threat to U.S. deployment, the weapons are an even more plausible and serious threat to our ally. The United States cannot offer a defense that only shows up when (and if) the United States deploys to theater. If that is the best the United States can do, the U.S. ally probably will have been successfully coerced long before the issue of U.S. deployment arises. There is a genuine need to provide the ally with either genuine protection from such weapons or genuine deterrence of the threat of their use.

U.S. declaratory policy on its response to the use of such weapons, both in general and in the specific case of the ally, is the starting point for deterrence. If the opponent cannot put the U.S. homeland at risk of such weapons, U.S. declaratory statements are inherently more plausible than if the United States itself is at risk. But declaratory policy alone may not be a reliable protection or, by itself, seem to our ally an adequate response, particularly if the United States has taken steps to protect itself from ballistic missile attacks. Active defense of the ally may be an obligation of the situation and the relationship.

There are a wide variety of Theater Ballistic Missile Defense systems under current development. These systems can be divided into lower tier and upper tier systems. The lower tier systems are intended to defend small areas by engaging incoming missiles in their last few seconds before impact. These systems include the Patriot Advanced Capability-3 (PAC-3); the Navy Area Defense, largely intended to cover naval task forces but able to reach out over land as well; and the Medium Extended Air Defense System (MEADS) being developed in cooperation with the Europeans to defend maneuver forces against tactical ballistic missile systems. Only the Patriot PAC-3 is built around an existing deployed system. Upper tier systems are intended to defend larger areas by reaching out farther into a missile's trajectory and engaging it above the atmosphere as it descends, or in particular instances, even while the missile is still ascending. These systems include the Theater High Altitude Area Defense System (THAAD) and the Navy Theater Wide Defense, to be based on AEGIS-equipped ships. In addition, the Air Force's Airborne Laser, a high-powered laser carried on a modified Boeing 747, is intended to fly in relatively close proximity to launch locations and engage missiles as they ascend.

Navy ship–based systems could be deployed to an area during a threat; if in a fast developing crisis they would be available on short notice from their forward presence locations, this might suffice. If, however, the mission is to maintain a long-running defense of an ally's key locations, land-based systems are both more visible to the ally and more economic in operation. If we want to reassure an ally, there seems little alternative to either selling or providing missile defense systems that can be kept in near-continuous operation as we now operate Patriot in the Persian Gulf and Korea. In order to cover a wider area and insure a higher probability of kill with a layered defense (that is, one that can both reach out and engage close in, thereby permitting multiple shots at single targets and thin out wave attacks), I would choose to develop THAAD and deploy THAAD in conjunction with PAC-3 as a combined missile defense.

With defenses deployed in advance along with sophisticated countermeasures, the entry into the theater by ship seems a feasible operation if the only threats to be dealt with are some tens of ballistic and cruise missiles rather than hundreds, and the Navy can concentrate TMD assets in the vicinity of the ports while Army forces are deploying.

Somewhat related to the question of weapons of mass destruction is the idea that the United States might have to deal with their consequences through terrorist use of such devices. The recent reports of the Hart-Rudman panel have proposed that direct attacks on the United States by terrorists using weapons of mass destruction are real threats that such weapons will almost certainly be successfully carried out in the future years. One of the consequences of this situation is said to be the need for military organizations, and particularly the National Guard, to be responsible for the effort to counter these attacks and to remediate their effects.[10] Remediating the consequences of an attack with weapons of mass destruction within the United States itself would have force implications. Current plans have directed the formation of Response Task Force organizations within the reserve components with particular special skills and capabilities augmented by the more generalized capabilities of other reserve component units.[11] The creation of small special purpose units to support existing civil organizations is underway, relying on full-time Guard personnel. Other capabilities useful to remediation in such situations are available within the reserve structure. Even though these units are not dedicated to such roles, they would be available if not deployed. The attraction of using the Guard and Reserve for these missions is only real if they need not be solely dedicated to them. If there is a genuine requirement for a capability to deal with large-scale effects of weapons of mass destruction, including the full-range of possible nuclear, biological and chemical weapons, and if this capability has to be maintained without regard to the state of mobilization or deployment of the reserve components, it might be better to reconstitute a special purpose civil defense organization. A special purpose civil defense organization would not impose the special obligations that must be met by service members, nor would it exclude those who do not meet the particular requirements for military service nor need it to provide compensation that includes military retirement pay—all of which seem unnecessary for a remediation organization.

THE GENERAL APPROACH TO DESIGNING A FUTURE FORCE STRUCTURE

In the following force structure sections, the particular services are reshaped according to the general beliefs described in the preceding section. Key choices about the future Army force structure spring from the answers to two questions: How small might Army forces for an MTW become, given technological choices about Army modernization? How large a force for SSCs might be sustained, given the design of forces for the MTWs? In addition, units for U.S. participation in NATO are assumed to be available for participation as part of smaller-scale contingencies within a European setting. The Army's reserve component forces are

---

10.   The United States Commission on National Security/21st Century, *Seeking a National Strategy: A Concept for Preserving Security and Promoting Freedom*, April 15, 2000.

11.   Department of Defense Tiger Team, Department of Defense Plan for Integrating National Guard and Reserve Component Support for Response to Attacks Using Weapons of Mass Destruction, January 1998.

sized to provide some heavy units that might be available for a second MTW within a reasonable time, and to provide a rotation base of light and medium units for protracted smaller-scale contingencies.

Much the same logic is applied to the Air Force. The force is modernized to provide a very capable air power force. Much of the power of this force is lodged in relatively short-range tactical aircraft that must be based within the theater of operations. Longer-range aircraft (B-1, B-2, and B-52) are modernized largely through improvements in their stand-off weapons rather than in new platform programs. Reserve forces whose obsolescent aircraft and low place on the modernization schedule make them unlikely to effectively contribute to any MTW are removed from the force structure.

The biggest changes in Navy force structure spring from a view that some reduction in U.S. carrier presence in the immediate vicinity of U.S. NATO allies is not only not a bad thing, but also probably a useful aid to greater cooperative behavior among all the NATO navies. A reduction in the number of carriers and its interactions with the shipbuilding and tactical aircraft procurement accounts produce large effects and significant acquisition savings.

The Marine Corps is transformed into a force that is dedicated to expeditionary operations with Marine Expeditionary Brigades and the myriad of smaller scale contingencies that can be accomplished by battalion-sized Marine Expeditionary Units. It is modernized in accord with its vision of how to accomplish such missions. It is, however, removed from operations that involve large, division-sized operations in major theaters of war. In removing these vestiges of the past, some force structure can be removed that does not match the vision.

Across all of the services, those forces that remain in the force structure are either modernized or primed to receive the first production models of new systems (as in units awaiting production of the Joint Strike Fighter). Rather than reuse systems that might be stretched to quite different roles (as in converting Trident ballistic submarines to cruise missile submarines), systems have either been kept on in exactly their current role, or removed entirely from service.

Army Force Structure

Over the next decade, the distinction between heavy forces—that is, forces predominantly equipped with armored and mechanized equipment, and light forces—forces that predominantly fight on foot—is likely to continue. The introduction of medium-weight forces—forces equipped with lightly armored vehicles that are not protected to the same degree as existing armor—will probably not in this decade provide a force that can be used in all situations. Therefore, the Army should be a mix of heavy, light, and now medium units, each of which has capabilities that can be mixed and matched to deal with particular situations.

Time is a crucial consideration in the proposed design of Army forces, particularly the drastic surgery that is performed on the Army's reserve combat components. In the event of major theater wars, even in the less likely second MTW, time will be at a premium. Units will have to be at high levels of training; even reserve units being readied for a potential second MTW will have to train at relatively high levels. This situation argues in favor of selecting a small number of reserve units designated for high-intensity conflict and keeping them at high levels of equipment and personnel readiness. In the more diffuse situations of smaller-scale contingencies, the demands may either be for large numbers at the start or for more modest numbers spread out over a long period time; the physical situation may also vary, from urban to rural, even to jungle. While the active forces should be prepared to handle some such operations on their own, the reserve component units will be needed in situations that become protracted. There may be time to train, retrain, or schedule units long in advance of their participation. This situation suggests that a larger number and a greater variety of units might be kept in the reserves to provide both a range of capabilities and also a depth of numbers, even though they might not be used all at once or in a particular situation.

THE HEAVY FORCES

This proposed Army force structure makes the First Digitized Corps (FDC) the centerpiece of the Army's MTW force projection capability. The First Digitized Corps is currently being constructed based on the existing heavy forces at Fort Hood.[12] These forces are incorporating new technologies to rapidly acquire, exchange, and act on information, and developing tactics and procedures to exploit information about opposition and friendly forces to be able to strike deeper, attack, or defend over more territory, and carry out operations with a faster tempo.

This process includes a succession of trials and field experiments that tests how the equipment itself performs in a tactical setting, and also shapes the development of tactics to exploit the equipment's capabilities. This process will extend to 2005; first a single division is being converted,

---

12.   Now the 4th Infantry Division, 1st Cavalry Division, and the 3d Armored Cavalry Regiment under the III Corps.

and then the process will gradually be extended to an entire corps of two divisions and an armored cavalry regiment.[13]

While these divisions will be able to exploit information in new ways, they strongly resemble existing formations.[14] At the completion of the experimental process and when the First Digitized Corps (FDC) is fully ready, it will be necessary to assess whether further redesign of the force is warranted, particularly whether divisions should be abolished in favor of a brigade-based Army in some form.[15] The divisions might be reorganized as two-brigade formations, with two modernized brigades able to carry out the missions of three older brigades. The division headquarters would still command the two brigades and coordinate the supporting units that are not within the brigades themselves: logistics, engineers, air defense, intelligence, and some artillery units.[16]

A more important question is whether the Digitized Corps (whether organized as three two-brigade divisions or two three-brigade divisions) contains by itself sufficient combat power to prosecute the major theater war requirements, given the joint and combined forces available in the theater and improved precision strike capabilities of the other services. In the existing MTW theaters, the FDC and forward-deployed forces or forces that deploy to pre-positioned equipment could rapidly build to nine heavy brigades. It is very likely that the enhanced capabilities of these units would permit a theater commander to create operations

---

13.   Even though this process still has years to run, some questions may not be completely answered at the time the units are declared ready. See Government Accounting Office, *Battlefield Automation: Performance Uncertainties Are Likely When Army Fields Its First Digitized Division,* GAO/NSIAD-99–150, July 1999.

14.   The Base Case Heavy Division (BCHD) will have about 15,000 soldiers including some integrated reserve component troops within the division support structure. The BCHD does, however, have the traditional battalion/brigade/division organization and command relationships with greatly enhanced information flows and capabilities. The operational concept of the corps itself directs a very broad mission and includes capabilities across the full range of military operations. TRADOC, *Force XXI Corps Operations and Organizational Concept* (Revised Draft), June 26, 1998.

15.   Robert L. Bateman, ed., *Digital War: A View from the Front Lines* (San Francisco: Presidio Press, 1999), collects a number of service authors who explore the implications of the digitization process. See also Douglas A. Macregor, *Breaking the Phalanx: A New Design for Landpower in the 21st Century* (Westport, Conn.: Praeger, 1997); John R. Brinkerhoff, "The Brigade-Based New Army," *Parameters,* Vol. 27, No. 3 (Autumn 1997), pp. 60–72; and David Fastabend, "An Appraisal of 'The Brigade-Based New Army,'" *Parameters,* Vol. 27, No. 3 (Autumn 1997), pp. 73–81.

16.   Two-brigade divisions have been used quite frequently. If a Korean War were to start tomorrow, the 2d Infantry Division would fight as a two-brigade formation. The 1st Cavalry Division fought in the Gulf War as a two-brigade formation.

plans that moved to decisive operations much earlier than previous plans.

The combat components of the corps only partially determine the size of the corps. At the current time, a rough rule is that for every soldier in a combat division (or a separate combat brigade or armored cavalry regiment), 1.6 more soldiers are necessary within the units that support the combat force. These supporting forces include medical, engineer, quartermaster, and transportation units.[17]

This redesign would produce a corps of roughly 100,000 soldiers organized in two or three digitized divisions (built from the six brigades of the FDC) and an armored cavalry regiment. This could be very close to a decisive force that could arrive in theater within a few weeks rather than months without dramatic additions of sealift. As this capability is realized, sometime shortly after 2005, an active heavy division could be stood down while retaining the capability of the present active force.[18]

A sizable number of the Army National Guard Heavy Divisions could also be drawn down. Numerous studies have pointed out that these divisions are not required under even a demanding 2-MTW force design.[19] Standing down two heavy divisions immediately would save $550 million annually and about $5.5 billion over the decade. In 2005, deactivation of two more of the heavy divisions would save a further $550 million per year, about $2.7 billion over the decade. This would leave two combat divisions in the Guard, one light and one heavy, and the two support divisions. Because of the reduced support structure requirements of the FDC, the corresponding corps support organizations lodged in the Army Reserve could also be drawn down, saving roughly $250 million annually. With the five divisions removed from the force structure, National Guard Field Artillery brigades and other nonorganic support units that would normally be associated with these divisions in active opera-

---

17. Fastabend, "An Appraisal of 'The Brigade-Based New Army,'" gives a good explanation of these rules of thumb for higher echelon formations.

18. It would be a good idea to reorganize all the digitized heavy divisions as two-brigade formations as a start on further reorganization; this would also keep the division count the same, even though three brigades had been removed from the force structure. Removing one unit out of three has a bad historical reference for the Army. The units that were committed to Korea in the first days of the war had been hollowed out in such a manner at every level from platoon to division. The capabilities and doctrine of these formations still depended on being filled out with all the missing subordinate units. The difference here is that it may be necessary to reduce the size of the units to realize the full effect of information operations.

19. Congressional Budget Office, *Structuring the Active and Reserve Army for the 21st Century,* December 1997.

tions are also removed from the force structure, saving about $400 million annually. The five attack battalions of these divisions currently pro-grammed to be equipped with Longbow Apache helicopter need not be modernized, reducing the program by about 120 aircraft and saving about $1.2 billion over the decade.

THE MEDIUM WEIGHT FORCES

There are two types of medium-weight forces in the proposed force struc-ture: the 101st Air Assault Division and the Army's new Brigade Combat Teams (BCTs). The 101st Air Assault Division is equipped with a hefty component of tank-killing Apache helicopters and a mix of helicop-ter-transported infantry also heavily equipped with tank killing weap-ons. In the Gulf War, the division was employed offensively against heavy forces. It has also been prepared to operate in other environments where the infantry would be used in more traditional roles. At the mo-ment, the 101st Air Assault Division is probably the only division in the Army that can or would be used in both high-intensity warfare against mechanized opponents and in light infantry roles. This chapter retains the division as a swing force to support both types of conflicts as needed.

The BCT concept is built around the idea of forces with light armored vehicles that can be transported by tactical airlift (that is, C-130 aircraft) and readily moved in brigade strength. Those forces forming now will be equipped with nearly off-the-shelf vehicles. With their initial equipment, these forces would not be able to engage heavy enemy forces offensively and would only be able to provide screening and delaying forces depend-ing on the terrain in defense. They would, however, be rapidly transport-able and capable against light forces, and thus useful in peace enforce-ment and stability situations such as Kosovo, where the force's tactical mobility would permit it to patrol roads and its light armor would be ad-equate in many situations. The force could also be useful in MTWs in the rear-area security mission, and to protect critical fixed installations like airfields and ports.

One BCT is forming now. This chapter proposes forming four active BCTs and converting three Army National Guard Enhanced Separate Bri-gades (ESBs) to this configuration, for a total of seven BCTs. The ESBs would be used to support a rotation base for the medium-weight units if they are committed to a protracted operation. Because these ESBs would never be used simultaneously, a single equipment set of medium-weight vehicles could be kept at a centralized location that would be used by the units during their annual training. Only a few combat vehicles would be available to the ESBs in their home locations, together with their own full equipment set of support vehicles (trucks, wreckers, etc). This concentration would permit the total cost for equipping the first-generation brigades to be kept to about $3 billion expended before 2010.

One of the first forming units should be deployed to Europe as part of our NATO-committed forces and go on a rotation to Bosnia or Kosovo for rapid feedback of operational lessons to influence the design and equipment of later-forming BCTs. Within Europe, the BCT could exploit its C-130 transportability to reach out a bit over 2,000 miles to the C-130's full range (at which the C-130 must refuel before returning) or on a combat radius of about 1,000 miles (in which the aircraft returns without refueling).

THE LIGHT FORCES

The light forces are largely infantry, some of whom arrive by parachute and some of whom arrive on foot, and a light cavalry regiment without heavy armored vehicles. Whatever their means of arrival, they fight on foot supported by the other arms. By some accounts, the infantry's principal contribution to armed conflict is to be casualties. And yet, every day the news from Chechnya, Kosovo, Ulster, or Sierra Leone drives home the immense difference in capability between good infantry and people with guns. Infantry will continue to be useful in a variety of situations, including the stability missions described above, some interventions, and the early-entry role as part of an MTW.

While the primary skills of these units will continue to be how they fight as infantry, how they move about in theater may sometimes need to be augmented, depending on the mission and terrain. To provide light units with armored carriers in these situations, three of the heavy ARNG Enhanced Separate Brigades should be converted to armored carrier units built from mechanized infantry battalions. These carrier units would retain their Bradley fighting vehicles but be manned only with drivers and associated vehicle maintenance personnel that do not have their own infantry. The training regimens of these high readiness units would prepare them to work with infantry from the airborne and light infantry divisions. Their summer training would consist of crew qualification and training with the light forces. This changeover could occur with existing stocks of non-upgraded Bradley fighting vehicles. The reduction in personnel requirements would save about $200 million annually.

In modernizing the light forces, the most important procurement program would be a continued Comanche program, to replace the aging Cobras and OH-58s of the light divisions' aviation battalions. This would give the light forces a readily transportable aircraft capable of providing real-time information to the digitized command networks of a light division while flying light attack missions.[20] In order to fund this program through the decade, money should be both added to and subtracted from the Comanche accounts. First, by reducing the Longbow Apache buy in accord with the reduced number of Apache battalions kept in the smaller force, some funds are freed early to complete Comanche development. However, once full production is ready to start, this chapter reduces the rate at which the Comanches are purchased, to about 48 aircraft a year rather than 72. This would save about $200 million annually in 2010. The reduced rate of production is adequate to modernize the light divisions at an acceptable rate.

The Army Force Structure over Time

Tables 7.1, 7.2, and 7.3 show the changes in the total force structure over time, reflecting the decisions described above. The sequence shows a migration of heavy force brigades into medium roles as the power of the individual heavy brigade increases. The light force is held relatively stable. The 2010 force could have two heavy brigades and a medium brigade stationed in Europe. It could project the FDC of seven brigades to an MTW and (depending on how many were forward-based in other countries) still have five heavy brigades (and as many as eight by drawing on the medium brigades of the swing force 101st Air Assault Division) either for commitment to the first MTW or available for a second contingency. By the rule of five, it would also be able to support three light or medium brigades (if the 101st were not committed to the MTW) committed to a protracted SSC, with 24 months between deployments, relying solely on the active units. (See Table 7.1.)

Reserve component heavy brigades are reduced consistent with a view that only the number that can be trained within a reasonable time for a second MTW should be retained within the force structure. Those heavy ESBs that remain in the heavy force structure would be called on, in the event of a MTW, to prepare for a possible second MTW in which they would be committed. The heavy ARNG division that remains in the force structure would be a true strategic reserve division: it would be called up for training on completion of the Enhanced Separate Brigades (ESB) training and would be able to cover assignments while the other

---

20. This mission does not argue against the use of drones for many missions. Drones are being developed and acquired. It does say that in the way we use light forces, the Comanche would integrate reconnaissance and strike and informing the command chain in a way that was unavailable in the past.

Table 7.1. Maneuver Brigades in Active Army.

	Active Component		
Year	Light Brigades	Medium Brigades	Heavy Brigades
2000	10	4[a]	18
2010	8	7[b]	14

a. Three of these are air assault brigades of the 101st Air Assault Division and one is the now forming Brigade Combat Team built around the 3d Brigade of the 2d Infantry Division at Fort Lewis.
b. Three of these are air assault brigades of the 101st Air Assault Division and four are Brigade Combat Teams. In 2010, the 101st Air Assault Division would be a likely candidate to be the first division to convert to the new style of combat built around the Future Combat System.

heavy units were deployed or redeploying. Some light and medium reserve component units are kept so that they can provide a rotation base for SSCs, with a relatively high probability that it would be a long time between call-ups for these units. (See Table 7.2.)

By drawing on the ESBs of the Army National Guard, three heavy brigades might be made available for a second 90–120 days after they were mobilized. If the nine light and medium ESBs were each called up only once in the sustained commitment of three brigades to an SSC, the time between deployments for the active brigades could be extended to 42 months. (See Table 7.3.)

A one-time call-up of the three additional light brigades of the ARNG light division would add an additional six months to the time between deployments for the active component.

The draw-down both clarifies the commitments of the units and their personnel and permits some specialization in their training. Personnel in the heavy ESBs commit to a prompt call-up for a definite commitment to any second MTW that occurs while a first MTW is underway. Personnel in the light and medium ESBs accept some greater probability that they will be called up for commitment to the later rotations of a protracted smaller-scale contingency. Personnel in the ARNG divisions have a lower probability of commitment after the respective heavy and light ESBs have been used for early MTW operations and rotations to SSCs.

ARMY PROCUREMENT

In support of the force described above, and in addition to the budget changes identified above, some procurements are also affected. First, the

Table 7.2. Maneuver Brigades in ARNG Enhanced Separate Brigades

Year	Light Brigades	Medium	Heavy
2000	7	0	8
2010	6	3	3 + 3 armored carrier

Table 7.3. Maneuver Brigades within Army National Guard Divisions

Year	Light	Medium	Heavy
2000	3	0	15
2010	3	0	3

Abrams and Bradley modernization programs, each of about 1000 vehicles, should be completed to provide all the retained active forces with digitized vehicles. In the course of these modifications, the key vehicles will also acquire a more fuel-efficient engine and improved mechanical reliability.

Second, the Crusader program should be cancelled promptly, and an existing self-propelled howitzer chosen and modified for the digitized environment, to equip the direct support field artillery battalions of the active divisions. The new gun might be the German PzH 2000 (recommended by the GAO and used as the basis for the CBO's estimate of savings) or it might be some other existing howitzer that could be integrated with the digital environment of the new corps. Using the CBO estimate as an initial basis, but buying fewer guns for the retained heavy forces while allowing additional dollars for integration, would save $1 billion in 2010 and about $7 billion over the decade. All of the money saved with this cut is redirected to fund the science and technology projects associated with the Future Combat System discussed below.

By drawing down the heavy forces at the end of the decade as described above, some of the expenses of modernization can be avoided. The procurement costs for the majority of the electronic equipment for digitizing one heavy division can be avoided at the end of the decade, which might amount to roughly $250 million in 2010. With the extensive reduction of heavy divisions, at the end of the decade the Army would reduce the rate at which it buys trucks by about a third (about 2200 trucks per year rather than about 3300), saving about $200 million annually.

ARMY RESEARCH AND DEVELOPMENT

In his first year as Army Chief of Staff, General Eric Shinseki laid out an ambitious goal of an Army Transformation, with the aim of creating a force with the deployability of a light force while having the capability to engage and defeat an opponent's heavy forces. This force would represent the ultimate convergence of light and heavy forces into a single new type of unit. The so-called "Objective Force" is meant to be achieved sometime after 2010.[21]

The BCTs discussed earlier are the first elements of the transformation to appear in the Army force structure. Over the period addressed by this volume—2000–2010 with a particular focus on the 2010 budget—the key elements of the Army Transformation and the Objective Force do not appear in the Army budget as either force structure or acquisition programs. Instead, they appear as a variety of science and technology programs. The central program of this is the Future Combat System (FCS) which begins as a joint demonstration program with the Defense Advanced Research Projects Agency (DARPA) to be conducted between 2000 and 2006. This first period is devoted to developing a networked advanced force structure with the capability to be lethal, strategically deployable, and highly survivable in combat even against modernized heavy forces. With the identification of the systems and technologies that will realize these goals, the DARPA/Army program will transition to the Army in 2006 for engineering development, acquisition, and an intended deployment beginning in 2012.

Preliminary work on the FCS concepts has emphasized the key areas of networked command, control, and communications, computers, intelligence, surveillance, and targeting (C4IST); robotics; precision indirect fires; and beyond-line-of-sight organic sensing and precision all-weather surveillance and targeting systems. While outwardly resembling similar lists associated with other new concepts, the scale of change and technological difficulty is much more dramatic. The Director of DARPA has already identified two technical areas—advanced networking and robotics—as significantly beyond the current state of the art in either the military or commercial worlds. The advanced networking among moving manned and unmanned platforms over a vast spatial extent involves a marked increase in scale over previous military and commercial net-

---

21.   General Eric R. Shinseki, Address to the Eisenhower Luncheon, 45th Annual Meeting of the Association of the U.S. Army, October 12, 1999; see also Department of the Army, The Honorable Louis Caldera and General Eric K. Shinseki, *A Statement on the Posture of the United States Army Fiscal Year 2001*, February 2000.

works. In robotics, the system requires not just remote operation by a human operator at a distance but endowing unmanned ground vehicles with autonomous capabilities based on interpretation of more general instructions. Both of these areas are identified as significant risk areas in accomplishing the program on its very demanding schedule.[22]

While the immediate funding needs of the FCS program in the current budget and the period of the DARPA/Army program have been resolved, the risks of the system are considerable. Accepting that this program will require more time and more money and is justified by the prospect of introducing an entirely new way of fighting on the ground, this proposal would cancel certain programs in favor of additional funding for the FCS and transformation projects, and accepts that the FCS will not be available for fielding in 2012 as intended. Thus, the Crusader program is canceled as described above and its out-year funding is moved to the FCS and transformation programs. At the same time, the key elements of the existing heavy force at Fort Hood that are being modernized around the digitization programs are kept modernized because they will probably be needed in the force until well past 2015.

Naval Forces: Doing Less with Less

Naval presence is a key tool of U.S. power and military diplomacy. It is an important element, indeed the decisive element, across a huge swath of the world. But there are areas of the world where its daily presence can and should be reduced.

This chapter proposes that the existing twelve carrier battle groups be reduced to ten, with nine air groups. All the surface combatants associated with the other two battle groups as well as the attack submarines that accompany it should be retained and freed for other naval presence missions. While others have pointed out that the same rate of presence in the Mediterranean might be supported with this reduced force by appropriate basing, I argue for keeping the ships homeported as they are, accepting reduced carrier time on station in the vicinity of U.S. NATO allies as relatively benign, and a bit of prod to those who share U.S. interests in the region to coordinate a more predictable presence of their own.

The reduction of carrier battle groups and the freeing of their existing escorts permit some further changes in the shipbuilding program. This chapter removes four DDG-51 destroyers intended as carrier escorts from

---

22. "DARPA Chief Warns Army of Risks in Developing Future Combat System," *Inside the Army*, July 3, 2000, p. 1.

the building program, saving $200 million in 2010, and $3.9 billion over the decade. This program also reduces the start rate of the DD-21-class from three per year to two per year when the class commences after 2005. This saves $750 million in 2010 and $2.25 billion over the decade.

Every carrier air wing should include a Marine F-18 squadron. As proposed in CBO documents, inserting six Marine squadrons into the carrier air wings would reduce the required procurement of the F-18 E/F. This takes advantage of the greater proficiency of Marine pilots at flying close air support (CAS) for the Marine forces that might be supported by the carrier air wing. The Marines work hard at CAS—that is, air action by fixed- and rotary-winged aircraft against hostile targets which are in close proximity to friendly forces and which require detailed integration of each air mission with the fire and movement of those forces—and are arguably its best practitioners. If ground Marines are committed, they should be supported by their own aviators; this insures that they will always have Marine CAS available. This proposal also saves a considerable quantity of money. By disestablishing nine Navy squadrons, about $450 million in operations and maintenance (O&M) costs are avoided annually, cumulating $4.5 billion over the decade if the cuts are carried out immediately. By swapping out airframes, this option reduces the need for the procurement of about 270 F/A-18. Slowing the procurement at the end of the decade by about 60 aircraft a year (from the Navy's intended purchase of about 120 aircraft a year) could reduce the annual procurement expenditure by $4.2 billion per year in 2010, and cumulatively $19 billion over the decade. This would also reduce the huge demand on the tactical aircraft accounts arising from having multiple aircraft programs in their acquisition stage at the same time.

As potent as the new *Virginia*-class attack boats may be, there seems little reason to rush the retirement of *Los Angeles*–class boats with considerable remaining life. Recommendations to slow the program would save $2.4 billion in 2010 and about $13 billion over the decade.

The Trident force currently consists of eighteen ships, ten equipped with the advanced D-5 missile and eight earlier ships equipped with the C-4 missile. Under the current administration plan, the Navy will have fourteen Trident submarines, all equipped with the D-5 missile. This chapter selects the option of retiring all of the C-4 submarines and increasing the number of warheads on each retained missile from five to seven. This choice accepts a somewhat reduced deployment area with a possible increased vulnerability to a resurgent Russian antisubmarine force. In making the change, the reduced operation saves about $300 million in operating costs in 2010 and about $4.9 billion over the decade.

AMPHIBIOUS FORCES

As important as amphibious presence is in some regions of the world, it can and should be reduced in other regions. Thus, consistent with the reduction of carrier battle groups, this chapter would reduce the fleet by two Amphibious Ready Groups (ARGs). This reduction in ARGs would provide O&M savings of about $550 million annually. The reduction of six ships would further mean that the commoncement of a number of new amphibious ship programs (Landing Helicopter Dock [LHD], and Amphibious Transport Dock) could be forgone, saving $200 million in 2010 and about $3 billion over the decade.

No changes are envisioned for the way the Marines provide Marine Expeditionary Units, apart from the somewhat reduced rate of deployment consistent with the reduction in the number of Amphibious Ready Groups. The Marines should focus on fulfilling their vision of warfare with innovative concepts in their particular specialty of expeditionary warfare, funding the MV-22 tilt-rotor, the Marine version of the Joint Strike Fighter (JSF), and the Advanced Amphibious Assault Vehicle (AAAV). However, this modernization does not create a Marine Corps that can wage high-intensity land combat at the scale of large units (division and above). This is most starkly the situation of the Third Marine Expeditionary Force (MEF) and its included 3d Marine Division based on Okinawa. While notionally an organic division, the division has only two regiments: one is actually based in Hawaii, while the regiment on Okinawa is made up of rotating battalions from other regiments. The primary reason for this deployment and the existence of the Third MEF is to provide a MEF to Korea in the event of war; all of the other key Marine deployments in the Pacific are provided from the First MEF and its 1st Marine Division.

Once the situation in Korea becomes clarified, perhaps within the next five years, the need for forces dedicated to Korea will diminish, and even within this period, the desirability of using a Marine division seems debatable. As the Marines move to a fully expeditionary model, the Third MEF and the 3d Marine Division should be dissolved, as should most of the Marine force structure in the remaining MEFs associated with heavy force operations: tanks, artillery, higher-level engineer formations, etc. This would amount to about 10,000 personnel and would save about $1 billion a year in personnel and O&M costs.

There is a compelling reason to have a Marine F-18 squadron in every carrier air wing—as mentioned above, this way ground Marines can always be supported by Marine Close Air Support. But there seems little reason for the remaining nine Marine F-18 squadrons: they don't fit on carrier decks in this force structure and they have no place in the vision once Korea is no longer a design point for the force. This chapter therefore proposes removing them from the force structure, saving $450 million in O&M costs annually.

The Air Force

No one would argue in favor of operating ground forces without U.S. air superiority, and few would argue against the proposition that the Air Force can provide rapid striking power in many regions of the world. Indeed, in some instances air power and strike warfare—air or naval—may be all that is necessary to convince some opponents, but in others, the Army will have to be deployed. However, modernization of the Army is not an alternative to modernizing the Air Force for those missions it can do best. The approach is to modernize the elements of the Air Force while increasing the number of dual-capable platforms and removing force structure that would arrive late or have little effect on the Air Force's contribution to an overall campaign.

FIGHTER AND ATTACK FORCES

The Air Force argument that the F-22 is necessary may be overstated, but the decision to acquire some of the aircraft now can be supported as a longer-term investment by a nation that places a very high value on air superiority. However, this has limits: the proposal is therefore to reduce the F-22 buy to 120, saving about $3.2 billion in 2010, and $22.2 billion over the decade. As Karl Mueller argues in Chapter 8, a portion of the savings should be used to increase the number of dual-capable aircraft within the air superiority force. Some $9 billion of this money should therefore be redirected to equip two fighter wings with F-16/60 aircraft, a dual-capable aircraft with air capabilities superior to the current F-15C. With the upgraded force of F-22 and F-16/60, one fighter wing equipped with the single-purpose air superiority F-15C can be removed, producing an annual saving of about $400 million annually and about $1.2 billion over the decade.

The Air Force possesses a few units that are unlikely to be deployed to combat or, if deployed, would make very little contribution because of their equipment limitations. The least effective of these are early-model F-16s lodged in the Air National Guard. Given the rate at which modernization will be carried out, these units are unlikely to change status over this decade. Taking 2 ANG F-16 wings out of the force structure saves about $480 million annually.

CLOSE AIR SUPPORT AND THE A-10 FORCE

Close Air Support (CAS) has been an item of contention between the Army and the Air Force. The Air Force has not wanted to fly CAS with its high-performance aircraft, and in response to Congressional pressure, it acquired the A-10, a dedicated CAS aircraft. It has gone largely unmodernized since its acquisition in the 1970s and may go on much this way until the end of its service life sometime around 2030. The A-10, and more particularly its pilots, can carry out the CAS mission when they are permitted to employ tactics that bring the aircraft close to the ground. However, these tactics expose the aircraft to a loss rate that was considered unacceptable in the Gulf War. In both the Gulf War and the operations in Kosovo, the aircraft were therefore kept at high altitude. Keeping the aircraft at altitudes above 10,000 feet reduces risk, but also seriously reduces effectiveness. If U.S. ground forces actually were in a difficult situation, A-10s would undoubtedly be used without regard to attrition. However, Army attack helicopters would probably be more effective in exactly the same situation, accepting the same class of risks while being more useful to the ground forces in normal situations. Therefore the Army helicopter force should be modernized, and used to carry out the A-10 CAS mission. The two wings of A-10s (one active and one Air National Guard) and the single wing of OA-10 forward air controllers associated with the mission (this wing is not counted as fighter wing in the count of Air Force fighter wings) could be removed, saving about $600 million annually.

AIRLIFT

The Army is devoting large efforts to make a portion of its force fit within very stringent limits on weight and form to fit tactical airlifters. However, all airlift is expensive, and military airlift can be excessively so. Of all airlift programs, perhaps the most difficult choice is whether to make yet another attempt to make the C-5A Galaxy a reliable airlifter by a major modification program. The C-5A Galaxy has been a disappointment throughout its entire career. It has been refitted and modified and still embarrassed everyone who promised to make it better. Even though it is a primary carrier for oversize or outsize military cargo (of which the Army has had a great deal), further effort should not be devoted to this aircraft.[23] Instead, the $3 billion that might be saved by not modifying the aircraft can be redirected. Concentrated over the last six years of the de-

---

23. "Outsize cargo" is cargo that is so large or bulky that it can fit on only two types of U.S. cargo planes—C-5s or C-17s. "Oversize cargo" is smaller than outsize and can fit on some military and commercial transports.

cade, this would be $500 million annually; $1 billion of those savings could then be spread across all the services to modify or replace equipment to reduce the need for particular items to be treated as oversize or outsize items, and Civil Reserve Air Fleet (CRAF) aircraft could be identified that would have the most effect on reducing the need for C-17/C-5 with the modified equipment. A reserve aircrew experiment (with as much as $200 million over the decade) could create an AF Reserve for civilian transport pilots so that CRAF aircrew might be activated and directed to hostile environments. Many civilian transport pilots already have military service and could fit easily into such a program. A budgetary discipline that did not add further C-130 tactical airlifters to the force would not damage the airlift fleet, would prevent needless retirement of aircraft with considerable remaining service lives, and could save about $600 million in 2010.

Budgetary Implications

This program of force and program restructuring would reduce anticipated defense expenditures by about $25 billion in 2010, and total about $140 billion over the decade. Adding the $10 billion that might be realized from the defense management savings identified by Cindy Williams in Chapter 3, this would hold the defense budget essentially flat for the decade.

The budget cuts are distributed unequally over the services. In the $25 billion cut from the 2010 budget, about 45 percent comes from the Navy, largely driven by reductions in the buy of the F-18 E/F, slowing of the Virginia-class submarine buy, and removal of two carriers from the force structure. The Air Force contributes about 32 percent, largely provided by reductions in the F-22, the slowing of the JSF program, and the reduction of two A-10, two ANG F-16, and one F-15C tactical fighter wing (TFW). The Army contributes about 17 percent of the cuts, almost entirely from reductions in Army National Guard heavy divisions and one active heavy division. The Marine Corps contributes about 6 percent from force reductions in the Third MEF and the F/A-18 force.

STRATEGIC CHOICES

The force structure designed here is a balanced force that has a great deal of combat power available for major theater wars and is consciously designed for a greater tolerance for potentially large or protracted smaller-scale contingencies. Underlying the design of this force is a great degree of uncertainty on what the future might require of the U.S. military. Certainty about the identity of the next peer competitor would provide a lot of focus. Even certainty on the geographic region of conflict would set distance scales that would influence force design: the Pacific is broad and places are far apart, while Europe is small and cities are separated by no more than a day's walk. This chapter cannot provide that certainty.

Judgments about how the United States participates in alliances lead to certain key decisions. One such judgment is that working with NATO allies would permit sharing carrier coverage in places like the Mediterranean, permitting a reduction in the total number of U.S. carriers, while simultaneously requiring some U.S. ground forces in Europe, if for no other purpose than to ensure familiarity in working together.

This chapter shares the premise that spending military modernization money wisely can have big effects. Indeed, this chapter proposes very large expenditures on science and technology programs to investigate and develop new methods for waging ground war. On the other hand, it does not share a buoyant optimism that improving the technology of spotting and striking targets of various sorts, fixed or moving, at greater and greater ranges will by itself solve the military demands of the next decade.

Perhaps the most prominent difference between this proposed force structure and the others in this volume is allowing a greater weight to the demands of smaller-scale contingencies on the Army's general purpose forces. The crude tools of policing ratios and a "rule of five" do not allow a great deal of precision in the calculation, but they suggest a need for fair numbers in the force structure if deployment demands on individuals are to be kept within bounds. Someone with more belief that U.S. allies are willing, or can be induced, to bear most of these burdens would make a different choice. So would someone who believed specially trained and dedicated international policemen could solve these problems much more efficiently than military forces. Similarly, someone with the same concerns about sea time for sailors and who believed that sailors would simply be placed at sea longer to make up for any lack of carriers would not choose the reduction of the carrier force.

Different assessments about the time that will be available for military operations figure prominently in the choices of the various authors, including this one. People who believe Army National Guard heavy units can be kept at very high readiness levels and quickly readied for deployment might make different judgments on the number of reserve units that might be available for a second MTW.

While other programs might be devised, this program seems to provide a set of forces both well matched to the particular requirements of the coming decade and also well positioned to adjust to the development of new competitors and new methods of war while keeping budgets flat. It is not likely to fail because of an over-reliance on a particular method of war or a single view of the future.

Chapter 8

Flexible Power Projection for a Dynamic World: Exploiting the Potential of Air Power

Karl Mueller

This chapter prescribes an approach for transforming U.S. defense investment and force structure during the coming decade that centers on increasing the role played by air power within the U.S. military. During the last generation, the capabilities of modern air power have increased dramatically, even relative to the impressive advances that have occurred in land and sea power. It is particularly important to take advantage of this trend as the United States enters the twenty-first century, for the flexibility of air power is ideally suited to the current security environment, in which demands on U.S. military resources are high, while the location and even the nature of future conflicts remain highly unpredictable. To provide the flexible power projection capabilities that the United States requires while simultaneously limiting U.S. defense spending, this proposal calls for a shift in resource distribution from the Army and Navy to the Air Force, and for all of the armed services to maintain a wide variety of capabilities while increasing their ability to respond rapidly to unforeseen crises and wars.

The author wishes to thank Christopher Bence, David Burbach, Dennis Drew, Thomas Ehrhard, Eugene Gholz, J.D. Harris, Richard Hilberer, John Horner, Wray Johnson, Chaim Kaufmann, Steven Kosiak, Timothy Lindemann, Stephen Luxion, Lane Pierrot, Barry Posen, Daryl Press, Michael Rampino, Tony Valle, Lee Wight, Harold Winton, and the other members of this project for generously providing extensive and invaluable comments, suggestions, skepticism, and advice. Although many of their best ideas have found their way into this chapter, the opinions and misconceptions expressed here are those of the author alone; moreover, to the best of his knowledge, they do not reflect the views of the U.S. Air Force, the Department of Defense, or the U.S. Government. At least not yet.

The first section of this chapter describes the premises that form the philosophical foundation for the flexible power projection strategy. This is followed by a more concrete overview of the proposed force structure, including the contingencies that it is and is not designed to deal with, and the relationship between land, sea, and air power within the strategy. The subsequent sections then detail the proposed changes in each of the services' force structures and acquisition plans, and the chapter concludes with discussions of the budgetary and strategic implications if the United States adopts such a strategy during the coming decade.

A Chaotic Strategic Environment

Contemporary international politics is unpredictable. This cliché is repeated incessantly, and nowhere more frequently than in military vision statements, where it all too often serves as a justification for strategic indecision and for promulgating innovative jargon in lieu of actual substance. Yet this facile briefing-slide mantra does reflect a key feature of the strategic environment that currently faces the United States: foreseeing the identities of its enemies ten years from now, and correctly anticipating the types of military operations most likely to be required to deal with them, is considerably more difficult today than it was during the height of the Cold War. This inevitably presents problems for strategists and force planners who must make decisions that will shape U.S. military capabilities years and even decades into the future.

Of course, it is all too easy to overlook the origins of this uncertainty, and to overstate its extent. First, the apparent simplicity of the Cold War world existed more in the minds of U.S. and Soviet policymakers than in the reality of the international system. The bipolar rivalry between the superpowers was real enough, but it did not in fact subsume virtually every other international confrontation or civil war. The Cold War political scene appeared far less well ordered when viewed from Paris, New Delhi, or Jerusalem than it did in Moscow and Washington. That the world now seems complicated and turbulent by comparison is due as much to a change in our preoccupations as it is to the objective collapse of Soviet power, or any resurgence of ethnic and religious animosities around the globe.

Second, the new world order is not quite as disorderly as pundits often suggest. It is chaotic, but not in the pre-Creation "all was chaos" sense of the term. Rather, it tends to resemble—at least metaphorically—the sorts of natural systems typically studied by chaos theorists, in which extreme unpredictability does exist, but within bounds, in certain places, and at certain times (especially as one looks far into the future). A butterfly flapping its wings in China may eventually affect the weather in Virginia, as non-linear meteorological models suggest, but no amount of Asian insect activity will cause snow to fall on the Pentagon in July. Similarly, and luckily for the strategymaker, despite much hand-wringing over the complexity of an international system that is moving towards multipolarity, it is still possible to predict much about what will happen in the near future—and even more about what will *not* happen.

However, the problem of strategic uncertainty does persist, and in order to make coherent strategy with limited resources it is necessary to choose a plausible set of premises upon which to build. The force structure proposed in this chapter is based on a cluster of interrelated assumptions about the political and technological conditions likely to face the United States in the next decade, which can usefully be organized according to five policy themes.

THE QUANDARY OF THE UNCHALLENGED SUPERPOWER

One of the central reasons the current strategic environment seems highly unpredictable for the United States is that U.S. power is so great relative to that of most potential adversaries. Vital U.S. interests—security of the national homeland and of principal U.S. allies, and a reasonably peaceful international environment in which to conduct commerce—face very little threat, giving the United States great freedom of action to choose where, when, and why to use military force in the pursuit of less critical objectives.[1] The asymmetric power of the United States relative to the rest of the world means that military planners cannot easily assume that U.S. armed forces will be called upon to conduct only certain types of operations, though of course an overall resource limit does prevent intervening militarily in every situation where the whim might strike. In short, from a foreign policy perspective, there are many things that U.S. military power

---

1. Many critics of past or current U.S. intervention policies argue that military force should only be used in the pursuit of vital national interests, and only as a last resort when all other policy instruments have failed. These are attractively simple principles that have been most visibly advocated in the so-called Weinberger/Powell Doctrine. However, even as ideals, these rules of thumb are obsolete—and arguably both immoral and un-American—in a world where military force is often less expensive and less destructive than alternative tools such as economic sanctions. See Karl Mueller, "Politics, Death, and Morality in U.S. Foreign Policy," *Aerospace Power Journal*, Summer 2000, pp. 12–16; and John Mueller and Karl Mueller, "The Methodology of Mass Destruction: Assessing Threats in the New World Order," *Journal of Strategic Studies*, Vol. 23, No. 1 (March 2000), pp. 163–87.

can do, and many perhaps that it *should* do, but few difficult ones that it *must* do. For the U.S. armed forces, on the other hand, this means there are many things that they must be prepared to do if called.

During the coming decade the U.S. military must continue to be prepared not only to protect vital U.S. interests from the limited threats they face, but also to conduct a wide range of operations in the pursuit of more peripheral objectives, including military interventions motivated by moral or humanitarian concerns. Moreover, it must be possible to conduct such operations at relatively low cost, since unlike defending vital interests, actions to protect less important ones will not merit the expenditure of many American lives.[2] Even if the U.S. defense budget remains constant during the next ten years, as this volume advocates, it is unlikely that U.S. military forces will be called upon to do substantially less than they have in the last decade, regardless of their well-founded desire not to be overstretched. Thus it becomes imperative to maximize the amount that limited U.S. defense manpower and spending can sustainably accomplish. This imperative drives the proposal to emphasize investment in military forces that have the greatest possible flexibility to perform a variety of missions, some of which may turn out to be quite unanticipated.

THE DILEMMA OF COOPERATION

The question of whether the United States should, and will, fight its wars alone or in alliance with other states is critical for many aspects of strategy and force structure design. The simplest option, of course, and arguably the safest, is to assume that the United States must be able to fend for itself without relying on the support of fickle allies or dubious coalition partners. With such a worst-case premise, any foreign support that does materialize will come as a pleasant surprise, and if potential allies are not cooperative enough, a self-sufficient United States can take them or leave them.

The problems with this conservative assumption are three-fold. First and least important, it is unrealistic. The United States has consistently sought the cooperation of other states before applying force in even the most trivial conflicts. Second, seriously underestimating the likely mili-

---

2. See, among others, John Mueller, "Public Opinion as a Constraint on U.S. Foreign Policy: Assessing the Perceived Value of U.S. and Foreign Lives," paper presented at the International Studies Association National Convention, Los Angeles, March 14, 2000; and Eric V. Larson, *Casualties and Consensus*, MR-726-RC (Santa Monica: RAND, 1996).

tary contributions of U.S. allies will lead to overspending on defense, an excessively timid foreign policy, or both. Finally, assuming that U.S. forces will be fighting alone when they in fact will not squanders the opportunity to design those forces for maximum effectiveness in alliance or coalition operations. Since the forces and capabilities provided by U.S. allies are not just miniature versions of those of the United States, the balance of U.S. military investment should be shaped by an awareness of what its partners will bring to the fights in which it engages, as Gordon Adams notes in Chapter 4. Although the experiences of the 1990s, particularly NATO's 1999 war with Serbia, have led to much soul-searching in the United States about whether allies might tend to be more trouble than they are worth, there is little prospect that the next decade will see any profound change in this fundamental pattern of U.S. foreign policy that has been sixty years in the making.

This chapter does not assume that the U.S. military will never need to act alone. There may be occasions in the near future when the United States will need to fight entirely without allied support, although far more likely are cases in which Washington will assemble enough of a coalition to provide a suggestion of international consensus for an operation like the invasion of Grenada or Panama, without actually receiving substantial military assistance from allies. However, in any conflict that might reasonably be described as a major theater war (MTW), significant allied support can be considered virtually certain, not because of the staunchness of U.S. allies in every case, but because U.S. choice to intervene militarily in any major conflict that does not involve either the defense of an important ally (such as South Korea or Taiwan), or partnership with one or more of them, is effectively inconceivable. Therefore this chapter makes conservatively realistic rather than maximally pessimistic assumptions about the contributions of allies in both major and minor conflicts during the coming decade.

THE DREAM OF TECHNOLOGICAL REVOLUTION

The capabilities of modern military forces, primarily through the use of air power broadly defined, have undergone a revolutionary increase during the past generation. This transformation is not due to a single technological innovation, but rather to an entire constellation of developments, some revolutionary and others more incremental in nature. Most of them can be classified in three broad categories. First, and perhaps most importantly, precision weapons—guided missiles, bombs, and other weapons in air, land, and sea warfare—have become extremely effective in the past thirty years, enabling small numbers of launch platforms to have destructive abilities that are quite disproportionate to their size by historical standards. Second, electronic warfare and stealth technologies have dramatically widened the capability gap between more advanced and less advanced aircraft, submarines, and increasingly, other types of systems. Third, innovations in the broad area of battle management, ranging from advanced surveillance and reconnaissance systems to satellite navigation technology, have multiplied the capabilities of sophisticated combat forces by an order of magnitude.[3]

These three areas of innovation will continue to loom large in the coming decade; some trends in them can already be anticipated. In many respects, precision weapons have reached a level of relative maturity, able to destroy almost anything their launch platforms can detect and identify, and the greatest changes now taking place in this field relate to weapons becoming less expensive and smaller, enabling more to be procured by a nation and more to be carried by an aircraft or ship. Stealth will increasingly spread to surface naval and land forces, while the protection that it provides to aircraft erodes as non-radar sensors such as advanced infrared search-and-track systems become widespread. As with most other revolutionary technologies, such countermeasures will inevitably gain ground, but stealth will continue to be valuable. Surveillance and reconnaissance capabilities stand poised to be the single most important arena of military innovation in the coming decade: as more and more countries acquire ultra-lethal precision weapons, and more battlefields become places where "if it can be seen, it can be killed," the ability to see, or not to be seen, is likely to separate winners from losers to an even greater degree than it has in the past. More revolutionary developments in fields such as robotic, directed energy, and non-lethal weapons will also shape these capabilities, probably in ways that are more difficult to predict.

But while accelerating technological change will make many types of weapons more effective, and some less so as countermeasures to them improve, none should be expected to become a panacea for U.S. strategists. Instead of investing heavily in particular systems that promise revolutionary advances in military capability, the United States is more likely to find dramatic benefits through investment in a wide variety of innovative systems. This hedges against unforeseen change, and takes advantage of opportunities for important operational synergies between even superficially unrelated forces and systems.

---

3. A fourth, usually less visible category might well be added to this list: that of advanced simulation technologies for military training, which can greatly enhance the capabilities of warriors in forces that are able to exploit them.

THE QUESTION OF ACCESS

Closely related to the preceding questions of technological change and the availability of regional allies is that of access to useful bases within a theater of war, a topic that has loomed especially large in recent years as fears of weapons of mass destruction (WMD) and ballistic missile proliferation have seized the popular imagination. If one assumes, as Owen Cote does in Chapter 6, that in-theater basing will generally be unavailable to U.S. forces during regional conflicts, due to some combination of unfavorable geography, uncooperative allies, primitive local infrastructure, and effective enemy WMD, then a strategy that relies very heavily on naval forces (for non-landlocked theaters) and even more on intercontinental air and space power becomes relatively attractive. (This does not provide a perfect solution, however; if the problem is that enemies are able to pose serious WMD or other military threats to friendly forces in theater, the same states are also likely to be able to mount significant threats to surface naval forces and to airbases within the United States.)

In contrast, this chapter is less pessimistic about the availability and security of regional bases, although it stops far short of assuming the problem away altogether. First, except in the unique case of the United States unilaterally helping to defend Taiwan from a Chinese attack so powerful that bases on the island were unusable, there is no plausible theater of war where substantial local basing possibilities simply do not exist due to geography. Second, the likelihood of the United States choosing to engage in a major regional conflict without allies in the region seems vanishingly remote, since it is the presence of allies that invariably motivates such interventions in the first place. Third, while inadequate local infrastructure may indeed limit the size of the air and land forces that can be deployed to and sustained at bases in theater, it will not alone prevent useful amounts of force being deployed; moreover, the theaters about which we care the most are generally well-developed, while more primitive areas tend to feature potential enemies against which even relatively small forces will be able to perform quite well.

Finally, and most important, the threat posed to U.S. forces deployed into theaters of war by enemy missiles and WMD is not as prohibitive as pessimists often suggest.[4] In very few cases is it likely that the United States would face regional adversaries both capable of mounting a truly sustained and effective WMD attack against U.S. fielded forces and willing to do so in the face of very plausible threats of apocalyptic retaliation.

---

4.   For a lengthier discussion of this point, see Mueller and Mueller, "The Methodology of Mass Destruction."

The sorts of primitive chemical and biological weapons and delivery capabilities likely to be available to lesser powers during the next decade or two will represent little more than a serious nuisance to U.S. power projection capabilities, provided that the United States takes reasonable steps to minimize its vulnerability to such attacks, as this chapter recommends.

THE WINDOW OF OPPORTUNITY

The final premise that underpins this chapter is that we should not assume that the current global imbalance of military power in favor of the United States will continue indefinitely. In forecasting the international distribution of power over the long term, there are a large number of important unknowns, particularly relating to economic development and military investment in China and India, the possibility of European defense unification, the shape of the resuscitation of Russia, the uncertainty of Saudi political stability, the eventual foreign policy trajectory of Japan, and similar questions about other potentially powerful states such as Brazil, Mexico, and Iran. Although it is not certain that the military power of any of these states will increase dramatically relative to that of the United States within the next generation, it is certainly prudent to prepare for the likelihood that the current low-threat international environment is an anomaly. Therefore, the force structure proposed in the following sections is based on the assumption that the U.S. armed forces of the next ten years may have to serve as the basis for a larger and more expensive force structure to deal with a more dangerous world in the decades beyond 2010.

Air Power and the Flexible Power Projection Strategy

Each of the considerations discussed above—the overarching need for functional and geographic flexibility, the need to maximize the military effectiveness of multinational forces, the profound changes in military technology during the past generation, the significant but manageable problem of regional basing, and the need to prepare for a longer term in which threats are likely to increase—shapes the force structure proposed in this chapter. Among their various influences, each of the factors favors adoption of a strategy for U.S. power projection that places increased reliance on air power.

THE RANGE OF CONTINGENCIES

The existing principle that the United States requires sufficient military force to be able to fight two nearly simultaneous major theater wars

(MTWs) has justifiably come under heavy fire in recent years. Surprisingly, however, most criticism leveled against it questions the plausibility of either the number of conflicts or the degree of potential simultaneity between them, rather than the underlying assumption regarding what forces are necessary to deal with an MTW. The possibility that two geographically separated aggressors—usually pictured as North Korea and a player in the Middle East to be named later—might through accident or design mount serious attacks against important U.S. interests at roughly the same time is fairly remote, but military leaders have been right to resist assuming that it will not happen. What we should reconsider instead is how much military capability the United States might actually need to deal with each of the wars in such a two-MTW scenario.

As Cindy Williams notes in her introductory chapter to this volume, the current MTW unit of measure is strikingly disproportionate to the sort of threats now posed by states like North Korea and Iraq, especially considering the military capabilities of their neighbors and traditional enemies. South Korea ought to be able to fend off an attack by the deteriorating North without much help from abroad, although U.S. assistance would be appropriate and would certainly reduce the defenders' losses.[5] There is no realistic prospect that China would be able to invade and conquer Taiwan successfully using conventional weapons in the near future, even if the United States refused to send substantial assistance. Iraq's military capabilities are but a pale shadow of their former might, let alone of the inflated strength mistakenly attributed to Iraq before the Gulf War. Among the so-called "rogue states," only Iran could realistically be described as militarily robust, while many key U.S. allies are increasing their force-projection capabilities even while downsizing their overall military forces.

Taking into account the decline of many formerly ominous regional threats, along with the likely contributions of probable U.S. allies, requires adjusting the assumptions that underlie the sizing of U.S. military forces. The United States should maintain the ability to deal with more than one substantial regional conflict at the same time, but in general each such conflict requires a deployable force on the order of two to three Army divisions and two to three carrier battlegroups, rather than the four or five of each that are currently envisioned. MTW requirements for land-based air power should be scaled back less, since this is an area in which contributions from allies are likely to be less helpful than those of

---

5. See Michael O'Hanlon, "Stopping a North Korean Invasion: Why Defending South Korea Is Easier than the Pentagon Thinks," *International Security*, Vol. 22, No. 4 (Spring 1998), pp. 135–169.

their land forces. Obviously, the ability to conduct two such scaled-down theater wars would also be more than sufficient to mass forces for a single MTW of the traditional, exaggerated size. However, maintaining a multiple-conflict planning criterion differs from a simple shift to a one-MTW rule in that it requires greater strategic lift capacity and larger numbers of certain types of low-density, high-demand systems, such as airborne warning and control system (AWACS) and reconnaissance assets.

In addition to being able to fight substantial theater wars, the United States needs to be able to respond to a variety of "smaller scale contingencies" (SSCs), even while dealing with the larger-scale ones. Exactly what capabilities are required to handle SSCs usually remains vague in budget and force structure discussions, since the SSC concept covers such a wide range of possible but unforeseen events, as James Quinlivan describes in Chapter 7. Although this seems to fly in the face of sound requirements-based planning, it is probably unavoidable. In the end, there will often be more SSCs in which we might like to intervene than our capabilities will support, no matter how large the U.S. armed forces are. Therefore, inelegant though it may be, it seems appropriate to fall back on capabilities-based planning for dealing with SSCs, making the policy question one of deciding whether and where to employ whatever amount of surplus military capability we decide to build and maintain. Although it is unlikely that the United States will desire less SSC intervention capability in the coming decade than it has had in the past one, the increasing (though still limited) expeditionary military capabilities of other states should expand U.S. opportunities to shift more of the burden for deploying ground forces, in particular, to allies and coalition partners in some such operations.

It is worth emphasizing that reducing the U.S. force requirement for MTWs does not place a new threshold on the maximum size of the conflicts in which the United States is prepared to intervene; it merely shifts a threshold that already exists. Broad though the current MTW concept may be, it still falls well short of encompassing the full range of possible contingencies in which U.S. intervention might occur, for there is a class of larger potential conflicts in which five U.S. divisions, ten fighter wings, and the rest would likely prove far from comfortingly sufficient: we might call these "contingencies too awful to contemplate." In such an event—a Russo-Ukrainian or Indo-Pakistani war, for example, or a full-blown civil war in Colombia or Nigeria (let alone Russia)—the United States would likely be faced with a choice between nonintervention or assembling a very large multinational force in which U.S. forces would be prominent, but far from a majority.

THE BALANCE OF FLEXIBILITY AND SPECIALIZATION

In order to provide the forces to handle a large, broad, and substantially unpredictable set of future military contingencies within a constrained defense budget, it is desirable to invest in forces with great flexibility so that they will be useful in a variety of situations; however, because no single type of weapon or unit can do everything well, it is also necessary to build a variety of forces. There is an intrinsic tension between flexibility and specialization in both military hardware and personnel. If the requirements for two missions differ, a system optimized to perform one must necessarily be less than optimal for the other, and the same is true of time and resources invested in training personnel for one mission rather than another. Yet a limited repertoire becomes problematic if there is no call for one's narrow expertise. How best to strike the balance between these two pressures depends on the strategic circumstances. At one end of the spectrum is a force posture like that of Norway during the Cold War: Norway faced only one security threat, an attack by the Soviet Union, the potential shape of which was quite clear. As a result of this certainty, Royal Norwegian Air Force F-16 fighter units, for example, were able to spend virtually all of their time practicing air-to-air combat, and developed an impressive reputation for excellence at it. However, so did the U.S. Air Force's single-role F-15C air superiority fighter units—only to discover after sweeping the Iraqi air force from the skies in January 1991 that there was now little for them to do to contribute further to Operation Desert Storm.

In the United States today, such trade-offs are the subject of much debate, as in the struggle over whether or not to build F-22 fighters that are optimized for (though not limited to) air-superiority missions, and whether the next generation of Navy surface combatants should be specifically designed for inshore warfare. Most visibly of all, the U.S. Army has embarked on a program to replace its force of functionally differentiated divisions with a single type of medium-weight division, more heavily equipped than current light forces but lighter than existing armored and mechanized infantry units.

How much to generalize or specialize—or, more specifically, how much one can afford not to specialize—also depends heavily on technological conditions. For example, it is far more feasible to build a true multi-role fighter aircraft today than it was fifty years ago, when the bulky early radar systems required for night or all-weather interception severely limited the performance of night fighters and made them ill-suited to most other missions. Meanwhile, new classes of specialist aircraft have appeared to perform roles such as defense suppression that were conducted by multi-role aircraft in the 1950s.

All military forces are subject to the flexibility-specialization trade-off, but for some it is more severe than for others. The Flexible Power Projection strategy's great emphasis on forces that are effective in a wide variety of situations is a principal reason why air power, particularly multi-role land-based air power, is its centerpiece. Since the early days of air power, its proponents have lauded its ability to fly over topographical obstacles and strike an enemy anywhere, and this geographic flexibility continues to be an important consideration when balancing investment in naval and air power. In general, naval forces cannot directly exert their influence far beyond the coastline of an enemy except as platforms for aircraft (including cruise missiles), and in most cases aircraft can conduct sustained operations more efficiently from land bases than from ships at sea.

Even more important, however, is the advantage in functional flexibility that both land-based and sea-based air power currently enjoy relative to land forces: the vast majority of modern combat air power is useful in contingencies ranging from full-blown major theater wars down to smaller scale conflicts of fairly limited intensity. In contrast, and notwithstanding the plans of the current U.S. Army leadership, it does not appear possible with the types of weapons available in the coming decade to develop land forces that are well-suited for deployment to SSCs such as peace enforcement missions in the Balkans, and still capable of conducting offensive operations against a competent and heavily mechanized enemy at an acceptable cost. Although this state of affairs may change with the development of revolutionary new generations of ground combat systems, for the coming decade it will be necessary to continue to maintain both traditional heavy mechanized ground forces and lighter forces suitable for use in lower intensity conflicts. Thus, to the extent that air power can efficiently substitute for ground forces across much of the spectrum of conflict, investing in the former will increase the overall flexibility of the U.S. armed forces.

THE SPECTRUM OF RESPONSE

In addition to varying with respect to the kinds and amounts of force that they can apply and where they can apply it, different types of military forces differ fundamentally according to the speed with which they can respond to an event or decision. Exactly what constitutes a "response" depends on the force in question, of course; in some cases this means traveling from a home base or deployed location to the scene of a crisis, while in others it refers to the length of time required to plan and launch an attack against an enemy.

In many cases, there are trade-offs between the speed and weight of a response, with heavier, more powerful forces taking longer to arrive or to strike than lighter ones. However, this is not at all a universal pattern, and it has become less generally true as military technology and technique have improved during the twentieth century. For example, capital ships are now far from being the slowest vessels in the U.S. Navy, and large forces of land-based aircraft can usually deploy to distant locations more quickly than less capable aircraft carriers can steam there (if they are not already deployed to the theater). With the development of pre-positioned unit equipment sets, even heavy land forces may not always be slower to deploy than lighter forces.

Although the range of possible response times of course varies continuously, it can be useful to classify the response times of conventional military forces informally according to whether a response to a distant crisis requires months, weeks, days, hours, or virtually no time at all.

PREEMPTIVE RESPONSE. At one end of the response spectrum are those forces that can deploy preemptively, thus reducing response time to zero. In most cases, these are land forces that physically interpose themselves in front of or among a potential enemy. On occasion, naval or air forces can do the same, by taking up positions on patrol past which an aggressor cannot sail or fly, but preemptive deployments of air and naval forces are more typically a means to reduce the time it will take these forces to respond to an enemy action or a commander's decision to attack.

IMMEDIATE RESPONSE. Immediate response forces can arrive or attack within hours. These traditionally include air, naval, and amphibious forces already deployed to locations in a theater that are within aircraft, weapons, or assault range of an enemy, or local ground forces that are alerted but not yet deployed. More recently, this category also includes intercontinental bombers capable of attacking distant targets from bases outside the theater. One could also distinguish an even faster "instantaneous response" category—for space-based directed energy weapons or conventional ICBMs capable of striking within minutes rather than hours—but, apart from exceptional circumstances, above the tactical level these differ little in function from slightly slower immediate response capabilities.

RAPID RESPONSE. Among U.S. forces capable of responding in a matter of days, air forces predominate. Assuming a sufficient level of alert, most U.S. fixed-wing air power can deploy transoceanically within days, given sufficient tanker aircraft or bases for refueling en route (for shorter-range types), enough airlift resources to carry necessary stores, support equipment, and personnel, and adequate bases into which to deploy. The rapid response category also includes naval forces that are not already on scene but are not far away, ground forces stationed elsewhere in the theater that can move overland, and alert ground forces that can be airlifted into the theater by virtue of being small or lightly equipped, or by having equipment pre-positioned with which to join up upon arrival. Expanding and improving the response capabilities of ground forces is a central preoccupation of current U.S. Army reform efforts.

DELIBERATE RESPONSE. The majority of regular U.S. ground forces, along with naval and amphibious forces deploying from U.S. bases or distant theaters, will have response times measured in weeks, provided, for ground forces, that sufficient sealift capacity is immediately available. Among these, deployment times can be considerably reduced through having equipment pre-positioned afloat on ships that are either maintained in theater or whose deployment is begun preemptively. Reserve air units at lower levels of alert will also have deliberate response times, as will rapid response air or ground units whose deployment is delayed due to logistical constraints.

DELAYED RESPONSE. The final important response category includes those forces requiring months to deploy. These consist primarily of reserve ground forces that require considerable time to mobilize and prepare, or regular ground forces whose deployment is delayed because sealift is not immediately available. Beyond deliberate response lies a further theoretical category that might be called "eventual response," consisting of forces whose response time is measured in years; this would principally be troops recruited and equipment built once the crisis or hostilities have begun. This characterized the bulk of forces in large, prolonged wars of attrition such as World War II or the Vietnam War, but is of little relevance in an era of limited threats and "come-as-you-are" wars.

TIME IS POWER. Of these categories, it is rapid response forces that appear to be the most important in the sorts of contingencies to be expected in the coming decade, followed by immediate and deliberate response forces. A strategy that emphasizes preemptive and immediate response might be attractive insofar as the faster a response is, the better. However, crises and other key events will often be difficult to anticipate, which will limit the opportunities for preemptive deployments, while focusing on responding to events within hours is often unrealistic given the pace of national decisionmaking under conditions of limited and ambiguous information. In practice, the ability to respond to an enemy's actions within a matter of days will usually be sufficient to avoid being presented with *faits accomplis,* particularly if sufficient immediate-response forces are available to impede the adversary's initial actions. At the other end of the spectrum, deliberate response forces are important, but focusing investment on them to the point of having military capabilities that give an adversary weeks to act before decisive U.S. force can be brought to bear would invite actions—such as the Serbian ethnic cleansing of Kosovo—that might be accomplished before the United States could effectively respond.

This set of response priorities provides further incentives to place heavy emphasis on air power, supported by long-range bombers and pre-deployed ground and naval forces to provide immediate response capabilities. It also suggests reducing U.S. investment in forces whose response is extremely slow, especially Army National Guard forces at low levels of readiness.

THE CENTRALITY OF AIR POWER

Together, the current imperatives for flexible armed forces that can respond both quickly and effectively even to unforeseen contingencies calls for a fundamental shift in U.S. military investment. The technological changes of the late twentieth century, together with the strategic conditions of the early twenty-first, provide the opportunity to use the increased potential of land-based air power to provide some of the capabilities for which the United States has traditionally relied on land and naval forces.

This is *not* to say that improvements in air power have rendered other types of forces obsolete. The variety of capabilities provided by different services and combat arms provide enormous synergies. For example, air power operating alone has difficulty attacking dispersed and concealed enemy ground forces. However, the coordinated use or threat of attack on the ground will force the adversary either to move and concentrate its forces, increasing their vulnerability to air attack, or to leave them dispersed, in which case friendly ground forces could overwhelm them. Similarly important hammer-and-anvil techniques apply to joint operations between air and naval forces, even as land-based air power becomes increasingly capable of performing sea control missions. Moreover, land forces remain the predominant military instrument for combat in urban environments, and above all for a wide variety of "peace operations," where advances in aerial sensors and precision weapons do nothing to alter the fundamental requirement for troops to be able to communicate and interact with the populations they are protecting or controlling.

However, because air power is now far more capable of providing firepower and surveillance against surface targets than it was a generation ago, the optimal mix of air and surface forces has shifted. Smaller land forces can provide the anvil for the improved hammer of air power, which means that land forces can deploy more quickly and at less risk. Similarly, while the ability of aircraft carriers to deploy into a maritime area of conflict when land bases are not available remains important, it has become decreasingly significant in recent years, as the operational effectiveness of U.S. land-based air power at longer ranges has grown.

There are two other important reasons to embrace greater reliance on air power broadly defined. The first is that doing so reduces the risks of U.S. casualties by placing fewer U.S. troops in harm's way. Although the apparently widespread belief that the U.S. public will "no longer" support costly wars is supported by neither empirical evidence nor sound logic, it is true that Americans have traditionally been unwilling to support wars in which large amounts of U.S. blood are spilled in the pursuit of goals that appear either unimportant or unattainable. Because most U.S. military interventions in the next decade or two are likely to be in defense of interests that are far from vital, even level-headed decision-makers who do not exaggerate the casualty aversion of the electorate will place great importance on minimizing the risk of U.S. casualties, and this will call for heavy reliance on air power.

The final reason to shift a greater proportion of U.S. defense investment into air power and the forces that support it is that this will help to maximize the military effectiveness of multinational forces. During the next decade at least, most U.S. allies will be able to contribute somewhat more in the way of land and naval forces than air power to alliance and coalition military efforts. Of course, this is more true of some states than others, and not at all true for a few, but the general pattern is consistent, and sensible. Because air power can deploy relatively rapidly, as discussed above, it is logical for the distant United States to invest heavily in it, while land forces that take longer to move from one continent to another are provided disproportionately by countries that are located in theater.[6]

Force Structure and Procurement for Flexible Power Projection

The sections that follow describe in detail the changes in force structure and acquisition of major systems that would reorient the U.S. armed forces to a posture for flexible power projection in the early twenty-first

---

6. Other factors also contribute to this pattern, of course, ranging from the historical importance of, e.g., the British navy or the German army, to the relatively high expense of air power, which tends to make investing in it less attractive to less affluent allies than to the United States. Finally, there are some ground force missions—notably in peacekeeping operations—where the specialization and experience of certain U.S. allies appear to make them better at performing the job than U.S. forces are, while only a few air forces can truly rival the effectiveness of U.S. air power in any major mission areas.

century, while holding the U.S. defense budget constant in real terms for the coming decade. The central elements of this transformation are a major reduction in the size of active-duty Army and National Guard ground forces, elimination of three aircraft carrier battlegroups, a modest reduction in the size of the Air Force's combat component, and substantially increased investment in a variety of weapons and enabling systems that would increase both the strategic deployability and the combat effectiveness of the resulting force.

LAND POWER: SMALLER FORCES, NOT LIGHTER
Under the Flexible Power Projection proposal, the U.S. Army would undergo a substantial reduction in force structure during the coming decade, amounting to some 30 percent of its regular combat forces, and two-thirds of the slowest mobilizing heavy units in the Army National Guard; in this connection, several major weapons procurement programs would be cancelled. In contrast to the prevailing trend in current discussions of Army transformation options, however, instead of making heavy units lighter, this plan principally calls for making light units heavier.

HEAVY FORCES. The Flexible Power Projection force structure would gradually reduce U.S. Army armored and mechanized forces from their current six divisions to four during the decade, finally resulting in a force of twelve heavy-brigade-equivalents. It would also eliminate one of the three existing armored cavalry regiments (ACRs) and, in keeping with these reductions, one of the Army's four corps headquarters, ultimately saving a total of $5.3 billion per year in operation and support (O&S) costs. However, these heavy forces would remain heavy: in spite of the difficulties they pose for rapid deployment and for maneuver in unfavorable terrain, no other type of force can provide the same concentrated firepower in a conventional land war with the technology that is currently available.[7]

This reduction in forces is justified by the strategy's emphasis on rapid response, realistic threat assessment, and multinational warfare. For the scenarios that are plausible in the coming decade, the total combat capability of the U.S. Army is less important than is the amount of capability that can be deployed reasonably quickly. With smaller heavy

---

7. Ideally, the remaining forces would be organized as independent brigades, with the divisional echelon serving only as a headquarters and intelligence organization to command combat forces assembled for particular operations (the logistics functions currently handled by the division would revert to being corps responsibilities). This would increase the flexibility of Army forces, and seems likely to produce O&M efficiencies as well, but no savings from such an organizational change are assumed here.

mechanized forces, the land power that the United States can project by sealift within the first one or two months of a crisis will be essentially unchanged, while in most cases the limited but significant expeditionary forces of major U.S. allies will provide additional capabilities sufficient, along with U.S. forces, for even the largest plausible regional wars. It is no longer necessary to have two mechanized brigades deployed in Korea, so one can be eliminated while preserving the U.S. tripwire on the peninsula, with the other reductions coming from forces based in the continental United States (CONUS) and Europe. Some of the equipment of the forces to be eliminated should be used to form additional pre-positioned sets for units that would deploy to Europe, Korea, or the Middle East in the event of a crisis ($900 million is allocated for this purpose in the plan), enhancing the Army's ability to deploy quickly.

The same argument applies in even greater measure to the Army National Guard (ARNG). Although their outright elimination would be a sound policy decision (though probably a prohibitively costly political one), this proposal calls merely for the reduction of each of the ARNG's eight combat and support divisions to an independent brigade. The existing National Guard divisions are maintained at such a low state of readiness that they are only suited to participate in a serious crisis or war lasting for years; this limited capability is entirely out of place in the current security environment. This reduction would leave the Guard with a total of twenty-one ground combat brigades, including its existing fifteen enhanced readiness brigades, which should be more than sufficient to enable ARNG forces to continue contributing usefully to peacekeeping operations and other low-threat missions such as domestic disaster relief. The force reduction would save $2 billion per year by the end of the decade.

LIGHT FORCES. Two principal changes would be made in the Army's four light divisions. First, two brigades of the 82nd Airborne Division (AD) and one brigade of the 101st Air Assault Division (AAD) would be eliminated, with the remaining components of these units being consolidated into a single division or, preferably, established as three independent brigades (one airborne and two airmobile). This change would acknowledge the fact that these forces provide potentially important niche capabilities that should be preserved, but that the need for such large forces to perform them is limited by the combat fragility of the 82nd AD and the expense and deployment difficulties posed by the bulky equipment of the 101st AAD. The change would save $1.2 billion per year.

Second, the two light infantry divisions, the 10th Mountain and 29th Infantry divisions, along with the two remaining armored cavalry regiments, would be reequipped over the next ten years to form the eight "medium-weight" brigades that the Army currently intends to build from some of its heavy forces.[8] The existing light divisions are not heavily armed enough even for most peacekeeping operations; for deployments to relatively low-risk environments such as Bosnia and Kosovo they are routinely augmented with tanks and infantry fighting vehicles from other units. Converting these forces into motorized or light mechanized units would make them well-suited for such missions, and also as screening forces for heavier units, protecting the bases of expeditionary air units, and other purposes that do not require main battle tanks and mechanized artillery. Smaller units of these brigades would be rapidly deployable by air, although their equipment would still be bulky enough to make deployment by sea preferable when possible. However, the Army's hope that such forces would be capable of conducting not only defensive but also offensive warfare against hostile heavy armor at an acceptable cost, thus enabling the entire Army to be standardized as a medium-weight force, does not appear realistic with the technology that will be available in the coming decade.

Converting light infantry forces into motorized brigades will require the acquisition of large numbers of light armored vehicles, and this proposal allocates for this purpose the $700 million per year by which the Army currently falls short of the acquisition funds necessary for equipping eight medium brigades. It also provides an additional $200 million in annual O&S funds for each of the brigades converting from light to medium weight.

This proposal would also downsize each of the Army's five Special Forces Groups (SFGs) by approximately half, at an estimated annual savings of $400 million, by eliminating their unconventional warfare (UW) mission, since organizing partisan forces to operate in the rear of an advancing enemy is now of little strategic relevance. Instead the SFGs would concentrate on their important role of foreign internal defense (FID) with allied countries, appropriately leaving the direct attack aspect of Army special operations to the Ranger Regiment.

PROCUREMENT. In connection with this reorganization, three major weapons procurement programs should be terminated or cancelled. First, the M1 Abrams main battle tank upgrade program should be halted (preserving the tank-producing industrial infrastructure for eventual future requirements), saving a total of $2.1 billion. Second, development of the escalatingly expensive Crusader self-propelled artillery (SPA) system, in-

---

8. This is, of course, logically equivalent to converting two mechanized divisions to medium-weight brigades and disbanding the two light infantry divisions, instead of the reverse.

tended to replace the M109 Paladin self-propelled (SP) howitzer, should be cancelled. Because the downsizing of Army heavy forces reduces the number of Crusaders that would be required for the active force, it will be far more efficient instead to acquire some 300 modern 155 mm/52 calibre SPA systems from abroad, such as the German PzH2000 or the British AS90, to replace M109s in the twelve armored and mechanized brigades; the new motorized units would employ lighter SP howitzer, mortar, and rocket systems for indirect fire. Net savings on SPA procurement would amount to some $7.2 billion by 2010.

The third program termination would be the RAH-66 Comanche scout/attack helicopter. The Comanche offers a number of attractive features, most notably including radar and acoustic low-observability, and far better air transportability than the AH-64 Apache. However, the expense of the program and its somewhat questionable mission—to fly scout missions for Apaches in environments too dangerous for other manned helicopters to venture into—justify its cancellation in light of the tight defense spending limits anticipated late in the decade. Instead of the Comanche, this option would purchase additional OH-58D Kiowa Warrior scout helicopters to replace aging OH-58As and Cs, and would replace the soon-to-retire AH-1 Cobra attack helicopters with AH-64s made redundant by the proposed force structure reductions, saving a total of some $8.1 billion by the end of the decade. (The additional savings resulting from a reduced need to upgrade the Apache force due to the smaller force structure can be devoted to modernizing and upgrading the Army's long-suffering utility and transport helicopter force.) In the slightly longer run, it appears inevitable that the RAH-66's primary mission of scouting for attack helicopters in high-threat environments will fall to tactical unmanned aerial vehicles (UAVs).[9]

SEA POWER: DOING MORE WITH LESS

A Flexible Power Projection force calls for considerable naval power, but recognizes that naval forces make their greatest strategic contribution by providing in-theater presence prior to or early in hostilities. Once substantial land-based air forces can be brought to bear, the striking power of aircraft carriers and ships equipped with land-attack cruise missiles remains useful but is relatively limited, particularly in sustained operations. Therefore, this proposal advocates a substantial reduction in the number of Navy carrier battlegroups (CVBGs), coupled with changes in

---

9.   On each of the U.S. armed services' experiences with UAVs to date, see Thomas P. Ehrhard, *Unmanned Aerial Vehicles in the United States Armed Services*, Ph.D. dissertation, Johns Hopkins University School of Advanced International Studies, 2000.

operational practices to enable the reduced fleet to provide proportionally greater forward presence than today's Navy, which maintains eleven operational CVBGs in order to keep an average of less than three (carrying some fifty attack aircraft apiece) on station at a time.

SURFACE FORCES AND NAVAL AVIATION. This proposal would gradually reduce the U.S. aircraft carrier fleet by three ships over the course of the decade, deactivating CV-64, CVN-65, and CV-67, along with two active and one reserve air wings.[10] Together with the scheduled replacement of CV-63 by CVN-76 in 2003, this would result in a force of nine *Nimitz*-class aircraft carriers and eight air wings. Twelve of the eighteen cruisers and destroyers associated with these CVBGs would also be deactivated, the others remaining in service for other missions, including air and theater ballistic missile defense and escort and fire support duty for amphibious forces. The six attack submarines usually detailed to support these CVBGs would remain in service. This force reduction would also permit a modest reduction in the size of the Navy's underway replenishment fleet, on the order of three of its thirty-four ships. Total annual O&S savings from the force reduction would amount to $2.9 billion by 2010.

Reducing the number of CVBGs would also reduce the need for ship procurement in the near term. Six of the last nine DDG-51 destroyers should be cancelled (saving $5.4 billion), along with one ADC-X dry cargo ship (saving $350 million). Most significantly, both of the Navy's planned next two carriers, the modified *Nimitz*-class CVN-77 and the further modified CVNX-78, would be cancelled, saving $8.8 billion (beyond the funds already spent to begin the construction of CVN-77). There are two principal reasons for this. First, with a fifty-year life span, the oldest remaining CVN, *Nimitz*, will not need to be replaced until 2025 (although the need for carriers with smaller crew complements will make producing new carriers attractive before that date). Second, the Navy's strategy of gradually transitioning from the *Nimitz* class to a revolutionary new carrier design (CVX-79) by building two non-standard and less evolved intermediate designs is not justified if the current rapid pace of carrier construction does not need to be maintained. Instead, there is plenty of time to follow the far better course of developing and standardizing a

---

10. The EA-6B Prowler electronic warfare aircraft of the three deactivated wings would be kept in service, expanding by some 20 percent the often hard-pressed expeditionary EA-6B force, which provides tactical jamming and air defense suppression support for Air Force and Marine aircraft. If it is necessary to maintain a conventionally-powered carrier in the fleet because homeporting a nuclear carrier (CVN) in Japan is unacceptable, CVN-69 (scheduled for a refueling-complex overhaul in 2001–03) would be retired instead when CVN-76 is commissioned, leaving CV-67 in service, potentially until as late as 2018.

truly revolutionary new carrier design before construction of the next carrier is required, well after 2010.

In contrast to some other shipbuilding programs, this proposal calls for only a slight reduction in the rate of acquisition for the new DD-21 "land attack destroyer," from three ships per year to 2.67 per year once full-scale production begins in 2005, saving $750 million every three years. In a striking contrast to current carrier construction plans, the DD-21s do promise revolutionary advances in propulsion and other systems that will make them the first U.S. major naval combatants to operate with crews dramatically smaller (and thus less expensive and presumably happier) than those of current vessels. The plan suggests no reduction in the Navy's force of twelve active-duty and seven reserve squadrons of land-based P-3 Orion maritime patrol aircraft.

Finally, with the reduction in the size of the carrier fleet, the unfortunate F/A-18E/F Super Hornet fighter/attack aircraft program should be cut back substantially.[11] This proposal would cancel procurement of 198 of the 548 Super Hornets the Navy plans to acquire, saving $14.1 billion, while it provides $2.7 billion in additional procurement funds to complete 54 of the rest as EA-18G "Growler" tactical jamming variant currently favored by the Navy as a successor for the EA-6B. One hundred and fifty of the cancelled Super Hornets are rendered redundant by the elimination of three air wings. The absence of the others can be comfortably offset by the drawdown reducing the age of the remaining Navy and Marine F/A-18C Hornet fleets, and through keeping the Navy's 120-strong force of invaluable F-14B/D "Bombcats" (with far better payload/range capabilities than the F/A-18E/F) in service until the arrival of the stealthy Joint Strike Fighter; $300 million is allocated to pay for the higher maintenance costs of continuing to operate the F-14s beyond their planned retirement later in the decade.

Surprisingly, eliminating three CVBGs need not reduce the current forward presence of U.S. Navy carriers. Each of three different options for changes in basing or operational practices could enable the smaller fleet to maintain as much—or more—carrier presence in the Mediterranean Sea and the Indian Ocean as the Navy currently achieves with twelve CVBGs. One possibility, which the Navy has pursued in the past and for

---

11. The Super Hornet, marketed as a modified version of the F/A-18C/D Hornet but in fact an almost entirely new system, has proved to be a competent aircraft, but offers only marginal performance improvements over the Hornet in key areas such as payload and range. The alternative of building an improved, multi-role development of the F-14 Tomcat would have resulted in a less expensive aircraft far more capable of performing all of the Super Hornet's missions.

which this proposal allocates $2 billion in initial funding and $100 million annually for O&S, would be to establish a carrier homeport in Italy or Spain. Although this would be more expensive than basing a carrier at Yokosuka (for which Japan pays much of the cost), it would provide a constant CVBG presence in the Mediterranean Sea, which currently requires more than five U.S.-based carriers to achieve. If this were not feasible, for example because the host nation might unacceptably restrict the activities of ships based there, similar efficiencies in on-station time could be achieved by restructuring carriers' deployment schedules, or by keeping the ships deployed for much longer periods and exchanging crews on station, as the Navy has recently done on a smaller scale with great success for some vessels of other types.[12] The latter option would be greatly facilitated by the establishment of a single-class carrier fleet, and if implemented for other forces could produce similar efficiencies throughout the fleet, greatly increasing the forward presence that is the primary justification for a large U.S. surface combat fleet.

Thus the only loss of capability that need follow from this contraction of the fleet would be a reduction in the maximum number of CVBGs that could be deployed in wartime. However, in a major conflict, two land-based fighter wings can provide more air power at far less cost than can three aircraft carriers. Moreover, in general they can deploy more quickly than can a carrier not already in the theater. Thus enhancements to the capabilities of Air Force and Marine air power should be able to compensate for most of the effects of losing several CVBGs. The one situation in which this would not be true is a major theater war in which regional bases are not available. However, as noted earlier, such a critical absence of bases seems quite unlikely except in certain scenarios involving a Chinese attack on Taiwan, and China has years of military modernization ahead of it before it would be able to mount a credible threat of successful invasion of that island.

SUBMARINES. Because the U.S. Navy's attack submarine (SSN) force provides a number of unique capabilities, not only for sea control but also for a variety of surveillance and other covert missions, the Flexible Power Projection proposal does not reduce the size of the force. It would slow the rate of *Virginia*-class SSN procurement from two boats per year to 1.5 per year between 2006 and 2010, resulting in twelve vessels being authorized in the coming decade instead of fifteen. To maintain the size of the

---

12. For details of these options, see Congressional Budget Office, "Improving the Efficiency of Forward Presence by Aircraft Carriers" (Washington, D.C.: CBO, August 1996); and J.D. Oliver, "Changing the Peacetime Deployment of Aircraft Carriers," research paper, U.S. Naval War College, March 1993.

SSN fleet, it would cancel the planned early retirement of a corresponding number of *Los Angeles*–class submarines, for an average annual net savings of $1.2 billion beginning in 2005. Moreover, two elements of this budget proposal would reduce the current overtasking of the attack submarine force. The first is the reduction in the number of carrier battlegroups, each of which normally has an escort of two SSNs assigned to it. The second is the conversion of four ballistic-missile submarines into Tomahawk land-attack cruise missile (TLAM) platforms, which would substantially reduce the need to keep SSNs deployed to areas such as the Persian Gulf in order to provide the ability to fire TLAMs at targets in the region on short notice.

The U.S. Navy now operates eighteen *Ohio*-class ballistic missile submarines (SSBNs), of which eight are armed with the Trident C-4 ballistic missile and ten carry the newer and larger Trident D-5. Current plans call for retiring the four oldest *Ohios* because the START II arms control treaty limits the United States to a force of fourteen SSBNs, and converting the other four C-4 boats to carry D-5 missiles. Considerable enthusiasm has developed both within and outside the Navy for a proposal to cancel the retirement of the first four vessels, and instead convert them into cruise missile–carrying submarines (SSGNs), each equipped with 154 conventionally-armed Tomahawk missiles, along with space in which to carry special forces SEAL units. Converting these submarines would not only avoid the waste of scrapping four very capable and expensive vessels long before their time, but would produce a set of stealthy, high-endurance ships, each capable of providing as much short-notice land attack firepower as five or more TLAM-equipped SSNs. A fleet of four *Ohio*-class SSGNs would be sufficient to keep one on station in the Middle East and one in the Far East at all times. However, after conversion to SSGNs, the submarines would still count against the fourteen-vessel SSBN limit in START II unless the treaty provision is renegotiated, which appears unlikely, or the conversion is made far more radical and expensive.

Therefore, this proposal offers a different recommendation: to retire the first four *Ohios* as scheduled, and convert the other four Trident C-4 submarines into SSGNs, at a modest cost of $725 million per submarine, including the price of the cruise missiles. This would leave the United States with a very robust force of ten SSBNs, each carrying twenty-four ballistic missiles with four or more warheads apiece, enough vessels to keep at least four on patrol at all times.[13] In addition to providing an

---

13. The remaining ten SSBNs could, if desired, carry between them the maximum number of warheads that START II allows the United States to deploy at sea, by modi-

SSGN capability likely to prove far more useful to U.S. security than would the four extra SSBNs during their lifetime, this plan would also permit the early termination of Trident D-5 missile production, saving some $4 billion between 2001 and 2005 (not included in the calculations of the total costs and savings from this proposal).

AMPHIBIOUS FORCES. The Flexible Power Projection proposal includes only a marginal reduction in the size of the U.S. Navy's amphibious forces. It accepts the Navy's planning principle that twelve amphibious ready groups (ARGs) are necessary in order to provide adequate forward presence of rapid response amphibious forces around the world, especially for missions such as short-notice noncombatant evacuation operations. In many cases, forward deployment of an ARG and its Marine ground and air forces to a region of potential crisis is far more useful than sending a CVBG because of the greater variety of capabilities embodied in the former.

However, the twelve-ARG planning requirement does not take into account the rapidly expanding amphibious capabilities of major U.S. maritime allies. This proposal would reduce the number of U.S. ARGs by one in 2003, to eleven, in recognition that the Anglo-Dutch Amphibious Force now possesses capabilities virtually equivalent to those of a U.S. ARG. In addition to this force, the cooperative development of expanded Spanish, French, and Italian amphibious capabilities, along with those emerging in Japan and Australia, will further increase the West's resources to perform such operations. Elimination of one U.S. ARG would permit the cancellation of the helicopter carrier (LHD-8) currently scheduled for construction in 2004–05, and of one *San Antonio*–class (LPD-17) dock landing ship, saving $2.1 billion in procurement, in addition to the $160 million per year saved by eliminating the ARG.

However, this proposal would not reduce the size of the U.S. Marine Corps, which already fits well into the model of small expeditionary land forces capable of rapidly responding to a wide variety of contingencies, and would preserve funding for both the advanced amphibious assault vehicle (AAAV) and V-22 Osprey tilt-rotor transport aircraft acquisition programs.

AIR POWER: A BETTER, MORE BALANCED DIET
Under the Flexible Power Projection proposal, the U.S. Air Force would become a slightly smaller but far more capable force, and would bear a greater responsibility than ever for projecting U.S. military power around

---

fying current plans to deploy only four Trident D-5 warheads per missile in order to comply with the treaty while operating fourteen submarines.

the world. Since the 1960s, revolutionary advances in munitions guidance, aircraft sensors, stealth and electronic warfare, avionics, flight simulators, and battle management, together with more evolutionary developments in airframe, engine, and other technologies, have brought modern air power to a point of maturity that is not yet reflected in the defense budget and force structure of the United States. With the arrival of the F-22 fighter, the modernization of older aircraft types so that all USAF fighters and bombers are capable of night and all-weather operations and of delivering a variety of guided weapons, and the appearance of new types of ordnance, the capabilities of U.S. conventional air power will continue to increase dramatically during the coming decade, both in absolute terms and relative to land and sea power.

Two general approaches are possible for reorienting U.S. defense investment toward a greater emphasis on airpower. One would be to focus on the ability of modern aircraft to project force on a global scale by shifting ever greater resources into weapons such as the B-2 Spirit stealth bomber that can fly from bases in the United States to strike at enemies anywhere in the world. Alongside B-2s and other long-range bombers, investment would focus on national ballistic missile and air defense, aircraft carriers, space weapons, and other systems that would contribute to the ability to project power from an impregnable U.S. citadel. Such an approach would look familiar to early U.S. airpower advocates such as Billy Mitchell or Alexander de Seversky, and would be well suited to an insular grand strategy that concentrates on direct defense of the U.S. homeland while retaining the ability to mount limited-intensity attacks against distant states in order to protect U.S. interests overseas.

The opposite course would be to focus on expeditionary air power capable of deploying rapidly to distant theaters, and then conducting sustained operations at a much higher level of intensity than is possible for aircraft based in the United States or aboard aircraft carriers. This approach would involve great emphasis on joint operations with land forces, close cooperation with allies, strategic airlift, tactical reconnaissance, and theater air and missile defense, all of which would be essential to assure the security of local bases and to take advantage of the force application capabilities of forward deployed air power.

Flexible Power Projection combines these two themes, but leans towards the expeditionary end of the spectrum. The assumption that the United States will remain actively engaged in a variety of military contingencies around the world, and must be prepared to help defend its allies, makes the insular approach to air power untenable. However, long-range capabilities remain important, both to provide immediate response capabilities and to deal with situations in which there are severe limits on U.S.

access to in-theater bases or the capability of the local base infrastructure to support major air operations. Fortunately, it is not necessary to neglect one approach entirely in order to embrace the other, for long-range aircraft have much to contribute to expeditionary air operations, while aerial refueling enables many modern "tactical" aircraft to operate from bases far from their targets when necessary.

FIGHTER, ATTACK, AND ESCORT AIRCRAFT. "Tactical" fighter and attack aircraft, and the defense suppression and electronic warfare aircraft that protect them, form the core of the Air Force's combat capabilities, although in many situations they are a less important element of air power than, say, transport or surveillance aircraft. However, air warfare experience in the 1990s indicated clearly that the U.S. Air Force has overinvested in fighters relative to many of the supporting systems that make their jobs possible, ranging from reconnaissance platforms to electronic jamming aircraft to the planning and intelligence resources necessary to run an air campaign. Because capability shortages in such rate-limiting areas can negate the utility of an abundance of fighters or bombers, this proposal calls for a limited but significant shift in resources into making key "high-demand, low-density" assets more dense, and places a higher priority on maximizing the capabilities and flexibility of combat aircraft than on increasing their numbers. Under this plan, Air Force fighter and attack aircraft numbers would decline from a nominal force of twenty fighter wing equivalents (FWEs) to eighteen.[14]

Although the U.S. Air Force has done a shockingly poor job of persuading the country that the F-22 Raptor program is worthwhile, this new and very expensive fighter does offer genuinely important advantages over the aircraft it is intended to replace, the F-15C Eagle.[15]

---

14.   The standard count of slightly more than twenty USAF FWEs (some thirteen active duty and seven reserve and Air National Guard) does not count an additional FWE of OA-10 forward air control aircraft (identical to the A-10 "Warthog" tank-buster, which does appear in the FWE calculations) or the Air National Guard's Air Defense Force, consisting of approximately 0.8 FWE of F-15s and F-16s. An FWE nominally represents seventy-two frontline aircraft, plus some twenty to forty additional aircraft for backup, training, testing, and attrition replacement.

15.   The majority of the USAF's public campaign for the F-22 has seemingly revolved around incessantly repeating the fact that F-15C is an aging aircraft inferior to the most modern Russian and European fighters, which has culminated in officially describing the new plane's mission as one of "dominating" its opponents, a vapid term that would be more at home in the world of professional wrestling than serious strategic debate. This ham-fisted approach has justifiably rung hollow to audiences aware of the severe weaknesses of potential adversary air forces, and has communicated neither the other factors that justify building the F-22 nor the true nature of the advantages the Raptor will offer over its predecessor.

Most obviously, the F-22 is stealthy, while the Eagle is decidedly not, enabling the Raptor to operate within range of advanced surface-to-air missiles, such as the Russian-made S-300 (SA-10) and S-400. It is also faster, and it has much greater range, partly because of its ability to cruise at supersonic speeds. This is not only a vital asset in certain scenarios such as a defense of Taiwan, but means that together with the F-22's advanced radar and datalinks, a small number of these aircraft will be able to provide more air superiority capability than a much larger force of F-15s. This in turn means that fewer aircraft need to be built, and that smaller numbers can be deployed, thus reducing demands on limited tanker support and potentially crowded bases. Moreover, the Raptor has a useful secondary role to perform as a stealthy, long-range strike aircraft, and although its payload is quite limited, new series of smaller precision-guided weapons that will appear later in the decade will greatly increase its value for attack missions. Because the F-22 is so much more capable than the F-15C, however, the number of aircraft to be procured should be reduced by one-third from the Air Force's current plans, to some 225, enough to equip two fighter wing equivalents (FWEs), which will save $11.1 billion by the end of the decade.[16]

Even more important than the F-22 is the Joint Strike Fighter (JSF) program, intended to produce the next-generation fighter-bomber for the Air Force, Navy, Marine Corps, and British Royal Navy, and scheduled to begin entering service with the Marines in 2008. If all goes well, the JSF will be a relatively inexpensive, yet stealthy and sophisticated replacement for the F-16, F/A-18C/D, A-10, AV-8B, and Sea Harrier and will be widely exported to major U.S. allies. Although the project has proceeded reasonably smoothly so far, there is good reason based on experience with other aircraft programs to anticipate that the current development and production schedule is overly ambitious. In order to avoid the expense of future delays, the Congressional Budget Office has proposed a preemptive slow-down of the JSF program by two years, which will also increase the opportunities to incorporate new technological developments into the plane. This proposal incorporates the CBO's suggestion, projected to save over $22 billion during the next ten years, mostly late in the decade.

Delaying the JSF will be hardest on its first planned recipient, the Marine Corps, which wisely declined to participate in the F/A-18E/F pro-

---

16. Two FWEs of F-22s could be organized into between six and ten squadrons, depending on unit size; with ten 15-plane squadrons, one could be assigned to each of the USAF's ten Air Expeditionary Forces.

gram in favor of waiting for an aircraft offering revolutionary advantages over its Hornets and Harriers. The blow would be softened slightly by the reduction in the number of carrier air wings, permitting retirement of older F/A-18Cs. However, some additional refurbishment of the Marines' approximately 275 AV-8B Harrier IIs might be required to keep them in service for two years longer than is now planned, for which this plan allocates $500 million. Adjusting to a delay in JSF deliveries will be much easier for the Navy and Air Force.

To compensate for reduced numbers of F-22s and slower arrival of the JSF, this proposal provides funding to increase the Air Force's fighter and attack capabilities by supplementing the acquisition of entirely new systems with purchases of new models of existing aircraft types, and additional improvements to and modifications of some of those already in service. This three-pronged approach to modernizing U.S. air power serves to hedge against possible failures in a small number of vital programs, and it capitalizes on much of the value that exists in older but still useful aircraft.

First, this plan allocates $4.6 billion to buy one FWE of 110 F-16C/D Block 60 aircraft, an extremely capable advanced variant of the F-16 multirole fighter developed for export, particularly to the United Arab Emirates. Equipped with a radically new radar, an improved engine, and additional fuel capacity, the F-16C-60 will not only be more capable than U.S. F-16s, but also a notably more effective air-superiority fighter than the F-15C. The combination of these aircraft and two wings of F-22s will ultimately provide the USAF with much more primary-role air combat capability than it currently derives from its four FWEs of F-15Cs (while the new aircraft would be capable of performing other missions as well); thus it will be appropriate to disband one F-15C wing late in the decade, saving $400 million in O&S costs per year.

Second, this proposal provides $2.6 billion to procure forty new F-15E Strike Eagles equipped for the suppression of enemy air defenses (SEAD) mission.[17] It also provides $600 million to install similar sensors, HARM (high-speed anti-radiation missile) capability, and conformal fuel tanks on forty existing two-seat F-15D Eagles that will no longer be required for the air superiority mission when that role is taken over by the F-22. During the Kosovo War, F-16CJ SEAD aircraft were in very short supply, limiting NATO operations against an enemy with a relatively an-

---

17. Although F-15Es are already capable of employing the HARM missile against air defense radars, they lack the HARM Targeting System installed on Block 50 F-16Cs to make SEAD their primary mission. However, a more sophisticated SEAD sensor system with a 360-degree field-of-view was tested on an F-15C in 1996.

tiquated air defense system. With two-person crews, better sensors, and much longer on-station times, a force of SEAD-optimized F-15Ds and F-15Es would substantially increase the Air Force's defense suppression capability, which has never entirely recovered from the retirement of the F-4G Wild Weasel force in the 1990s.

Finally, to augment Air Force long-range strike capabilities, this plan allocates $400 million to provide air-to-ground targeting pods and ordnance capabilities for eighty F-15Cs that will be made redundant by the arrival of the F-22, using them to replace older F-16s. Although it is not stealthy, the F-15's long range makes it well-suited for the attack mission, much as the Navy's F-14 Tomcat air-superiority fighters proved to perform brilliantly when they were turned to the air-to-ground role late in life. It provides a similar amount to procure targeting pods for A-10s and Block 30 F-16s that still lack the ability to perform attack missions at night or in bad weather. Together, these three initiatives will substantially enhance Air Force strike capabilities, permitting the elimination of one Air National Guard FWE equipped with older Block 25 F-16s, resulting in a savings of some $240 million per year.

Of course, strike aircraft are no more useful than the ordnance they deliver. In the wake of the war in Kosovo, when inventories of some stand-off weapons ran troublingly low, the Air Force has already shown renewed interest in acquiring expanded stocks of key weapons such as air-launched cruise missiles. An especially important trend in aerial weapons technology that must be actively supported, especially if the various U.S. air and aviation forces are going to shift increasingly to flying stealthy aircraft, is the development of smaller guided weapons. Programs such as the LOCAAS anti-armor weapon, and a family of small laser-guided and GPS-guided bombs in the 100kg class along the lines envisioned in the USAF's "small smart bomb" technology project, will enable attack aircraft to carry far more weapons than they do today. For stealthy fighters such as the F-22 and JSF that carry their ordnance internally, this will mean being able to apply force efficiently against targets more numerous than traditional "strategic" ones. On a more general level, this will dramatically increase the effective firepower that a given number of any type of aircraft can bring to bear, making it more important than ever to base air power force structure requirements not on numbers of platforms, but on what those platforms can do.

LONG-RANGE BOMBERS. Even in a force structure that focuses on expeditionary air power, long-range bombers have important roles to play. They provide a capability for immediate response against enemies in situations where no forward-deployed forces are initially available, whether due to geography, political limitations on preemptive deployment, or simple surprise. Like naval forces, bombers also provide a longer-term strike capability against enemies who are far from any available bases, and when equipped with anti-ship missiles they are powerful tools for sea control. Naval forces embody a greater capacity to communicate commitment by establishing regional presence prior to conflict; on the other hand, the bases of intercontinental bombers may be safer from attack than surface naval forces are, depending on the circumstances, and bombers will almost always be a more efficient means of conducting missions such as cruise missile attacks.[18]

However, when in-theater bases are available, the supposed advantages of inter-theater bombing capabilities evaporate. Although much was made of the successful use of the B-2 stealth bomber for intercontinental attacks on Serbia in 1999, much of its value in that conflict was due to the simple accident that no other U.S. aircraft had yet been equipped with the new JDAM GPS-guided bomb. Because of the thirty-odd-hour sortie lengths and extensive tanker support required to bomb Serbia from bases in Missouri, a handful of F-117s or a pair of F-15Es carrying JDAMs from bases in Western Europe could have achieved as much as each B-2, and could have done so less expensively. Thus, it will often be worthwhile to deploy bombers into the theater where they are needed, where their long range and large payloads will enable them to substitute for much larger numbers of smaller aircraft.

This proposal does not suggest acquiring additional B-2s or other bombers during the coming decade; the existing force of some two hundred bombers (roughly ninety B-52Hs, ninety B-1Bs, and eventually twenty-one B-2s) should suffice. Although the Air Force's intention of keeping a modernized B-52 force in service into the late 2030s, when some of its aircraft will be approaching eighty years of age, has aroused much skepticism, the aircraft in question actually have suffered relatively little wear and tear, thanks to having spent most of their early careers sitting quietly on nuclear alert. Therefore, calls for the urgent development of the next generation of bombers are premature, particularly in light of the questionable value of developing a hypersonic heavy bomber.

The one change that this proposal does favor for the bomber force is the conversion of twelve B-1Bs into tactical electronic jamming platforms, for which it allocates $500 million. The EA-6B Prowler force, which bears

---

18.   A B-52 bomber can carry twenty air-launched cruise missiles, roughly comparable to the capacity of a TLAM-equipped attack submarine. Not only is the bomber much less expensive, but it can launch another load of missiles within a few days at most, while a submarine or surface vessel must return to port to be rearmed. Even a converted Trident SSGN would carry fewer cruise missiles than a force of eight B-52s.

sole responsibility for U.S. tactical jamming since the Air Force's fa-
mously ill-considered retirement of the superior EF-111 Raven, was badly
overstretched by the demands of the war in Kosovo even though most
U.S. air operations over Iraq were suspended during the conflict. One
useful response to this problem, along with the Navy's likely plan to buy
an EA-18G variant of the Super Hornet, is equipping a small force of
heavy bombers to serve as powerful and long-endurance stand-off jamming platforms, while retaining most of their weapons-delivery capabilities. Although the Air Force is moving in the direction of converting a
handful of B-52s along these lines, a B-1B conversion offers greater advantages: the B-1's smaller radar cross-section and greater speed would
make an EB-1 more flexible than an EB-52, and sufficient jamming requirements exist to justify a larger force, assuming that the early aircraft
prove successful. Over the longer run, it seems likely that the jamming
mission will be taken over by unmanned platforms, or else by systems
carried aboard strike aircraft, thus eliminating the need for specialized
electronic jamming escorts.

COMMAND, CONTROL, COMMUNICATIONS, INTELLIGENCE, SURVEILLANCE,
AND RECONNAISSANCE (C3ISR). Along with SEAD and electronic warfare
aircraft, a variety of command, control, communications, intelligence,
surveillance and reconnaissance (C3ISR) capabilities have consistently
limited the U.S. ability to project power, most recently in Kosovo.[19] In
short, air power has now achieved a very high level of effectiveness
at killing targets it can locate and identify; it is finding the targets
that poses the greatest remaining problems. This proposal calls for a
number of investment increases in ISR resources; a larger shift in the
Air Force mindset that extends far beyond budget allocations, to embrace these missions as being truly central to its capabilities, is also
required.[20]

As a result of the first Quadrennial Defense Review, the longstanding
U.S. Army–USAF requirement for nineteen E-8 Joint STARS battlefield
surveillance aircraft was reduced to thirteen planes, in the expectation
that a NATO Joint STARS force akin to the NATO Airborne Early Warning (NAEW) force would purchase additional E-8s. When this did not occur, two additional Joint STARS aircraft were authorized, for an eventual

---

19. To this grotesque abbreviation U.S. military jargoneers typically add a fourth, redundant C for computers, even though the era when computers were an arcane and
specialized element of military operations is long past.

20. Much of the required philosophical change relates to personnel management issues in an organization where battle managers and intelligence officers lack the prestige of fighter and bomber aircrews.

total fleet of fifteen. In the meantime, the system has proved itself over Iraq and Kosovo, providing detailed information on the location and movement of ground forces that was invaluable in efforts to strike them effectively from the air. The Air Force is now moving to re-engine the aircraft to increase their endurance and, more importantly, the altitudes at which they can operate, a critical factor in enabling the surveillance systems to detect and track targets in mountainous terrain. Because of its emphasis on theater air attack, including strikes against enemy military forces in the field, this plan provides $900 million to purchase three additional E-8s, for a total inventory of eighteen. Over the longer term, the battlefield surveillance missions of Joint STARS will shift to space platforms or a combination of satellites and unmanned aerial vehicles (UAVs). The Discoverer II satellite program is an essential element in this transition, and must continue to be fully funded.

This proposal does not advocate expanding the E-3 AWACS fleet, because U.S. AWACS capabilities can be augmented by the substantial British, French, and NATO E-3 forces, and by other airborne early warning (AEW) aircraft operated by Japan, Australia, and other allies. However, it does allocate $750 million to develop and begin procuring a new generation of manned stand-off reconnaissance aircraft to supplement the RC-135 Rivet Joint and similar platforms. Such a system would be modular, permitting the same aircraft to perform a wide variety of missions by switching sensors, and would probably be based on a long-range business-jet airframe such as the C-37 Gulfstream V.

Most importantly, this plan shifts an additional $10 billion into UAV research and development, with emphasis on three categories of systems: small tactical scout UAVs for the Army (and potentially the Marines), to perform the dangerous primary mission now planned for the Comanche; a fast, stealthy tactical reconnaissance platform for the Air Force capable of performing missions in high-threat air defense environments; and an ultra-long-endurance, stealthy, high-altitude UAV capable of maintaining the uninterrupted surveillance of enemy surface forces over long periods that neither satellites nor existing aircraft can currently provide.[21] Together, these systems would dramatically enhance the ability of air and surface forces to strike mobile and camouflaged targets. The same platforms might have utility in more direct force application roles, but it is in

---

21.   Such an ultra-long-endurance UAV would presumably require a nuclear rather than a solar propulsion system in order to carry an effective payload. Although revealing such a program would elicit intense political opposition from critics who would never accept the fact it could be built and operated safely, it would comfortably reside in the depths of the black world, far from public scrutiny.

the area of intelligence collection that UAVs can remedy the most serious deficiencies in current capabilities.

Space platforms will of course remain central to U.S. reconnaissance capabilities, as well as military navigation and communications, leading to growing concern about the possibility that U.S. space systems will be attacked by enemies in future conflicts. This fear is well-founded, although the satellites themselves are likely to be less attractive targets than other elements of space operations systems, such as terrestrial command, control, and communications facilities. While it is tempting to respond to this danger by investing more heavily in developing space weapons capabilities, it will be far more effective to emphasize defensive measures that eliminate the worrisome vulnerabilities in the first place, for example by developing redundant non-space-based capabilities, and where possible by replacing small numbers of critical high-value satellites with decentralized networks of many smaller satellites.[22] However, because of the importance of space-based C3ISR systems, it behooves the United States to establish a robust system for maintaining surveillance of adversaries' satellites. Therefore, this proposal allocates $590 million to establish and operate a constellation of space-based sensors for this purpose.

AIRLIFT AND BASING. A robust and versatile set of airlift capabilities is critical to any effort to develop the ability to rapidly deploy and sustain ground forces in distant theaters of crisis or war. It is equally important for expeditionary air power. This proposal assumes that Air Mobility Command will continue on its current trajectory towards an expensive but worthwhile rehabilitation of the C-5 Galaxy heavy transport fleet.[23] Beyond this, it provides additional funding to acquire a force of commercial freighter aircraft for the Air National Guard, while canceling scheduled procurement of C-130J tactical transports through 2010.

---

22.   See David Ziegler, *Safe Heavens: Military Strategy and Space Sanctuary Thought* (Maxwell AFB, Ala.: Air University Press, 1998); William L. Spacy II, *Does the United States Need Space-Based Weapons?* (Maxwell AFB, Ala.: Air University Press, 1999); Karl Mueller, "The Phantom Menace: Assessing Threats to American Interests in Space," paper presented at the American Political Science Association Annual Meeting, Atlanta, Georgia, September 4, 1999.

23.   The C-5 fleet includes approximately 75 C-5As and 50 C-5Bs, both of which—especially the As—have been woefully trouble-prone throughout their careers. The C-5s require at least $40 million per aircraft to replace their engines and hydraulic systems and to upgrade their avionics, but it appears inevitable that this will eventually be funded. The alternative of replacing the C-5s with additional C-17s cannot duplicate the lift capacity of the huge Galaxies, and the advantages of replacing an older aircraft with a newer one are smaller than they appear at first glance: ironically, the enormous amount of time that the C-5s spend on the ground waiting for repairs has kept their airframes relatively young.

Although the Air Force has long hewed to the principle of operating only distinctively military transport aircraft, there is much to be gained by adding to these aircraft a number of transport aircraft only minimally modified from commercial freighters. (Although the Civil Reserve Air Fleet includes hundreds of commercial cargo aircraft that can be mobilized in a national emergency, their crews cannot be ordered to fly into hostile environments.) Such "commercial off-the-shelf" (COTS) aircraft are far more economical to operate than military transports. Although they have limitations, such as requiring specialized cargo-handling ground equipment for loading and unloading, and being unsuitable for carrying bulky outsize cargo, they have heavier payload capacities than comparable military transports, they can fly much longer missions without aerial refueling, and they cost less to purchase and operate.[24] Thus, adding COTS freighters to the military airlift fleet will increase its flexibility, which has declined as fewer C-17s have replaced larger numbers of C-141s, and will prolong the service lives of more expensive specialized military transports. This proposal allocates $4 billion to purchase forty 767–300-class freighters, and $350 million per year to operate them.

While the U.S. armed forces have a critical need for greater strategic airlift capacity, the Air Force does not yet require new C-130 Hercules tactical transport aircraft. Nevertheless, Congressional supporters of the aircraft have consistently pressed new C-130J transports on the Air Force, resulting in the premature retirement of older C-130 models long before their scheduled life spans have elapsed. This proposal would cancel further acquisition of transport variants of the C-130J through 2010, saving a total of $3.85 billion over ten years, with annual savings rising to some $650 million per year late in the decade.

AIR AND THEATER BALLISTIC MISSILE DEFENSE. Access to, and the security of, in-theater bases is central to any strategy that relies heavily on expeditionary air power. This involves protecting not only forward bases themselves, but also the logistical chains that connect them to home bases and, perhaps less obviously, protecting allied states lest their fears of attack cause them to refuse to allow U.S. forces to operate from their territory. Because of the currently limited ability of most potential U.S. enemies to strike targets far beyond their borders with conventional weapons, such security concerns have increasingly come to center on questions of defense against nuclear, biological, and chemical "weapons

---

24. For a detailed discussion of the relative merits of COTS and traditional military transports, see Christopher Bence, "Bedding Down with COTS," Master's thesis, School of Advanced Airpower Studies, June 1999.

of mass destruction" (WMD), and the ballistic missiles and other systems that might be used to deliver them.

Although popular concerns about the potential effects of non-nuclear WMD are often remarkably overblown,[25] biological or chemical attacks on U.S. bases could seriously if temporarily disrupt operations, while attacks on civilian targets could in some cases weaken host-nation support for the presence of U.S. forces. Therefore, effective theater ballistic missile defense (TBMD) is critical for the Flexible Power Projection Strategy, as is the perhaps less glamorous but no less important issue of defense against aircraft, UAVs, and land-attack cruise missiles. Although a substantial measure of protection for U.S. forces can be provided simply by configuring their organizations and command and control systems so they can operate coherently from dispersed locations, thus denying an enemy a small set of extremely valuable targets to attack, active defenses remain important.

However, in the post–Cold War missile defense frenzy, the United States is pursuing more expensive TBMD programs than it needs. In addition to the Air Force's AL-1 airborne laser system, designed to shoot down TBMs during their boost phase, at least six TBMD missile systems are now being developed. Among these, the Army's THAAD is the best target for cancellation, in spite of some recent successful tests. Unlike the point-defense Patriot PAC-3, the struggling but worthy MEADS, and the Navy Area program, THAAD will be useful only against ballistic missiles, not aircraft or cruise missiles, which will probably represent a far more serious threat a decade from now than they do today. Alongside the other upper-tier TBMD programs that will offer similar capabilities, the U.S.-Israeli Arrow and the Navy Theater Wide system, THAAD does not appear essential, and its cancellation will save more than $5 billion over the course of the decade, while leaving the United States with a very robust set of systems to defend against theater missile attacks.

Budgetary Implications

This proposal for restructuring the armed forces of the United States based on a strategy of Flexible Power Projection would reduce anticipated defense expenditures by $25 billion in 2010, and a total of some $138 billion over the coming decade. It would thus maintain defense spending at 2000 levels for the next ten years, assuming that another $10

---

25. See Mueller and Mueller, "The Methodology of Mass Destruction;" pp. 163–169.

billion can be saved annually by 2010 through the sorts of defense infrastructure reforms that Cindy Williams describes in Chapter 3.

The budget cuts would not fall equally on each of the armed services. Of the net $25 billion cut from the baseline FY2010 budget, 43 percent ($10.8 billion) would come from Army force structure and acquisition programs (including THAAD). Navy forces and programs, excluding the Joint Strike Fighter, would account for some 29 percent of the cuts ($7.2 billion), while the Air Force would provide the remaining 27 percent ($6.8 billion, including the other services' shares of the JSF). The Marine Corps emerges relatively unscathed, except as the most anxious member of the JSF team. Distribution of the net budget reductions would vary over the decade, reflecting the large reductions in shipbuilding programs early in the decade, and the acquisition schedules for the F/A-18E/F, F-22, and JSF. Between 2001 and 2010, the Army would suffer approximately 53 percent of the cuts, the Navy (excluding JSF) 36 percent, and the Air Force and JSF 11 percent.

Naturally, the budget cuts could be less extreme if greater savings could be realized from other sources. For example, if spending reductions in defensewide programs, military infrastructure, and strategic nuclear forces and defenses amounted to an extra $5 billion per year by 2010, it would provide sufficient funds to restore the following useful though noncritical items to the services' budgets: two heavy armored cavalry regiments, one airborne brigade, the RAH-66 Comanche program, the Navy's reserve carrier air wing and 50 Super Hornets for it,[26] full production of DD-21 destroyers, the twelfth ARG plus two guided missile destroyers to escort it, and 56 F-22s to equip more than half a fighter wing.

Strategic Consequences

More important than the money that this proposal would save, however, are its strategic effects. The changes described here would provide the United States with a modernized and highly flexible military force capable of responding rapidly to a wide variety of contingencies around the world, even on very short notice. By exploiting the rapidly increasing capabilities of air power to substitute *in part* for other, less flexible types of military power, this approach generates substantially more useful combat

---

26. The idea of maintaining more Navy air wings than are always required for a carrier force that often has one ship laid up for overhaul has considerable merit if naval aviation becomes flexible enough to operate from bases ashore when appropriate. See Stephen P. Luxion, "From the Beach," *Armed Forces Journal International*, September 1999, pp. 85–88.

capability from a constant defense budget than would a business-as-usual continuation of the current U.S. defense establishment through the next decade.

The air power–heavy Flexible Power Projection force provides sufficient combat capability to deal with two realistically-sized regional conflicts or, far less probably, one truly massive theater war, realistically assuming some force contribution from allied states. It is also an agile force well suited to responding to the plethora of smaller-scale contingencies in which the United States is likely to become involved during the next decade.

As is true of the U.S. armed forces today, much of this force's flexibility is due to its diversity. The combination of heavy mechanized and medium-weight motorized Army brigades, along with Marine Corps forces, provides capabilities appropriate to tasks ranging from intense conventional warfare to air base defense and peacekeeping missions. A smaller but more efficiently deployed Navy provides critical forward presence where preemptive deployments ashore are not possible, or where sea power is needed to establish freedom of navigation or to interpose itself in the way of amphibious invasions. Together with pre-deployed forces, U.S.-based long-range air power provides immediate response capabilities in the first hours or days of a conflict, while a richly varied combat air force, with enhanced intelligence, surveillance, reconnaissance, and airlift support, has the ability to bring both more intense and more precise force to bear against adversaries.

Inevitably, however, there are trade-offs. Some of these can be eliminated through innovation, such as altering naval deployments or operational practices to produce more forward presence with a smaller force, or using air power to provide heavy firepower for smaller contingents of ground forces. Others cannot be avoided, and must be recognized by those who advocate the sorts of reforms proposed here.

Perhaps the most significant sacrifice this force structure involves is the major reduction in slow-mobilizing reserves in favor of rapidly deployable forces. Although the proposed cuts in the total size of the active-duty Army, the National Guard, and the surface Navy would have little impact on the amount of force the United States could project in the first weeks and months of a conflict, they would substantially reduce U.S. combat capabilities in a large war that lasted several years. Those who do not consider such a conflict extremely unlikely in the next decade will find such a drawdown of delayed response forces unacceptable, particularly if they believe that the United States needs to be able to fight such a prolonged major war alone.

Another significant trade-off follows from the assumption that the nature of future conflicts will vary unpredictably, although this does not represent a departure from current U.S. policy. A shift toward demanding multi-role capabilities from both equipment and personnel must have costs in capabilities for performing single missions, particularly for air power in all the services. The benefits of building no more single-role air superiority fighters, for example, appear to be worth this price, but planners who were certain of what the next war would look like would prefer different choices with respect to the specialization-flexibility trade-off.

Designing forces in order to maximize their ability to mesh efficiently with allied military capabilities also involves risks, for the resulting structure may not be well balanced if the United States has to fight alone. There is every reason to anticipate that future wars will be fought alongside allies, while retaining the ability to manage without them, but less ambitious strategists might prefer a more conservative set of assumptions about the reliability and utility of U.S. allies, even if it is less likely.

Finally, the procurement changes in the Flexible Power Projection proposal would involve significant costs for some sectors of the U.S. defense industrial base. Although most aerospace manufacturers would find only limited grounds for complaint here, the shipbuilding cuts in this proposal are profound in the short term, including the cancellation of two aircraft carriers, six destroyers, and two major amphibious ships during the next five years. Although the cuts later in the decade are less drastic, this would nevertheless raise significant concerns about preserving U.S. military shipbuilding capacity, which might require short-term governmental support in order to preserve capacity for future requirements (as with cancellation of the M1 tank upgrade program). However, some contraction of this industrial sector appears inevitable, as the Navy's ability to do more with fewer ships increases.

THE SCIENCE OF STRATEGY

There is another dimension to reorienting U.S. military capabilities toward greater reliance on air power that this essay has not yet addressed, because it is not primarily a matter of either budget or force structure. The more unpredictable the strategic environment, and the greater the flexibility of the forces the United States develops to deal with it, the more important it is that these capabilities be wielded by highly skilled and well-educated strategists, and not merely by brilliant tacticians.[27] This calls for an intense commitment by the U.S. armed services to education as well as training, yet it continues to be true that pursuing advanced education is more likely to threaten than benefit the careers of promising officers, and significant components of the U.S. professional military education system remain intellectually moribund. The fact that expertise about most of the regions in which the United States has fought recent wars has been quite scarce within the military is just one notable indication of this problem.

With this in mind, this proposal designates the final $1 billion remaining from the program cuts outlined above as a token investment increase in military education, ranging from strengthening intermediate and senior service schools to expanding Foreign Area Officer programs. However, the need for greater funding for the education of strategists is not as critical as is the requirement that the U.S. armed forces fully embrace the principle that developing smarter warriors is far more important than developing smarter weapons for them to wield.

FLEXIBLE FORCE PROJECTION BEYOND 2010

Continuing to hold the defense budget constant past 2010 is likely to become increasingly challenging due to a large number of procurement programs that cannot easily be deferred. The F-22, JSF, and V-22 aircraft will be in full-scale production in the early 2010s, along with DD-21 land-attack destroyers and *Virginia*-class attack submarines. The Air Force also plans to begin replacing its large force of KC-135 tanker aircraft; the Army will be ready to procure its projected family of light but powerful Future Combat Vehicles; and the Navy will need to buy replacements for the *Tarawa*-class amphibious assault ships, to name only those programs that are most visible ten years in advance. Waiting in the wings will be other programs including replacements for the *Nimitz*-class aircraft carriers, the F-15E, and a variety of naval aircraft, along with the systems that will emerge from current research in technologies such as UAVs and transatmospheric "spaceplanes." Rising acquisition costs may

---

27. On this point, see Bernard Brodie, "Strategy as a Science," *World Politics*, Vol. 1, No. 4 (July 1949), pp. 467–488. Brodie's assessment from fifty years ago remains apt today: "The strategist of the American armed forces has often in the past stressed the difficulty of his problems as compared with his opposite number of European military establishments. The latter has always been much less in doubt concerning the identity of the probable adversary and the probable theaters of operations. . . . It is all the more necessary, therefore, that we develop a conceptual framework adequate not only as a base of departure for specific strategic plans, but also as a means of weighing one plan against another" (pp. 474–475).

not be fully offset by trends such as radically smaller crews on naval combatants and the development of reliable technologies for unmanned transport aircraft.

Even if the U.S. security environment of the 2010s is quite similar to the one that exists today, technological changes may transform what an optimal flexible power projection force should look like. In addition to being shaped by continuing developments in precision weapons, stealth and electronic warfare, and battle management, the menu of military power could well be radically altered by major advances in areas such as unmanned aerial and undersea vehicles, directed energy weapons, and non-lethal weapons.

However, the possibility of international security stasis seems less probable than that international political developments may produce major strategic changes for the United States. One of the trends at least reasonably predictable, for example, is that significant new allied military capabilities are likely to appear after 2010, such as the planned British large-deck aircraft carriers. Far more significant and yet more difficult to anticipate, however, will be larger trends in the national growth rates, defense spending, and alignments of important states currently among the ranks of both allies and potential adversaries of the United States. Even if the world is not transformed by a single event as earthshaking as the democratization of China or the dissolution of the Russian Federation, the world of the 2010s may be a considerably more—or substantially less—dangerous place for the United States. Either of these possibilities would have a dramatic effect on the size of the armed forces required to protect U.S. security and overseas interests; continued constant defense spending might become simple to maintain, or might instead prove hopelessly out of reach.

Thus, we may now be entering a decade of decision: a strategic interregnum in which the forces and weapons the United States develops will need to be suitable for a demanding set of short-term security needs, while also providing a sound foundation on which to build even more potent but potentially very different military forces for subsequent decades. By emphasizing both flexible and diverse military capabilities, the set of proposals presented here offers both.

Chapter 9

Conclusion and Recommendations

Cindy Williams

The six-year budget plans that the military services submitted to the Secretary of Defense in the spring of 2000 call for taxpayers to spend another $30 billion on defense each year beginning in 2002. Service leaders argue that the ten percent increase over planned spending is urgently needed to cover critical shortfalls and ensure the military's readiness to deploy quickly and to fight and win wars. But adding money will perpetuate a more fundamental problem: today's military is not shaped properly to meet the challenges and capitalize on the opportunities of the new century.

Adding another $30 billion to annual military budgets would restore military spending to about 98 percent of the average Cold War level—this despite the fact that the United States is the world's only surviving superpower, that the Cold War enemy no longer exists, and that no new enemy has emerged to take its place. Even without additional money, the United States spends more on its military than all of the next six countries—Russia, France, Japan, China, the United Kingdom, and Germany—combined.

Part of what drove the services' request for another ten percent increase was election-year politics. The presidential candidates were formulating positions and offering promises; why not lock in some promises for the military? Another driving factor was the prospect of huge federal budgetary surpluses. But to some extent the services' requests reflect the very real budgetary pressure under which the military is working.

During the coming decade, the Defense Department plans to start producing major new weapons that have been in development for years: Comanche and Crusader, DD-21, F-22, Joint Strike Fighter, theater and national missile defenses. Independent cost analysts foresee large cost overruns on all these systems. In addition, the military raises in the department's budget plans as of this writing are lower than those stipulated by lawmakers for 2003 to 2006. The Pentagon has admitted defeat in the war against rising operation and maintenance costs, but its budget plans still reflect the presumption that those costs are under control. Moreover, the department assumes it will be able to cut back substantially on spending for research and development at a time when many observers believe more research is needed, not less, to exploit the opportunities created by a new world of innovative technologies.

The truth is that as operating expenses and weapons costs rise over the next decade, the nation will need to spend tens of billions of dollars more a year than it does now just to keep today's forces at current readiness levels and to carry out the Defense Department's plans for modernizing equipment. Adding on the services' wish lists would raise the price even higher.

In this chapter, I review briefly the approaches described in Chapters 3 through 5 that others have offered to hold budgets in check, and the reasons why those approaches will not come close to solving the Pentagon's money problems. Then I compare the strategic choices that Owen Cote, James Quinlivan, and Karl Mueller offer in Chapters 6 though 8, and the resulting military force structures and modernization plans. I end with a set of recommendations for decisionmakers.

There Is No Miracle Cure

The Defense Department hoped for years to offset growing budgetary pressures by instituting reforms of its processes for material acquisition and seeking efficiencies in infrastructure activities. But the savings the Pentagon currently projects from those efforts fall far short of the amounts that would be needed to hold budgets at today's levels, and may not be realized in any event. The department could save money through more extensive infrastructure reform. Consolidating and collocating laboratories, test facilities, classroom training, and other functions across services and components; eliminating the military's medical school and the elementary schools that are located on bases in the heart of solid public school districts; and substituting cash payments or other benefits for some of the compensation currently provided in kind to military families and retirees could save more than $9 billion a year. Combined with the $6.5 billion the Pentagon hopes to save annually by closing additional bases and allowing the private sector to compete for work currently handled by government employees, those savings would be enough to pay for all three expensive new tactical aircraft that the military plans to purchase in the coming decades. But overcoming the political barriers that block such changes will not be easy. Even if the nation adopts every one of them and they all bear fruit, the military will still not be able to dodge the coming budget crunch.

During the 1990s, formal arms control agreements and unilateral measures to reduce nuclear forces and lower their alert levels have saved the country significant sums. U.S. budgets for strategic offensive forces, nuclear weapons activities in the Department of Energy, and nuclear threat reduction in the former Soviet Union fell from about $60 billion in 1990 to $35 billion in 2000, freeing resources for other purposes. But further reductions in nuclear forces are unlikely to produce large additional savings. Depending upon the nature of future arms control agreements, the expense of new verification measures might offset whatever savings are possible.

Another avenue often put forward as a source of long-term savings for the U.S. military is to convince the nation's allies to pick up a greater share of the burden of international security and common defense. Some burden-sharing measures would result in immediate savings. For example, by pulling U.S. forces out of South Korea and Europe and disbanding those units, the United States could reduce troop levels by more than 10 percent and save $4 billion or more a year, enough to pay most of the incremental costs of the transformation that the Army's chief of staff has outlined for his service. A substantially more ambitious draw-down could save enough to hold the military budget at today's level for a decade or more, and might even allow the United States to restore budgets to the post–Cold War low point that they reached in 1998. But such a strategy seems unlikely in today's political climate.

Some policymakers hope to convince the NATO allies to spend more on defense, easing the military burden on the United States. But plans for greater military spending are sure to run into problems as Europe confronts its own economic concerns. It will take more than a decade for recently announced European investments in technology to bear fruit that might offset some U.S. spending in that area. Thus, greater allied burden-sharing is also not a cure-all for the military's budget problems.

Holding the Line on Defense Spending

Given that the medicines usually prescribed are not strong enough to cure the Pentagon's budget ills, is there an alternative to big increases in defense spending for as far as the eye can see? The answer lies in a fundamental reshaping of the nation's conventional forces. Such reshaping, in accord with a military strategy matched to the country's present and future security needs and interests, could put the armed forces into far better position to face the future at today's level of spending.

After the Cold War ended, the military made significant reductions in the major elements of conventional force structure. But the remaining forces look very much like a shrunken version of their Cold War predecessors. The Defense Department argues that today's conventional force posture and modernization program are appropriate to the current national security strategy. But a look at the history shows that the opposite is true: the current national security strategy was fashioned largely as a rationale for limiting the budget reductions and force structure cutbacks that military leaders during the Bush administration anticipated would take place during the 1990s. The current strategy is not much more than a justification for preserving Cold War forces; a new strategy based more closely on the nation's current and future security needs and interests is in order.

In matters that involve the military, the first priority of current strategy is to be able to fight and win in two major theater wars that occur at nearly the same time. But current forces are significantly larger than the ones the military would need to support today's economically strong and militarily capable South Korea against the weakened North, and at the same time to fight today's Iraq, weakened as it is by the Gulf War, daily no-fly patrols, and a decade of economic sanctions. Moreover, as argued by the recent bipartisan Commission on National Security Strategy/21st Century, reliance on the "two-war" yardstick is not producing the capabilities needed for the challenges that the military faces today and will face increasingly in the future. Clinging to the two-war standard no longer makes sense.

Another big driver of force structure is the military's involvement in activities to "shape the international environment." Much of what "shaping" entails would seem to be either old-fashioned diplomacy or a military substitute for it. As such, it seems fair to ask why the burden of it must fall so heavily on the military. Additional spending for the State Department's conduct of diplomacy, for support of international institutions, and for aid to foreign countries might allow the nation to shape the international environment at lower expense and less risk.

A telling indicator of the nation's failure to embrace fundamental change in the armed forces has been the continued near-constant apportionment of funding across the services. For decades during the Cold War, the three military departments each received virtually an unchanging share of the defense budget. It stands to reason that the end of the Cold War and a world of new technology might have sparked a change in the relative utility of or preferences for airplanes, tanks, rockets, ships, or helicopters. Yet the past decade has seen no real change in the budget share each service holds onto each year. Even within the services, shares continue to be apportioned in a nearly constant pattern across key communities. No wonder the U.S. military today looks like a smaller version of its former self.

The nation could fix the military's budget squeeze for at least a decade by perpetuating the pattern of constant shares, reducing conventional force structure across the board by 15 to 20 percent from today's levels and trimming procurement plans to match. The resulting force of eight active-duty Army divisions, ten aircraft carrier battle groups, about 250 Navy ships, and 16 tactical fighter wings would be more than adequate to handle a single major theater war of the exaggerated size that currently figures in Pentagon plans, and even, perhaps, two theater wars against the forces of any enemy that that actually exists today. The newly reduced forces would be large enough to handle a significant level of "shaping" activities at the same time, although the pace of such day-to-day commitments would likely have to be reduced from today's ambitious level. By lowering the priority (or relaxing the timeframe) for fighting a second major theater war against the unrealistic threat that the Pentagon envisions, the nation would also be assured that the military could continue to handle multiple smaller-scale contingencies at least as well as it does today—operations that run the gamut from humanitarian relief and interventions to peace operations. Moreover, by shearing procurement programs to be consistent with the force structure cuts, the remaining forces would be equipped just as the Defense Department currently desires.

Finding the Right Strategy for the New Century

Dropping the two-war standard in favor of more realistic priorities and threats would allow the military to get by with an affordable smaller version of its current force. But keeping forces designed for the Cold War and continuing with weapons programs that got started well before the Warsaw Pact collapsed leaves other problems unaddressed. For one thing, forces are not properly configured for the jobs they are now asked to do. The Army's problems in deploying attack helicopters to the war with Yugoslavia, and its complaints that it takes months to restore the readiness of forces engaged in peace operations, are symptomatic of a wider ill: the military has not restructured to handle the real missions it faces in the post–Cold War era and beyond. Second, forces that no longer make sense and procurements that are not needed drain resources from those that the nation cannot do without. Perhaps most important, retaining Cold War force structure and programs—even at reduced levels—fosters a business-as-usual attitude and stifles desperately needed innovation in every aspect of military affairs, from personnel management to organization to technologies and systems.

STRATEGIES AND FORCES FOR THE FUTURE

In Chapters 6 through 8, Owen Cote, James Quinlivan, and Karl Mueller explore military strategies and forces that look to the future instead of the past. In a break with Pentagon tradition, each author offers a military strategy, a force structure, and a modernization program that recognizes and plays to the unique strengths of one of the military departments: Cote for the Navy, Quinlivan for the Army, and Mueller for the Air Force. Each author recommends eliminating forces and cutting back projects that are not useful for the future he expects. By doing so, each author fashions a defense agenda that holds defense budgets in check at today's level, while opening the door to substantial innovation in military organization, operational concepts, and equipment.

Owen Cote describes a future world in which major theater wars are most likely to be fought along the Mediterranean-Indo-Pacific littoral, where the United States will not be able to count on access to a developed local base structure. To position the military for rapid power projection in the absence of such a base structure, he proposes a maritime-centered strategy. His recommended force structure emphasizes maritime forces, a longer-legged Air Force, and a smaller Army, better equipped for rapid deployment. His plan includes several important innovations that would increase the ability of U.S. forces to project power in an access-constrained security environment: reorganizing and re-equipping several Army light infantry brigades and armored cavalry regiments to deploy more easily, to be more useful in peacekeeping, and to provide more combat power in major wars; making the Army's planned medium-weight brigades fully air-mobile by purchasing a new type of airlift aircraft and establishing new procedures to pre-position material at sea; providing the Army and Marine Corps with a new type of attack aircraft that could deploy to a conflict on its own without external airlift, evade radar coverage, and conduct reconnaissance and attack missions; reducing the Air Force's dependence on local bases by providing it with fighter planes that can take off and land under primitive conditions; and substantially increasing naval firepower by converting eight ballistic-missile-carrying submarines to fire conventional precision weapons.

James Quinlivan portrays a world in which the United States continues to be drawn into peacekeeping and similar missions that last for decades, but may also face the challenge not only of defending allies against the threat of invasion but of having to counter-attack to expel adversaries from defended positions and occupy their countries. He recommends re-shaping the Army for better balance between the demands of major wars and the long-term commitment of forces to peacekeeping and similar missions. He also recommends a somewhat smaller Navy, a smaller Marine Corps that focuses more on expeditionary warfare using innovative tactics, and less on high-intensity land combat at the division level, and a somewhat smaller Air Force that emphasizes multipurpose tactical air-planes. Quinlivan proposes several key innovations in organization, equipment, and personnel management: changing the structure of Army divisions to capitalize on information technologies; converting and equipping Army National Guard brigades to form a rotation base for peacekeeping; enhancing Guard readiness and training; developing an advanced new army combat vehicle; modifying equipment in all the ser-vices to make it more transportable by air; and supplementing military airlift crews during wartime with civilians employed during peacetime by U.S. airlines.

Karl Mueller foresees a world that remains relatively safe for the United States, but in which unpredictable events require the military to project power rapidly in support of allies, and often with their assistance. Because he sees the location and nature of future threats as inherently un-predictable, he prefers the versatility that airpower provides. His plan trims the Air Force modestly but equips it with better munitions, com-mand and control, air-defense suppression systems, and space-based sen-sors. It substantially reduces the size of the Army, especially the divi-sional brigades of the National Guard. It reduces the number of carrier battle groups in the Navy but compensates with new operational prac-tices, and leaves the Marine Corps largely as it is today. Mueller's plan supports key innovations in command and control, reconnaissance from manned and unmanned platforms, electronic jamming, suppression of enemy air defenses, and strategic transport.

Table 9.1 compares the environments, strategies, forces, capabilities, and costs of each author's alternative with the world and the military that the Pentagon envisions, and with the one that might result if the ser-vices continue to share equally in the cuts required to hold budgets at to-day's levels.

Compared with the current plan, all three strategic alternatives pro-posed here result in smaller forces and less expensive modernization plans. But in each case, the resulting forces are better suited to the de-mands of the future than those under the current plan. In all three cases, the resulting forces would be highly capable in high-intensity warfare,

Table 9.1. Comparison of Three Alternatives with Current Plan and Constant Shares.

	Current Plan	Constant Shares[a]	Maritime Strategy	Flexible Ground Forces	Flexible Power Projection
Strategic Environment	Spectrum of threats and concerns; hierarchy of interests: vital, important, humanitarian; formal alliances important.	Not addressed	No need for major continental commitment; constrained access to bases ashore in key regions; less formal alliance relationships.	No single defining threat; sustained SSCs; alliances key to global security.	Relatively safe for U.S., but unpredictable contingencies require rapid response; continued importance of formal alliances.
Military Strategy	Engagement; shape, respond, prepare; overmatch in 2 MTWs as first priority; SSCs as second.[b]	Not addressed; affordable force structure determines strategy.	Rapid power projection along Mediterranean-Indo-Pacific arc.	Continued engagement in NATO; deterring presence in Korea, Gulf as long as necessary; balance for wars and SSCs.	Widespread and varied engagement, usually with or in support of allies.
Army Ground Combat Brigades[c]					
Active Component	32	26	26	29	23
Guard ESBs	15	15	15	15	15
Guard Div. Brigades	18	14	0	6	7

Table 9.1. Comparison of Three Alternatives with Current Plan and Constant Shares (continued).

Navy/Marine Corps[d]					
Ships	306	255	306	285	288
Carriers	12	10	11[e]	10	9
Trident SSBNs	14	14	10	10	10
Trident SSGNs	0	0	8	0	4
Amphib. Ready Groups	12	10	12	10	11
MEFs	3	2.5	3	2	3
Reserve USMC Div's.	1	1	1	1	1
Air Force					
Active Tactical Wings	13	11	12	11	12
Reserve Tactical Wings	7	5	5	4	6
Bombers	187	147	187	187	187
MTW and SSC Capabilities	Overmatch in 2 MTWs; MTWs crowd out SSCs; military accepts risk for second MTW caused by SSCs and other shaping.	Overmatch in 1 MTW; multiple SSCs; sufficiency in second MTW against realistic threat.	Overmatch in 1 MTW; multiple SSCs; sufficiency in second MTW against realistic threat.	Overmatch in 1 MTW; better balance of ground capabilities for MTWs and sustained SSCs; sufficiency in second MTW.	Sufficiency in 2 wars against realistic regional threats, usually with allies; plus multiple SSCs, often with short warning.
Cost (2000 $ billions)[f]	310–320	285	285	285	285

a Assumes $4 billion across-the-board reduction in defense-wide activities and 15–20 percent reductions in minor procurement programs.
b MTW is major theater war; SSC is smaller-scale contingency.
c Enhanced Separate Brigades; Divisional Brigades.
d SSBNS are submarines that carry nuclear ballistic missiles; SSGNs are submarines that carry precision conventional weapons; MEFs are Marine Expeditionary Forces.
e Assumes second overseas home port; otherwise 12.
f Lower estimate for current plan and other four estimates assume $10 billion in infrastructure savings.

even against a threat sized as unrealistically as the Pentagon currently envisions for a major theater war. All three would be more capable than today's forces of balancing the demands of major war and smaller-scale contingencies. All three would be more flexible and mobile, capable of projecting power more quickly than under today's plan.

With the smaller navies that Quinlivan and Mueller plan and the smaller Army proposed by Cote, the military might be less able than under today's plan to handle all of the shaping missions that the nation expects of it today. However, the State Department or other civilian organizations can, more effectively and at considerably lower cost, handle many of the shaping commitments currently taken on by the military: nation-building, spreading democratic values, providing a U.S. presence, conducting diplomacy.

Thus, all three strategic alternatives compare favorably to the current plan. Compared with holding service budget shares constant and trimming all service forces and modernization programs to meet budget targets in a balanced way, the three strategic alternatives seem vastly superior. Unlike the constant-shares plan, the strategic alternatives reshape the forces, eliminating elements that are not relevant to the world they envision and that may not be useful in any future the military really faces. All of them support a greater degree of innovation in the way the military is organized, staffed, and equipped than the constant-shares plan. All of them look to the future instead of hanging on to the structure and programs of the Cold War.

Of course, the services could make room for innovation even if their budgets are allocated in constant shares. They have done this to some degree over the past decade. But the continued mindless allocation of resources based on the Cold War pattern generally fosters a business-as-usual attitude that stifles innovative thinking. Changing the pattern of incentives and allowing the services to vie for budget dollars could open the door to creative new solutions to military problems, as Chapters 6 through 8 demonstrate.

COMPARING THE THREE FORCE STRUCTURES

Cote, Quinlivan, and Mueller all recommend a smaller force structure than the military maintains today. As expected, however, the reductions they recommend are not identical across the services. Of the three, Cote is the staunchest protector of his preferred service, recommending very little change in Navy or Marine Corps force structure or procurement plans. Rather, he recommends substantial reductions of Army forces, eliminating entirely the eight combat divisions of the National Guard, and wholesale cancellation of several Army and Air Force systems. In contrast,

Quinlivan recommends significant reduction and reshaping in all three services, including the Army, and concentrates most of his ideas for innovation in that service as well. Mueller recommends a small reduction in tactical wings of the Air Force and cutbacks in the Air Force's beloved F-22 fighter plane, but concentrates his proposed reductions in the other services. Yet considering that the three authors start with quite disparate views of the world, divergent military strategies, and strikingly different service preferences, the changes that they recommend to U.S. force structure have a surprising amount in common.

Consistent with the recommendations of several advisory panels since the end of the Cold War, the three authors all recommend substantial cutbacks from the eight combat divisions of the Army National Guard. These divisions are the slowest-mobilizing units in the Army and, as configured in 2000, seem to have little relevance to today's fighting concepts. The Pentagon's own Bottom-Up Review of 1993 urged eliminating three of them by 1999, but political factors have kept them in the force. New proposals for using these divisions in homeland defense, particularly to organize and manage recovery efforts in the aftermath of an attack involving nuclear, biological, or chemical weapons, may provide an argument that they are worth keeping. But as Quinlivan points out, the potential usefulness of these units in such recovery efforts is far from clear. Moreover, eliminating them might help the military solve its reserve component staffing problems.

All three chapters recommend retaining all of the National Guard's enhanced separate brigades. All three trim the Army's active forces to some extent. All three suggest reducing the number of aircraft carriers in the Navy—Cote by home-porting an additional carrier overseas, Mueller largely on efficiency grounds, and Quinlivan as a way of encouraging U.S. allies to take up the maritime challenge. Two of the authors recommend reducing the Marine Corps' amphibious ready groups. All three suggest eliminating at least one tactical wing from the active-duty Air Force and one from the Air Force reserve.

COMPARING THE MODERNIZATION PROGRAMS

Cote, Quinlivan, and Mueller all recommend adjusting the procurement programs of all three services, and all three suggest innovative new equipment that would help the military to change dramatically the way that it operates. As with their force structure recommendations, the suggested adjustments to the services' modernization programs are surprisingly consistent in some areas.

For example, the three authors all propose that the Army cancel the Crusader self-propelled artillery system, either relying on the existing

Paladin or by purchasing and adapting one of the new systems already developed by U.S. allies. Cote and Mueller both recommend canceling the Army's stealth Comanche scout and attack helicopter; even Quinlivan, who strongly supports spending for Army transformation and innovation, suggests cutting the Comanche purchase by half. In contrast, all three of the authors recommend that the Army purchase a light armored vehicle for its medium-weight brigades. Similarly, they all support the purchase of all the Marine Corps' planned MV-22 tilt-rotor transport aircraft.

In the area of tactical aircraft, all three chapters recommend substantially reducing the Air Force's planned purchase of F-22 air-to-air fighters; Cote urges canceling the program altogether. In addition, all of the chapters recommend delaying Joint Strike Fighter procurement, allowing this complicated program a longer period in development. Cote recommends scrapping the Air Force version of the new fighter, so that the Air Force will take advantage of the shorter takeoff and landing features of the Marine Corps or Navy version. Mueller and Quinlivan recommend reducing the Navy's F/A-18E/F procurement by about 50 percent, and also taking advantage of the opportunity to purchase the newest model of the Air Force's relatively inexpensive F-16 multipurpose fighter.

Except for Cote, who strongly supports most of the Navy programs, the authors recommend canceling the two aircraft carriers that the service plans to build during the decade. They also suggest reducing the shipbuilding programs for amphibious assault and transport ships, trimming the new attack submarine program, and retaining some of the *Los Angeles*–class submarines that the Navy currently plans to retire before the end of their useful lives.

Recommendations

The preceding chapters point to a number of recommendations for the nation to consider as the Defense Department embarks on the 2001 Quadrennial Defense Review (QDR).

RE-EXAMINE THE NATION'S SECURITY STRATEGY, MILITARY STRATEGY, AND MILITARY PRIORITIES

The QDR affords the nation and the Defense Department an opportunity that must not be taken lightly: to rethink national and defense priorities in light of the real world we face, not the world of the past or even the world that military leaders believed we might face as the Cold War wound down. The Cold War is well behind us; new challenges and opportunities have emerged. Yet the military's central priorities are the same ones established by the Base Force review, which began before the Berlin Wall fell and was completed before the nation came to a full understanding that the fight against the Soviet Union was over. The military strategies described in this book illustrate a range of possibilities for the future. Before the Defense Department settles again on a strategy designed to preserve the status quo, it is time for a serious national debate about foreign policy and the role and priorities of the military.

DROP THE CURRENT TWO-WAR STANDARD IN FAVOR OF A STRATEGY THAT REFLECTS MORE REALISTIC PRIORITIES AND THREATS
The Clinton administration's declaratory national security strategy sets the military's first priority on fighting in two major theater wars that unfold at about the same time. But the demands of smaller-scale contingencies and so-called "shaping" missions crowd out preparedness for the second MTW. As part of the reassessment of priorities, we need to decide as a nation how we mean to use our military. Assuming that the smaller-scale contingencies will continue, we should assign a lower official priority to preparing for a second MTW.

In addition, we should re-calibrate the measuring stick for major theater wars. The Defense Department currently demands that U.S. forces have "overmatch" in a major theater war, that is, that they be sized and shaped to win even if the enemy turns out to be much more powerful than any realistic threat assessement would show. Retaining such an insurance policy may be a good idea for one MTW, but keeping it for two MTWs is a waste of resources.

HOLD THE LINE ON DEFENSE SPENDING FOR A DECADE
Holding the line makes sense in a world where the United States still spends 85 percent as much as its Cold War average on the military, where U.S. military spending swamps the spending of all the nations considered to be potential adversaries, and where no new military threat has emerged to take the place of the Soviet Union. Although projections of huge federal surpluses might mean that the nation can afford to spend more on the military, other uses of the surpluses promise higher social and economic payoffs. Moreover, holding the line may have positive benefits for the military. As businesses have found, living with the discipline of a fixed budget can help leaders to set priorities and make choices that would otherwise be put off. As the strategies, force structures, and modernization plans recommended in this book illustrate, such discipline can also spark more innovative approaches to military problems—much

as lean corporations are often more agile in response to new challenges than the staid behemoths.

Holding the line is likely to require the military to trim force structure and rein in plans for modernization. But if the decision to hold the line is made early in the decade, then the services can conduct an orderly draw-down and possibly even avoid the programmatic difficulties that they faced during the previous decade, as procurement accounts had to be tapped repeatedly to pay operation and maintenance bills that exceeded expectations.

DISCONTINUE THE PRACTICE OF DIVIDING THE BUDGET PIE INTO CONSTANT SERVICE "SHARES"

Allocating money across the services in a consistent pattern is politically expedient and dampens inter-service warfare. But, as the examples in this book illustrate, competing for resources can stimulate people to explore more creative solutions to the military's problems. It is time for the nation to set military priorities, cut forces that are no longer relevant, eliminate programs that no longer make sense, and reward innovation, without regard to the budget shares that the services held during the Cold War.

WIDEN THE DEFENSE DEPARTMENT'S INFRASTRUCTURE REFORM EFFORTS

The department hopes ultimately to save about $6.5 billion a year by closing about fifty more bases and by implementing "strategic sourcing," and to reap unspecified amounts through reengineering and intra-organizational consolidations. But the department has not stepped up to the more politically difficult reforms that have the potential to save more money. Chapter 3 suggests a number of approaches, and some possible ways to reduce the political barriers that have stood in their way.

WORK MORE CLOSELY WITH ALLIES

As Chapter 4 explains, allied burden-sharing is not a pot of gold into which U.S. defense planners can dip. But allied forces are well suited to handle some missions with little or no U.S. help. Moreover, it is only by cooperating more closely as strategies are developed, force structures are planned, and technology and modernization programs are established that the United States and its allies will be able to reap the potential financial benefits of shared security arrangements.

REDUCE NUCLEAR FORCES TO START III LEVELS

The United States has already made substantial reductions in its nuclear arsenal. The financial payoff of the reductions amounts to tens of billions of dollars a year, compared with nuclear spending during the Cold War.

As Chapter 5 details, the savings from further reductions will be smaller. Nevertheless, some savings are possible. With the Cold War well behind us and no new vast nuclear power in sight, negotiating with Russia to reduce nuclear forces to a level of 1,000–2,500 nuclear warheads makes security sense and economic sense.

REDUCE AND RESHAPE CONVENTIONAL FORCE STRUCTURE
The United States should reduce conventional force structure and modernization plans at least enough to hold defense budgets in check for a decade. Force structure reductions will have financial payoffs and will also ease the military's recruiting and retention burdens. Three authors with quite varied views about military strategy and diverse preferences for military forces demonstrate in Chapters 6, 7, and 8 a surprising degree of consensus in some areas of their force structure recommendations. As a minimum, the nation should consider a substantial reduction of Army National Guard ground combat divisions, some downsizing of Army active-duty combat divisions, elimination of at least one aircraft carrier, and removal of at least two Air Force tactical wings.

REIN IN AND RESHAPE MODERNIZATION PLANS
Some of the modernization recommendations made by Owen Cote, James Quinlivan, and Karl Mueller in Chapters 6 through 8 are strikingly consistent with one another. They suggest that, at a minimum, the Army should cancel the Crusader self-propelled artillery system, relying instead on the existing Paladin or adapting a new system developed by NATO allies, and that the Comanche program should be canceled or cut back substantially. The Army should purchase a new light armored vehicle for use by the new medium-weight brigades.

The Navy should consider deferring further production of aircraft carriers into the next decade, taking advantage of the opportunity that a pause in 2001–10 would open to pursue innovative technologies that might make new carriers more effective and less labor-intensive. In addition, the Navy should consider trimming its shipbuilding programs for surface combatants, attack submarines, and amphibious ships, and reconfiguring at least four Trident SSBNs to carry conventional precision munitions instead of the nuclear-tipped missiles they currently hold.

The Defense Department should cut back and reshape its expensive plans for tactical air modernization. Specific recommendations include canceling or substantially reducing the F-22 program; and also delaying the purchase of the Joint Strike Fighter to allow more time for development and to reduce the financial burden of overlapping tactical aircraft procurements in the 2006–10 period. In addition, F/A-18E/F purchases might be reduced, and advantage taken of the opportunity to purchase new F-16 Block 60s not included in the department's current plans.

Most important, the nation should look for and devote more resources to innovative solutions to the problems that face the military: solutions that are well within reach but are often crowded out by spending for platforms invented for the Cold War and stifled by business-as-usual practices.

Summary

The United States needs a national security strategy that acknowledges the present and looks to the future instead of the past. It needs to reshape the conventional forces to reflect that new strategy and to take advantage of the opportunities afforded by new technologies, getting rid of forces and weapons programs that no longer make sense and emphasizing the ones that position the armed forces for the future. Such reshaping is both possible and affordable within today's budget levels. But it requires decisionmakers to take a fresh look at strategy, at the relative contribution of each element of force structure and each item of equipment to the security environment the nation actually faces, and at the opportunities afforded by new technologies, new ways of organizing and new ideas for attracting and holding the best people.

Contributors

Gordon Adams teaches international affairs and national security at the Elliott School of International Affairs at The George Washington University in Washington, D.C. He also directs the Security Policy Studies Program at the Elliott School. He was previously Deputy Director of the International Institute for Strategic Studies (IISS) in London, where he participated in management and planning activities and developed the IISS corporate membership program. He has also been Associate Director at the Office of Management and Budget (OMB), where he was responsible for oversight over all U.S. foreign affairs and national security budgeting for the Executive Office of the President, and was the principal adviser to the OMB Director on foreign and national security policy issues. He was previously founder and Director of the Defense Budget Project, a non-partisan research center in Washington D.C., which became a leading analytical institution working on the defense budget, defense economics, and defense policy issues. He holds a Ph.D. in Political Science from Columbia University and has been a Fulbright Fellow at the College of Europe in Bruges, Belgium, an International Affairs fellow of the Council on Foreign Relations, a senior staffer of the Council on Economic Priorities in New York, and a staff associate for European Programs at the Social Science Research Council. He is currently a member of the Defense Policy Board advising the Secretary of Defense, of the Strategic Advisory Board to the Raytheon Systems Company, the IISS, and the Council on Foreign Relations.

Owen R. Cote, Jr. joined the MIT Security Studies Program in 1997 as an Associate Director. Previously Assistant Director of the International Security Program at Harvard's Belfer Center for Science and International Affairs (BCSIA), he remains co-editor of the Center's journal, *International Security*. He received his Ph.D. from MIT, where he specialized in U.S. defense policy and international security affairs. He is working on one book that analyzes the sources of innovative military doctrine, comparing cases of U.S. Navy responses to Cold War nuclear vulnerability crises, and another book analyzing the sources of the U.S. Navy's success in its Cold War antisubmarine warfare effort. He has also written on naval doctrine, nuclear force structure issues, the politics of strategic mobility, and nuclear weapons in the former Soviet Union.

Lawrence J. Korb is Vice President and Director of Studies and holder of the Maurice Greenberg Chair at the Council on Foreign Relations. He has also served as Director of the Center for Public Policy Education and Senior Fellow in the Foreign Policy Studies Program at the Brookings Institution, Dean of the Graduate School of Public and International Affairs at the University of Pittsburgh, and Vice President, Corporate Operations at the Raytheon Company. Mr. Korb served as Assistant Secretary of Defense (Manpower, Reserve Affairs, Installations and Logistics) from 1981 through 1985, with responsibility for administering about 70 percent of the defense budget. For his service in that position, he was awarded the Department of Defense's medal for Distinguished Public Service. Mr. Korb is Chairman of the Board for the Committee on National Security, and a Board Member of the Washington Center, the Procurement Round Table, and the National Military Family Association. He is also a member of the Council on Foreign Relations, the IISS, the National Academy of Public Administration, and the Aspen Strategy Group. He was a member of the Defense Advisory Committee for President-Elect Reagan (1980) and a member of the Defense Issues Group for President-Elect Bush (1988). He received his M.A. from St. John's University and his Ph.D. from the State University of New York at Albany. Among his books are *The Joint Chiefs of Staff: The First Twenty-five Years; The Fall and Rise of the Pentagon;* and *American National Security: Policy and Process.*

David Mosher recently joined RAND as a Nuclear Policy Analyst after ten years in the National Security Division at the Congressional Budget Office (CBO). He has written papers, studies, and articles on a wide variety of issues including nuclear weapons and forces, ballistic missile defenses, arms control, reducing nuclear threats, and general defense budget issues. Before joining CBO he worked at the Johns Hopkins University's Applied Physics Laboratory, where he conducted research on ocean physics and remote sensing. He holds a Masters in Public Affairs from Princeton University's Woodrow Wilson School and a bachelors degree in physics from Grinnell College.

Karl Mueller is an Associate Professor at the U.S. Air Force's School of Advanced Airpower Studies (SAAS) at Maxwell AFB, Alabama, where he teaches international relations, defense policy, and strategic air power theory and application. He also runs SAAS's guest speaker and air power film programs, and directs the school's annual joint theater campaign wargame. He received his B.A. in Political Science from the University of Chicago and his Ph.D. in Politics from Princeton University. He has written on alliances, deterrence theory, nuclear strategy, economic sanctions, and the coercive use of military power. His current research projects deal with space weaponization, the role of air power in twenty-first century warfare, and the strategy and results of Operation Allied Force. He is completing a book about the deterrence strategies of European middle powers and small states from the 1930s through the Cold War.

James T. Quinlivan is a Senior Analyst at RAND working on strategic planning issues. He has been the Program Director for Aerospace and Strategic Technology in RAND's Project Air Force and Vice President of the Army Research Division at RAND. He has degrees in mathematics and physics and an Engineer's Degree in Operations Research. His articles have been published in *Parameters, International Security,* and *Marine Corps Gazette.*

Cindy Williams is a Senior Research Fellow of the Security Studies Program at the Massachusetts Institute of Technology. Her work at MIT includes a study of future U.S. spending for defense and an examination of the U.S. military's experiments on advanced warfighting concepts. She previously served as an Assistant Director of the CBO, where she led the National Security Division in studies of budgetary and policy choices related to defense and international security. Dr. Williams has also served as a director at the MITRE Corporation in Bedford, Massachusetts; as a member of the Senior Executive Service in the Office of the Secretary of Defense at the Pentagon; and as a mathematician at RAND in Santa Monica, California. Her research focuses particularly on the national security budget, command and control of military forces, and conventional air and ground forces, and her publications have examined command and control and the defense budget. Holder of a Ph.D. in mathematics from the University of California, Irvine, she is an elected fellow of the National Academy of Public Administration, a member of the Information and Command and Control Systems Technical Committee of the American Institute of Aeronautics and Astronautics, and a member of the Advisory Board of Women in International Security (WIIS).

Index

BCSIA Studies in International Security

Published by The MIT Press

Sean M. Lynn-Jones and Steven E. Miller, series editors
Karen Motley, executive editor
Belfer Center for Science and International Affairs (BCSIA)
John F. Kennedy School of Government, Harvard University

Allison, Graham T., Owen R. Coté, Jr., Richard A. Falkenrath, and Steven E. Miller, *Avoiding Nuclear Anarchy: Containing the Threat of Loose Russian Nuclear Weapons and Fissile Material* (1996)

Allison, Graham T., and Kalypso Nicolaïdis, eds., *The Greek Paradox: Promise vs. Performance* (1996)

Arbatov, Alexei, Abram Chayes, Antonia Handler Chayes, and Lara Olson, eds., *Managing Conflict in the Former Soviet Union: Russian and American Perspectives* (1997)

Bennett, Andrew, *Condemned to Repetition? The Rise, Fall, and Reprise of Soviet-Russian Military Interventionism, 1973–1996* (1999)

Blackwill, Robert D., and Michael Stürmer, eds., *Allies Divided: Transatlantic Policies for the Greater Middle East* (1997)

Blackwill, Robert D., and Paul Dibb, eds., *America's Asian Alliances* (2000)

Brom, Shlomo, and Yiftah Shapir, eds., *The Middle East Military Balance 1999–2000* (2000)

Brown, Michael E., ed., *The International Dimensions of Internal Conflict* (1996)

Brown, Michael E., and Šumit Ganguly, eds., *Government Policies and Ethnic Relations in Asia and the Pacific* (1997)

Elman, Colin, and Miriam Fendius Elman, eds., *Bridges and Boundaries: Historians, Political Scientists, and the Study of International Relations* (2000)

Elman, Miriam Fendius, ed., *Paths to Peace: Is Democracy the Answer?* (1997)

Falkenrath, Richard A., *Shaping Europe's Military Order: The Origins and Consequences of the CFE Treaty* (1994)

Falkenrath, Richard A., Robert D. Newman, and Bradley A. Thayer, *America's Achilles' Heel: Nuclear, Biological, and Chemical Terrorism and Covert Attack* (1998)

Feldman, Shai, *Nuclear Weapons and Arms Control in the Middle East* (1996)

Forsberg, Randall, ed., *The Arms Production Dilemma: Contraction and Restraint in the World Combat Aircraft Industry* (1994)

Hagerty, Devin T., *The Consequences of Nuclear Proliferation: Lessons from South Asia* (1998)

Heymann, Philip B., *Terrorism and America: A Commonsense Strategy for a Democratic Society* (1998)

Kokoshin, Andrei A., *Soviet Strategic Thought, 1917–91* (1998)

Lederberg, Joshua, *Biological Weapons: Limiting the Threat* (1999)

Shields, John M., and William C. Potter, eds., *Dismantling the Cold War: U.S. and NIS Perspectives on the Nunn-Lugar Cooperative Threat Reduction Program* (1997)

Tucker, Jonathan B., ed., *Toxic Terror: Assessing Terrorist Use of Chemical and Biological Weapons* (2000)

Utgoff, Victor A., ed., *The Coming Crisis: Nuclear Proliferation, U.S. Interests, and World Order* (2000)

Williams, Cindy, ed., *Holding the Line: U.S. Defense Alternatives for the Early 21st Century* (2001)

The Robert and Renée Belfer Center for Science and International Affairs

Graham T. Allison, Director
John F. Kennedy School of Government
Harvard University
79 JFK Street, Cambridge, MA 02138
(617) 495-1400

The Belfer Center for Science and International Affairs (BCSIA) is the hub of research, teaching, and training in international security affairs, environmental and resource issues, and science and technology policy at Harvard's John F. Kennedy School of Government. The Center's mission is to provide leadership in advancing policy-relevant knowledge about the most important challenges of international security and other critical issues where science, technology, and international affairs intersect.

BCSIA's leadership begins with the recognition of science and technology as driving forces transforming international affairs. The Center integrates insights of social scientists, natural scientists, technologists, and practitioners with experience in government, diplomacy, the military, and business to address these challenges. The Center pursues its mission in four complementary research programs:

- The International Security Program (ISP) addresses the most pressing threats to U.S. national interests and international security.

- The Environment and Natural Resources Program (ENRP) is the locus of Harvard's interdisciplinary research on resource and environmental problems and policy responses.

- The Science, Technology, and Public Policy (STPP) program analyzes ways in which science and technology policy influence international security, resources, environment, and development, and such cross-cutting issues as technological innovation and information infrastructure.

- The Strengthening Democratic Institutions (SDI) project catalyzes support for three great transformations in Russia, Ukraine, and the other republics of the former Soviet Union—to sustainable democracies, free market economies, and cooperative international relations.

The heart of the Center is its resident research community of more than one hundred scholars: Harvard faculty, analysts, practitioners, and each year a new, interdisciplinary group of research fellows. BCSIA sponsors frequent seminars, workshops, and conferences, many open to the public; maintains a substantial specialized library; and publishes books, monographs, and discussion papers. The Center's International Security Program, directed by Steven E. Miller, publishes the BCSIA Studies in International Security, and sponsors and edits the quarterly journal *International Security*.

The Center is supported by an endowment established with funds from Robert and Renée Belfer, the Ford Foundation, and Harvard University, by foundation grants, by individual gifts, and by occasional government contracts.